The
Criminal Records Book

The Complete Guide to the Legal Use of Criminal Records

by
Derek Hinton

Edited by Michael L. Sankey and Peter J. Weber

©2002 By Facts on Demand Press
Post Office Box 27869
Tempe, AZ 85285
(800) 929-3811
www.brbpub.com

Criminal Records Book
The Complete Guide to the Legal Use of Criminal Records

©2002 By Facts on Demand Press
PO Box 27869
Tempe, AZ 85285
(800) 929-3811

ISBN: 1-889150-28-2
Cover Design by Robin Fox & Associates; Derek Hinton Photo by Mark Moore
Derek Hinton; Edited by Michael L. Sankey, Peter J. Weber.
First Printing, 2002

Cataloging-in-Publication Data

    Hinton, Derek.
      Criminal records book : the complete guide to the
    legal use of criminal records / Derek Hinton ; [edited
    by Michael Sankey, Peter Weber] – 1st. ed.
      p. cm.
      Includes index.
      ISBN: 1-889150-28-2

      1. Criminal registers–United States. 2. Criminal
registers--Access Control--United States. 3. Police--
Records and correspondence--United States.   I. Title.

    KF9751.Z9H56 2002   345.73'052
                    QBI01-201478

Acknowledgements

This book is dedicated to my family and friends.
I especially thank my wife and children for their
tolerance of the time this book took away from them.
I would also like to thank my parents and brother,
who, complete and honest truth be told, probably
suspected that I might someday become familiar
with criminal records.

My friends know who they are. If there is any doubt,
the fault is mine.

Finally, I would like to thank the individuals who
reviewed drafts of the book. Your help is sincerely
appreciated. To Mike, Mark and Peter at Facts on
Demand Press, thank you, too. It's been fun.

Derek Hinton

It ain't no sin if you crack a few laws now and then, just so long as you don't break any.

—Mae West

Contents

Section 2:
Where Criminal Records Are Found

Section 3: Employer & Vendor Guidelines to Using Criminal Records

Section 4: Government Agency Profiles

This chapter consists of detail pages for each state. The following information is included: access requirements, restrictions, fees, online modes, policies and procedures for state criminal record agencies; analysis of county courts; statewide court systems; profiles for obtaining records from state prisons; state sexual offender registries and how to access them

How to Access Federal Records by Mail or Phone; Online Access to Records; PACER Access; U.S. Party/Case Index; CM/ECF-Case Management/Electronic Case Files; Federal Record Centers and the National Archives; Locations of the U.S. District Courts

Section 5: Appendix

Compact Memberships; State Criminal Records Required Data; Prohibited Access to Records

Prescribed Summary of Consumer Rights; Prescribed Notice of Furnisher Responsibilities; Prescribed Notice of User Responsibilities

Evaluation of employer's policy of refusing to hire individuals with conviction records; Commission's procedure for determining whether arrest records may be considered in employment decisions; Job advertising and pre-employment inquires; A business justifying the exclusion of an individual from employment on the basis of a conviction record

Introduction

All serious conversations gravitate towards philosophy.

—Ernest Dimnet

I wish it were so.

I wish all individuals really were created equal, or at least behaved in a responsible manner, that given the same stimuli, individuals would exhibit, within a massive spectrum of possibilities, enlightened behavior.

The problem is that there are some people who, to quote a Southern friend of mine, "just ain't right." All the wishing in the world will not change that fact. Nothing can change that fact. The vast majority of us behave as responsible members of society—but lock our doors at night. We avoid going to certain areas at certain times. We spend a lot of money on everything from police protection, jails, prisons, court systems and security systems to airport metal detectors, department store surveillance equipment and gated communities.

We also order criminal records before hiring individuals who will spend half their waking life among us. W. C. Fields once said there's not an adult alive, who at one time or another, has not wanted to boot a child in the ass. There's probably not a working adult who at one time or another has not wanted to wring a co-worker's neck. And yet, of course, we don't do it. Frustration goes hand-in-hand with work. 98.7% of us never go past daydreams in which we have a co-worker in a headlock and are giving them a good and true Dutch rub.

And yet, there are those who "ain't right." And so, criminal records are ordered. Of the criminal records ordered by the private sector, the vast majority are used by employers. Usually, these records are ordered from service providers and vendors, such as pre-employment screening companies and investigators. This book is written to benefit all —the public, employers and vendors.

I especially hope this book helps the small employer who can't change the world, but is tending his own garden, who is using criminal records in the hiring process because he believes in his gut that it is the right thing to do; who is ordering criminal records in an effort to insure that other employees and the general public are not exposed to someone that would do them harm.

At the same time, most of us believe a criminal record should not inevitably disqualify an individual from all future employment. I hope this book gives guidance to the employer that knowingly hires the individual with a criminal record, who doesn't automatically reject anyone with any past transgression, regardless of severity and age.

And for the individual who has committed a crime in which there was no victim and is trying to find a job? Keep looking. Employers are out there who will hire you and the employers who won't? Think about it: do you really want to devote whatever you have to offer to them anyway?

Finally, to the felon who committed a crime—who hurt, stole or defrauded another—I'll work up all the sympathy I can for you with what sympathy is left over for your victims.

In general, most readers will probably just want to know more about how the various justice systems in the United States gather, process, and release criminal record information. The goal of this book is to help you fully understand and correctly utilize criminal record information.

Section 1

What Do You Really Know About Criminal Records?

This section defines essential criminal record terms and phrases; examines the differences between records ordered by criminal justice agencies and the private sector; and touches on the privacy concerns regarding the use of criminal records and the purposes for which they are used.

Chapter 1

Testing Your Criminal Record Quotient

Somebody once said that in looking for people to hire, you look for three qualities: integrity, intelligence, and energy. And if they don't have the first, the other two will kill you. You think about it; it's true. If you hire somebody without the first, you really want them to be dumb and lazy.

—Warren Buffet

Here is a true story to demonstrate why it is important to always conduct criminal record checks. At the end are questions to see how much you know about conducting these record checks.

Jean and Harvey's Dream

Jean and Harvey already had one thirty-year career behind them when they decided to start their own business. They eased into opening their new business and it had done well. Over several years, the business grew and they found themselves working harder and longer than ever. On the positive side of the ledger, they were within a decade of retirement age and the business was becoming a true asset and would help fund their retirement. A leisurely life of family, hobbies and travel was within sight.

As the business grew and began adding more employees, management of the office staff, dealing with suppliers, and addressing the "small business infrastructure crisis of the day" began to lay claim to their days. The solution was not difficult to see: hire an office manager.

One applicant for their new office manager position swept them off their feet. Marilou was conversant about basic accounting, payroll software, human resource issues and customer service. Her college degree was confirmed, the references listed on her employment application checked out.

To work she went, with a bigger salary than the owners themselves had commanded until recently. Marilou was a fast learner. She was obviously intelligent, had a sense of humor, and the owners noticed that she was no pushover for the office staff under her. Employees showed up for work on time, smoke breaks didn't last all morning, and morale was good. By year's end, revenues were the highest they had ever been.

The first cloud on the distant horizon was the next year's mid-year numbers. Gross revenue was higher, but the net was disappointing. At year-end, they were surprised to find themselves with yet higher gross revenues, but essentially no net. Despite all their new accounts and greater gross revenue, the business was just breaking even.

For the next several weeks, the Jean and Harvey found themselves back in the office. With Marilou's help, strategic plans were made to cut costs. The office manager was a Godsend. She tactfully negotiated significant discounts for goods from suppliers that the owners would not have imagined practical.

Revitalized, Jean and Harvey promptly landed several huge Fortune 500 accounts. Net revenue leaped and the mid-year net figures were a little higher than break-even.

Then, one night, Harvey picked up a fax from the machine. It was an inquiry from a client concerning some goods that had been ordered. It wasn't rude, but there was a hint of testiness that prompted the husband to log on to the computer to check on the order's status. He couldn't find the client, which was not unusual. Many of their clients had several operating divisions, sister companies, or operated under various d/b/a's. Tired, he left the fax with a short note on Marilou's desk, and went home.

The next day, while he drove to an appointment, Harvey checked in on his cell phone. He asked Marilou if she had seen the fax and taken care of company "XYZ." Overhearing the conversation, Jean remarked that she would sure like to get "XYZ's" business. Harvey informed her they apparently had it. Jean was surprised, explaining that she had called on XYZ only two weeks previously and couldn't meet their price.

Nightmares are peculiar in that you almost never remember the start of it—just the middle and end. Jean and Harvey didn't remember much of their next few appointments with potential clients. Their next few days were filled with first open —and then surreptitious— inquiries of employees, clients and suppliers. Records and accounts were checked. Then, one morning, Marilou didn't show up. A voice mail from her said there had been a sudden parental sickness and she was resigning—effective yesterday. The next day her telephone was disconnected.

As the facts became known, Jean and Harvey determined that Marilou had set up her own thriving business within their business. Here is how it worked: Marilou would offer a client the same goods offered by Jean and Harvey's business, but at a lower price. Marilou would obtain the goods herself for free by ordering through the business, but she would bill the clients herself. Her cost of goods sold was zero. As a result, she had netted well over $100,000. Meanwhile, the business for which she worked was buying much of the product at a 100% loss.

Jean and Harvey went to an attorney but concluded that there would probably be no money left to recover. Plus, the recovery process would be extremely expensive in legal fees. Next, they talked to a detective about criminal charges. The detective was sympathetic but honest about how long the process might take, how much of the owners' time would be involved, and all the interviews that would have to be made with hesitant clients.

The deeper that Jean and Harvey dug into the damage, the more it yawned into every aspect of their business. The numbers that had shown the business breaking even had been skillfully manipulated. They faced bankruptcy. They had a hard decision to make. They could spend their time and money pursuing the office manager, or they could attempt to salvage their business. They obtained a second mortgage and went back to doing what they did best: work the business.

Something like this is hard to forget. One day they decided to make an inquiry. It was an easy inquiry to make, as it was their business. During Marilou's tenure as office manager, the company had branched out into criminal records—and it was criminal records that the office manager had been obtaining and selling at the owners' expense. So, they ordered a criminal record check on Marilou. The record check showed that she had previously been arrested for felony embezzlement and she had pled it down to a misdemeanor. With that blemish on her record, she had decided that a change in venue was in order. Thus she moved across country, and later managed to land the office manager position with Jean and Harvey.

I got a call from Jean within the past year. She asked if I had read a certain newspaper story about a successful business in a small town. The article gushed on the prospects of the business and had a photograph of the top managers. One was a sharp, professional-looking lady. It was Marilou.

You can't help but feel sorry for Jean and Harvey. They got taken to the cleaners. On the positive side, they did save their business. Think of the emotions running through their heads when they saw Marilou being touted in print!

This story breezes over several issues that will be discussed in this book. For starters, consider the following questions—

A Criminal Record Quiz

Using the Jean and Harvey story as a starting point, let's test your knowledge of criminal records. The good news is that this is an open-book quiz. For some of the questions, an assumption is made and an answer is given. In others, there is no answer until more questions are answered. The chapter that discusses the pertinent questions is referenced.

1. Would it have been legal for Jean and Harvey (the employers) to order a criminal record before they employed the office manager?

    It would have been legal to order a criminal record provided, of course, that they obtained the information from a legal source. On the other hand, if they happened to have had a friend in law enforcement and this friend had inquired surreptitiously into the FBI's files, it would have been illegal. (See Chapter 2 for which records are public and which are not.)

2. Would they have had to have the office manager's permission (Marilou) to order a criminal record?

    While certainly not a bad idea, the legal question depends on whether they obtained the information themselves or through the use of a service and from what state the record was obtained. If they obtained the record from a service (and there are excellent reasons to do so), then they would have needed permission. (See Chapters 13 & 16 for details.)

3. Would it have been legal to use the information received to deny the office manager a job?

    Jean and Harvey would have had to make several determinations regarding the information. See Chapter 15 for what some of those determinations are. Given the circumstances, Jean and Harvey almost certainly could have used the information to deny the manager a position.

4. Was it legal for the owners to order a criminal record on the office manager after she had already left their employ?

    Criminal records obtained from counties and most states are public records. Jean and Harvey obtained the information from a public source. It was legal. However, in some states a signed release or fingerprints may be required. See the Chapter 17 to learn each state's nuances.

5. What are the legal ramifications of the felony arrest for embezzlement evolving into a misdemeanor conviction?

    This is a tricky one in that it mingles two different considerations, that of an arrest versus a conviction, and a felony versus a misdemeanor. The first step is to understand the differences. These terms are defined in Chapter 2.

    The legal ramifications are myriad, and it's best to separate the question into two parts:

    -   To what degree may arrest records be used as compared with conviction records?

In general, more care must be used when using arrest records. The EEOC's guidelines are more stringent (see Chapter 15), and on the state level, the use of arrest records may be restricted. (See Chapter 16)

- Felonies versus misdemeanors: are felonies more important?

  Not necessarily. There are several reasons why. See the "Pros and Cons of Using Misdemeanor Records" discussion in Chapter 12. Find out which states forbid or restrict the use of misdemeanor records in Chapter 16.

6. Would the fact that the office manager was a female have affected the owners' use of the criminal record?

   Probably not in this case. However, if Jean and Harvey were to learn a false lesson from their experience and institute a policy of only ordering a criminal record on female applicants, this disparate practice might cause them future peril.

7. If the office manager were African-American, would it have affected the use of the record?

   It may have. The issue of race has affected policy regarding employers' use of criminal records. See Chapter 15 for the EEOC guidelines.

8. Would it have made any difference if the previous act had been committed twenty years ago instead of recently?

   It could have in several ways. First, the court or repository may simply not have made the record available to search because of the record's age. If so, then Jean and Harvey would not have found the record.

   Second, one consideration to be considered before *using* a record from employment purposes is the length of time that has elapsed since the act was committed.

9. Do you think the owners wish they had ordered the criminal record before they hired the office manager, then dealt with any legal ramifications later?

   The answer, of course, is that if the owners had known what was about to transpire, they most certainly would have ordered a criminal record and rejected the applicant.

   However, they didn't have the requisite knowledge to acquire, evaluate and legally use the criminal record information that would have averted their ordeal. And that is the goal of this book—to impart the knowledge on how to acquire, evaluate and use criminal record information.

Chapter 2

Essential Criminal Record Terms and Phrases

*You can get much farther with a kind word and a gun
than you can with a kind word alone.*

—Al Capone

Before going on, it would be wise to define some important terms.

A ***Criminal Record*** is a paper or computerized accounting that includes individual identifiers and describes an individual's arrests and subsequent dispositions.

Keep in mind that this "accounting" may be complete or incomplete. Also, not all parts may be available to the public, depending on the administering jurisdiction's rules. Criminal history records do not include intelligence or investigative data or sociological data such as drug use history.

In most states, the available criminal records can include information on juveniles only if they are tried as adults in criminal courts. Even then a juvenile criminal record does not usually include all the data describing that subject's involvement in the juvenile justice system.

Felonies and Misdemeanors

There are two broad categories of criminal severity—felonies and misdemeanors. While in the United States the distinction between the two has been blurred, these general definitions are common.

A *Felony* is the more serious class of offense and punishment ranges from imprisonment for over one year up to the death penalty.

A *Misdemeanor* is an offense of a minor degree and is anything less than a felony.

Some people believe that misdemeanor records should be ignored, that misdemeanors really don't mean anything, and to base any kind of decision on a misdemeanor is wrong. They have a good point, but nothing a good barber couldn't disguise.

Seriously, there are several scenarios in which misdemeanor records might prove useful: Do I like the moral character of this job applicant? Is my daughter's boyfriend really okay? Has this potential babysitter committed an offense I should worry about? Having knowledge from a misdemeanor record might help to clear the muddy waters.

Whatever the scenario, there are two cogent reasons why misdemeanors should be considered:

- A misdemeanor record may be as pertinent as a felony, or more. From a human resource viewpoint, this is especially true if the misdemeanor is job-related.
- Many recorded misdemeanors are originally the result of felony crimes.

Even so, it is important—sometimes legally necessary—to understand the difference between felonies and misdemeanors. The distinctions between felonies and misdemeanors, and the reasons that felonies are not necessarily more important or significant than a misdemeanor, are discussed in Chapter 12.

With or Without a Disposition?

The terms "arrest" and "disposition" were used in the definition of a criminal record.

An *Arrest* is the taking of an individual into custody by law enforcement personnel (i.e. the person's behavior is arrested) in order to charge the person with an illegal act.

An arrest differs from a *Conviction*. A conviction is a finding of guilt after a judicial trial. In some states, it includes deferred sentences and in some it does not. A *Disposition* is the final outcome of the arrest. This may or may not be a conviction.

It is important to note that many criminal records may not contain a disposition. Some states will purge a record (at least from the public file) if there is no disposition after a specified time frame. About one-half of all state criminal record repositories do not release records without dispositions after a period of time, usually one year; or will not release records without dispositions at all. On the other hand, there are times when a case is dropped but the record without disposition remains on the books because the court fails to notify the record center.

The Distinction Between *Public* and *Non-Public* Criminal Records

One of the most significant keys to understanding the US criminal record system is to know the differences between *public record* and *non-public record* criminal records.

Non-Public criminal records are available only to law enforcement or criminal justice agencies, or other groups who have been granted statutory authority to access the records.

Public criminal records are those that can be obtained by a private citizen without some form of government authorization. The vast majority of criminal records found at the county level are public records. Public access to state criminal record depositories is somewhat more complicated.

FBI Records are Non-Public

Perhaps the most prolific of the non-public criminal records are those at the Federal Bureau of Investigation (FBI). The FBI makes its records available to law enforcement agencies nationwide and to certain approved entities. Even so, these entities' access to these records is not carte blanche. For example, gun dealers have access to FBI records in order to screen potential gun purchasers. Over the telephone (via modem going through the FBI state gateway), dealers can usually obtain an answer within minutes. However, they are only allowed to use the system for potential gun purchasers. A gun dealer may not use the system to open up a pre-employment screening business on the side.

A key component of the FBI's records is that they are nationwide. While the FBI does not have record of all crimes—let alone dispositions—they do have records from across the country. A search of the FBI's system—even when it is conducted through a local state repository—is a linked search that encompasses much of the other state and Federal law enforcement records. For more information about the FBI system, turn to Chapter 7.

Non-Public State Repository Criminal Records

While central criminal record repository data is available to the general public in most states, other states have classified their repository criminal records or portions thereof as non-public information.

Tennessee is good example of a state whose central repository considers criminal records non-public. Record access from their Nashville repository is limited only to agencies that have specific authorization by law. California, Louisiana, Mississippi, New York, North Carolina, and Vermont have similar restrictions.

Another factor to consider is that most states cloak or mask certain portions of their records to the public, but do provide full information to those with statutory access.

Public Criminal Records

Nearly all county courts and most state record repositories classify their records as public.

As a counter-example to Tennessee, with their restrictions, Florida is "open." Florida state records are available without restriction to the general public by mail, in-person or by computer. Florida can offer records going back to the 1930's, their fee is $15.00 each.

Hybrids: States with Release Requirements

Anyone who has conducted nationwide criminal record searches knows that there are states where the repository records are not strictly public or non-public. While these states do not have statutory prohibitions at the state level as Tennessee does, neither do these "hybrid" states follow Florida's example of open records for all.

The most common requirement is a signed release by the subject of the request. And, as with many aspects of criminal records, there may be no other consistency between the states that require a release. Some states, Indiana for example, require a release go so far as to mandate a specific, state-approved form. Ohio has no state-numbered form, but requires the release to be signed and a witness signature. Virginia has a special form that must contain the notarized signature of the subject as well as the notarized signature of the requester.

The second most common type of hybrid access requires the subject's fingerprints. A record request must include a set of the subject's fingerprints at thirteen state repositories, or merely a thumbprint as they do in West Virginia. In essence, the supplying of fingerprints means that the subject has given approval for the record search. Nearly all states that process fingerprints as part of a record request will also submit the prints to the FBI to determine if the subject may be "wanted" in another state or by the feds. By the way, the submission of fingerprints is an option in an additional thirteen states.

> **Author's Tip—**
>
> To find the individual search requirements and options for each state, turn to Chapter 17 - *State Profiles*.

Betwixt and Between

Criminal records often contain a myriad of unfamiliar terms. Each state has a veritable dictionary of crimes and penalties. While it is true that the definitions of most common crimes and penalties are fairly uniform from state to state, arcane state-unique terms are frequently found. In one state a pyramid scheme is a fraud; in another, that same crime might be known as a Ponzi scheme.

Unfortunately, these and other inconsistencies have led to the development of great gray areas in the use of criminal records. In one state, a family-related court matter may result in a publicly-accessible criminal record, but in a neighboring state, a family court record is not public. These gray areas are why individuals, particularly employers, now have a much more difficult time making well-informed decisions from what is, or what is not, available.

Adding to the mix, there have developed other "quasi-dispositions" such as:

- **"Prayer for Judgment"** A request of the court to give leniency in which no finding of guilt by the court is found.

- **"1st Offender Act"** After fulfilling the terms of probation, and release by the court prior to the termination of the period thereof, upon release from confinement, the defendant is discharged without court adjudication of guilt. The discharge completely exonerates the defendant of any criminal purpose and does not affect any of his civil rights or liberties. The defendant is not considered to have a criminal conviction.

- **"Diversion Programs"** A court direction which calls a defendant, who has been found guilty, to attend a work or educational program as part of probation. Usually, a "diversion" will "set aside" the criminal record.

- **"Deferred Adjudication of Guilt"** The final judgment is delayed for a period of time. This can be likened to probation before a final verdict. If probation is completed without incident, the charges are usually dropped and the case dismissed. During the "probationary period," the disposition is not necessarily considered a conviction, and may or may wind up on the record of the subject's criminal history.

Author's Tip—

If you will be ordering many criminal records from various locales, chances are you will be using a public record provider. Ask your record provider for a glossary of common criminal record terms.

Other Significant Criminal Record Terms

Listed below are certain words and phrases used frequently in the criminal record process.

Arraignment	A court hearing in a criminal case where a defendant is advised of the charges and asked to plead guilty or not guilty.
Bench Warrant	A process initiated by the court or "from the bench" for the arrest or the attachment of a person.
Class	Within government jurisdictions, the severity of a felony or misdemeanor is ranked by classification, moving from most serious to least serious.
Consecutive Sentence	Two or more sentences which run one after another.
Concurrent Sentence	Two or more sentences which run at the same time.
Docket	A book containing entries of all proceedings in a court. A *Docket Sheet* contains the case history from initial filings to the current status.
General Jurisdiction Courts	These courts hear felony cases. Some also hear misdemeanor cases.
Limited Jurisdiction Courts	These courts are limited in the types of classes of criminal cases they may hear.
Non-Biometric Identifiers	Non-physical (e.g. non-fingerprints, non-photographic) criteria used to determine the correct identity of a person when doing a criminal record check. In addition to name, may include aliases, date of birth, address, Social Security Number, etc.

Chapter 3

Who Uses Criminal Records?

Against the suffering which may come upon one from human relationships, the readiest safeguard is voluntary isolation, keeping oneself aloof from other people.

—Sigmund Freud

Well...okay. Meanwhile, back here on planet Earth in our 21st century, "keeping oneself aloof from other people" is quite a trick to pull off.

The FBI began maintaining its criminal history files back in 1924. Presumably, forward thinkers at the federal level had noticed that some of the ne'er-do-wells were repeat offenders and somebody really ought to keep score on this kind of thing.

By the late 1990's the FBI had over 200 million fingerprint cards on file. Clearly, keeping oneself aloof is impractical. For the better, various entities have decided to research the histories of those individuals from whom, for one reason or another, we are unable to keep aloof. A discussion of these entities who research the background of others is in order.

The Most Prominent Users

Many different entities order and use criminal records. These general users can be subdivided into three primary categories:

- Criminal justice agencies (federal and state law enforcement, and courts systems)
- Other than criminal justice agencies who are required by law to use criminal records, and;
- Other than criminal justice agencies (the private sector) that order and use criminal records on their own accord.

These are not idle category distinctions. The records obtained by the first two groups are more national in scope than the last group. The first two broad groupings are criminal justice agencies or groups that have been granted statutory authority to use non-public criminal records.

There is a perhaps confusing but important point to be made here. Criminal justice agency records are maintained for criminal justice purposes and are part of the FBI system (see Chapter 7). But, criminal justice agency criminal records can be either public or non-public. Whether or not they are open—or partially open—to the public is dependent upon the inherent restrictions of that criminal justice agency.

Criminal Justice Agencies

Among the more prominent criminal justice agency users of criminal records are:

- Court systems, e.g., judges, prosecutors
- Government agencies involved in the justice system

These users have unfettered access to all non-public and public criminal record databases.

Non-Criminal Justice Agencies As Required by Law

Three types of prominent private agencies use criminal records due to statutory requirements.

- Government Regulatory Agencies, e.g., FAA.

- Occupational Licensing Bodies, e.g., teaching, nursing, casino or racetrack workers, liquor sales.

- Financial and Commerce Agencies, e.g., financial institutions, insurance and securities related institutions.

The General Public

As described earlier, this group includes entities that order and use criminal records on their own accord. Typically, this group includes:

- Leasing institutions—both residential and commercial

- Businesses, for "relationship" purposes, e.g., mergers and acquisitions, evaluating business partners

- Personal users, e.g., checking out daughter's new boyfriend, father's new girlfriend, great-grandpa's new young girlfriend

- Miscellaneous uses such as genealogy (no, not the study of automatic garage door openers) and skip tracing

However, by far and away, the **largest group** of non-criminal justice users of criminal records is:

- Employers

Not only are they the biggest group, they are the fastest growing group.

Clearly, the two biggest users of criminal records are governments (federal and state law enforcement and courts systems) and employers. While this book can be used by governmental entities or the idly curious, most discussion will concentrate on employer use of criminal records.

When Non-Criminal Justice Agencies are Granted Access to FBI Records – The Fingerprint Dilemma

As explained in Chapter 2, The FBI's cache of criminal records is extensive, nationwide, but not easily accessible by non-law-enforcement entities. Employers who have been granted access to FBI records have not been granted the silver bullet it might seem. The reason is that in most instances, the search must include "positive identification." This means fingerprints. Fingerprints are messy in the figurative as well as literal sense. To begin with, they're physically messy if the standard ink and paper method is used; there is also an art to getting good prints. The transfer and verification process is messy. There's the problem of obtaining an acceptable set of prints. Next, there's getting those prints into the proper hands at the FBI. Then, there is the waiting for the response. All this is time consuming and expensive.

Automated Fingerprint Identification Systems

If you do not meet the fingerprint requirements, don't bet that the FBI will give you the records. Hope appears on the horizon for non-criminal justice agencies, though. **Automated Fingerprint Identification Systems (AFIS)** are coming and the War on Terrorism has helped speed up their development. At its heart, an AFIS is an automated system for searching fingerprint files and transmitting fingerprint images. AFIS's computerized equipment can scan fingerprint impressions and automatically extract and digitize ridge details and other identifying characteristics in sufficient detail. This enables the AFIS computer's searching and matching components to distinguish a single fingerprint from innumerable fingerprints previously scanned and digitally stored. Digital fingerprint images generated by AFIS equipment can be transmitted electronically to remote sites, eliminating the necessity of mailing fingerprint cards. Remote access to AFIS will make fingerprint files accessible to more users. So, this new system reduces the need for manually searching fingerprint files, while the new scanning capability increases the speed and accuracy of ten-print processing, the old standard which includes arrest fingerprint cards and non-criminal justice applicant fingerprint cards.

There are three types of AFIS finger scan capture devices. Current AFIS systems only use optical scanners while the other simple identification systems are developing. The three scanning methods are:

1. **Optical**

    The finger is placed against a platen (usually made of glass, often with a soft coating), and a picture of the finger is captured. These devices have become much smaller and less expensive over the past few years. There are more than fifty vendors of optical scanners.

2. **Ultrasound**

    While ultrasound technologies have been around for many years, their use in fingerprinting is not widespread. When a finger is placed on the glass platen, a buzzing is heard and a vibration felt as the ultrasonic scan is taken. Since sound is used, direct contact with the platen is not needed. The scanning will work through a thin latex glove or on very dirty fingers.

3. **Chip-Based**

    Users place their fingers directly on silicon chip-based sensor. The sensor has the surface area of a postage stamp.

Until these AFIS and other new technologies become less costly, many employers in industries with mandatory criminal record fingerprint checks will, initially, obtain the much faster and cheaper state or county criminal record using non-biometric identifiers (name, date of birth, address, etc). Then, once the hiring decision has been made, there is a follow up fingerprint check to remain in compliance with the law. So, an employer might hire an individual after obtaining the faster criminal information and ask the applicant to affirm that they had no disqualifying offenses. In the rare instance in which the subsequent fingerprint search discloses a disqualifying offense, the employer would terminate the employee for falsification of the employment application.

In any event, if you are an employer in a specialized or regulated industry, you will probably wish to order a cheaper and timelier criminal record. If so, look for a service provider with expertise in your industry (see Chapter 10 – *Advice on Using a Criminal Record Vendor*).

Chapter 4

Should You Use Criminal Records ... The Great Criminal Record Debate

Memories are the key not to the past, but to the future.

—Corrie ten Boom

I believe that men, at heart, are good.

—Anne Frank

These are amazing statements considering the sources.

Corrie ten Boom, a Dutch woman, was born in 1892 and put into a concentration camp for sheltering individuals—Jewish individuals who had done nothing wrong—from certain death. Her most noble, selfless and courageous deeds were rewarded with a stint in Ravensbruck Concentration camp. There she watched her sister die. Her father also died, and Corrie's brother died of a disease contracted at the camp. In a time and place of profound hunger, betraying the locale of hiding Jews meant sacrificing one's food. Hiding Jews brought hideous reprisals. And yet, Corrie and her family hid Jews on principle.

The story of Anne Frank is well known. Anne died in a concentration camp, and yet, her amazing statement: "I believe that men, at heart, are good." She was a better person than I.

And yet, we can agree with her. The problem is, the quote is not speaking in absolutes, but rather in "averages." The average person is good. The heck of it is, averages are averages. An old mentor of mine was fond of saying "a man can drown in a river that, on average, is an inch deep." While on average, man is good, there are some deep, deep holes out there that will drown you.

The Debate Over the Use of Criminal Records

And so, to paraphrase Corrie ten Boom's quote, are "memories—perhaps court-recorded criminal record memories—the key not to the past, but to the future?" Or, is Anne Frank's sentiment correct, that "men, at heart, are good"—good and perhaps undeserving of having past transgressions interfere with their unfettered pursuit of life?

This is the debate played out in American society and legal systems today: "given that most individuals are good, even those who have previously done bad, should we not let bygones be bygones and suppress previous records of criminal behavior?"

Why shouldn't we? We have a system that is pretty decent at catching wrongdoers. Crime usually does not pay. Thus, wrongdoers are usually caught. They are put before a jury of their peers and guilt or innocence is—correctly or incorrectly—adjudicated. Provided the individual is deemed guilty of the offense with which he has been accused, a penalty—too harsh, just right or too lenient—is rendered. The individual serves whatever penalty is meted out (if any) and is judged to have "paid his debt to society." Justice has been served. The victims have received retribution in relation to the offense. The slate has been wiped clean. While law enforcement, in case of a repeat offense, might need to have record of this information, why in the world should this information be "public information?"

As will be seen in Chapter 16, not all states have come down on the same side of the fence on this issue.

Private Individuals Ordering On Other Individuals

On a more practical level, let's look at the parties who may want to access criminal information on others: a single, working mother hiring a nanny, an employer hiring a delivery person, and a government agency dispensing aid. Each has different needs.

There are instances when a private citizen may wish to determine whether another citizen has a criminal record. This can be done fairly easily because criminal records are *public records*. See Section 2 for access methods.

The Privacy Objection

Thus far, the discussion has centered on the *use* of criminal records, not the question of their *availability*. Availability questions actually precede the use question and are easier to answer.

Public Records and Privacy

Criminal records are a matter of public record. The accusation, trial and sentencing are public record. The Supreme Court, in a 1976 decision (Paul v. Davis, 424 U.S. 693) effectively ended debate on whether the records were public or private. Interestingly, this case revolved around a criminal charge that was dismissed. In the Paul v. Davis case, a flyer identifying "active shoplifters" was distributed to local merchants. The flyer included a photograph of Edward C. Davis III, who had been arrested on a shoplifting charge. When the charge was dismissed, Davis brought an action against Edgar Paul, the local chief of police. Davis alleged that the distribution of the flyer had stigmatized him and deprived him of his constitutional rights.

In a 5-to-3 decision, the Court held that Davis had not been deprived of any constitutional rights under the Due Process Clause. The Court also emphasized that constitutional privacy interests did not cover Davis's claims. The Court stated that the constitutional right to privacy was limited to matters relating to "marriage, procreation, contraception, family relationships, and child rearing and education." The publication of records of official acts, such as arrests, did not fall under the rubric of privacy rights.

And so, criminal records are, as a rule, accessible. Some may find this lack of privacy disturbing, almost "Orwellian." After all, government agencies have collected all this sensitive information and it is available to the general public. I believe the public debate on this aspect of privacy has become somewhat convoluted.

Originally, the information was public to protect citizens. The thought was that the government could not secretly charge a person, convict them, and put them away. The charges, court decision, and penalties were public.

Consider the former Soviet Union. Now there was a society with a lot of privacy. A person could be accused, sentenced, shipped to refrigerator country and be worked to death in privacy. The crime of which the person was accused? Private information. The verdict? The sentence? Private. The point is, privacy is not an automatic good. If you are considering in-home care for an elderly parent, a business venture with a neighbor or thinking about hiring a nanny for your child, you may well appreciate the fact that these records are public rather than private.

This doesn't mean you can use the records for any purpose once you obtain them. If you use them or attempt to use them for an illegal purpose such as blackmail, you may join the ranks of potential blackmailees. Generally speaking, criminal records are accessible by private citizens on other private citizens. These records may be used for any legal purpose.

Employers and Job Applicants

The workplace—this is where the real debate rages. Is it moral, ethical…or just *right* for employers to order criminal records?

Let's get down to brass tacks. No one objects to an employer *ordering* a criminal record on a job applicant. The objection is really that the employer may *use* the information, i.e., refuse to hire the applicant based on information on the criminal record.

So, why do some people believe employers should never use information obtained on a criminal record to discriminate against an applicant? The reasoning is this: if the person is applying for a job, then that must mean they have completed their punishment. This of course assumes they have not fled prosecution, escaped from incarceration or a seeking a job they are barred from holding. They have paid the price for their offense and their debt to society is over. Furthermore, to deny them a job is to nudge them into obtaining the money they need in one of two undesirable alternatives:

1. They depend on the state or the kindness of family, friends or charity for the rest of their life.

2. They steal or otherwise unlawfully obtain what they need to live.

So, in other words, the argument is that after someone has paid their debt to society, it would be immoral, wrong or at a minimum, vindictive to continue to punish an individual for something they've already paid for.

And, not only is it wrong from a moral standpoint, it's wrong from a public policy standpoint because the continued punishment for past undesirable behavior will not only fail to deter but may *cause* future undesirable behavior.

It's a compelling, logical argument. Do you buy it? What would your reaction be in the following scenario? Assume you had your children in a daycare that—in a spirit of progressive rehabilitative fervor—hired a convicted pedophile who had done his time. Remember, the pedophile has paid his debt to society. Would your kids be at the daycare come Monday morning? Humph. Societal Neanderthal.

While most states have enacted laws to prevent convicted pedophiles from working with children, the example is instructive. This is not a cut and dried issue—although job-relatedness is a key consideration and is discussed at length in Chapter 15. Consider another angle to the debate: the nature of the offense.

Ann Frank and Corrie ten Boom were not just ushered off to prison camps. They were arrested, found guilty and shipped off. Their "crimes" were documented—and their crimes were "on the books." So, the fact that something is on the books and the person has been found guilty is something for the beholder to consider. And if you think this is something that could never happen here, think again, maybe about Rosa Parks—or another person writing a letter from a Birmingham jail—and the "crimes" for which they were "guilty."

We aren't all fighting for universal justices. Consider this fellow. He was ticketed one night after he went to help anther person who had been knocked down by a police horse. The police use the horses to control crowds, but when the horse rears up—as horses are wont to do—the police start arresting people and say it is to protect their officers from getting hurt.

We might laugh at a criminal record for "failure to yield to a police horse." An employer, however, might not laugh when reading a criminal record of "obstruction of police duty." In Chapter 15, federal hiring guidelines will be discussed. These guidelines emphasize that employers have some responsibility to ascertain that the individual actually committed the crime for which they were arrested or convicted.

The point here is that once it has been determined that the individual actually committed the action of which he was accused, the nature of the crime itself should be considered. "Obstruction of police duties" sounds pretty bad, but not determining the facts of the situation could cause an employer to reject the best candidate or deny a promotion to a deserving employee.

This issue is subjective. It is not a matter of law so much as it is judgment, common sense and fairness. Subjective as it may be, there are several cut and dried circumstances relating to the record that can be used as a factor in your decision making process, either as an employer or individual thinking about where you stand on the issue.

There are also several other criteria that, perhaps while they are not so clear cut, can be used, again, either to evaluate an applicant if you are an employer or to think out where you stand on the issue the next time this aspect of privacy comes front and center as a political issue. Several schools of thought advocate considering the criteria of whether there was a *victim* of the crime and if so, were they the victim of a *violent* crime.

Victimless and Non Violent Crime

Outside of the job relatedness, fairness and the true facts of the record itself—and another way to view the seriousness of the crime—is to consider who or what was injured. Was there a victim? Was the victim injured by violence or "merely" inconvenienced?

Victimless Crime

Some dispute there is such a thing. Others insist that an illegal transaction between two consenting adults is, by definition, victimless.

Drug possession, prostitution and sexual mores offenses are the most common crimes described by some as victimless. Proponents argue that there are no victims of this "crime." Others insist that there are indeed victims such as the Drug Enforcement Agent killed in the line of duty or the society as a whole through the degradation of morals (as defined by them, of course.) The victimless crime proponent would argue that these alleged victims were victimized by bad law, and not by the lawbreaker.

Violent Crime

More and more, a distinction is being made today regarding whether a crime was "violent." For example, some "3 strikes and you're in prison" laws take into consideration whether one or all of the strikes were violent.

There is some credence to classifying a crime as violent or non-violent. However, the distinction has its limitations. Consider the following true story.

Violent Crime, Victimless Crime and Damned Crime

I have a co-worker friend who brought her two-year old to daycare before coming to work. She parked her car, ran her daughter into the room right inside the door, and came back to her car within four minutes to find her purse had been stolen. Inside her purse was the typical stuff: drivers license, credit cards, cell phone and checkbook—as well as an undeveloped roll of pictures taken over the course of a month of her daughter and family. Also, on this day, she had a ring that had belonged to her husband's grandmother. The diamond ring wasn't worth a fortune, but it was the only thing of the grandmother's they had.

Within the hour, the thief was video taped purchasing over $500 of merchandise using one of the stolen credit cards. $4,000 in bad checks followed in the days and weeks to follow.

Everyday at lunch, my co-worker drove across town to her credit union to sign affidavits as the bad checks rolled in. She worked with all her credit card issuers and spent some pleasant time in the State Department of Health making sure her birth certificate was notarized in all the right places so she could move on to the lines and waiting rooms of the friendly, helpful and courteous Department of Motor Vehicles to replace her driving license. She also spent some quality time at the local office of the Social Security Administration getting her social security card replaced. While without identification, she needed lots of cash for purchases—from a bank account soaked by bad checks.

Meanwhile, she visited the businesses that had accepted the bad checks and asked for video and witnesses to identify the thief. The police were bemused by these efforts—it happens all the time and the thief is rarely caught. In this case, thanks to my co-worker's prodding, cajoling—and frankly, investigative work—the thief was arrested and received a $200 fine and a suspended sentence for writing a bad check. There were no charges filed for the actual theft, and the film, ring, purse and billfold were never found.

I dare you to tell my co-worker that we should really be spending more money on law enforcement in eradicating wild marijuana plants and enforcing moral turpitude in desolate areas at 2:00 AM.

I double-dare you to tell her that a non-violent, suspended sentence, fraudulent check charge is no big deal.

Section 2

Where Criminal Records Are Found

This Section presents an in-depth analysis of the three primary government levels where criminal records can be accessed; county, state, and federal.

This Section also presents an overview of criminal-related records including prison, parole, probation, sex offender, and military records.

Finally, this Section examines how to access criminal records, the criminal record vendor, what services they may offer, and how to tell the difference between a good one and a not-so-good one.

Chapter 5

Criminal Records at the County Level

We have a criminal jury system which is superior to any in the world; and its efficiency is only marred by the difficulty of finding twelve men every day who don't know anything and can't read.

—Mark Twain

Court Basics

Before trudging into your local county courthouse and demanding to view a criminal record document, you should first be aware of some basic court procedures. Whether the case is filed in a state court, county court, municipal court, or federal court, each case follows a similar process.

In a **criminal case**, the plaintiff is a government jurisdiction. The Government brings the action against the defendant for violation of one or more of its statutes.

Statewide Courts Structure

The county courts that oversee felony cases are actually part of the state court systems. Misdemeanor cases are held at local courts that can be either be part of the state court system or a municipal or town court.

The secret to determining where a state court case may be located is to understand how the court system is structured in that particular state.

The general structure of all state court systems has four parts:

1. Appellate courts

2. Intermediate appellate courts

3. General jurisdiction trial courts

4. Limited jurisdiction trial courts

The two highest levels—appellate and intermediate appellate courts—only hear cases on appeal from the trial courts. Opinions of these appellate courts are of interest primarily to attorneys seeking legal precedents for new cases.

General jurisdiction trial courts usually handle a full range of civil and criminal litigation. These courts usually handle felonies and larger civil cases.

Limited jurisdiction trial courts come in two varieties. First, many limited jurisdiction courts handle smaller civil claims (usually $10,000 or less), misdemeanors, and pretrial hearings for felonies. Second, some of these courts—sometimes called special jurisdiction courts—are limited to one type of litigation. For example, consider the Court of Claims in New York. This court only handles liability cases against the state.

Some states, Iowa for instance, have consolidated their general and limited jurisdiction court structure into one combined court system. In other states there may be a further distinction between state-supported courts and municipal courts. In New York, for example, nearly 1,300 Justice Courts handle local ordinance and traffic violations, including DWI.

Generalizations should not be made about where specific types of cases are handled in the various states. Depending on the state, misdemeanors, probate, landlord/tenant (eviction), domestic relations, and juvenile cases may be handled in either or both the general and limited jurisdiction courts.

How Courts Maintain Records

Case Numbering

When a case is filed—or a warrant is issued—it is assigned a case number. This is the primary indexing method in every court. Therefore, in searching for case records, you will need to know—or find—the applicable case number. If you have the number in good form already, your search should be fast and reasonably inexpensive.

You should be aware that case numbering procedures are not consistent throughout a state court system. One district may assign numbers by district while another may assign numbers by location (division) within the district, or by judge. Keep in mind, case numbers appearing in legal text citations may not be adequate for searching unless they appear in the proper form for the particular court where you are searching.

Docket Sheet

All basic case information is entered onto docket sheets.

Information from cover sheets and from documents filed as a case goes forward is recorded on the docket sheet. Thus, the docket sheet contains an outline of the case history from initial filing to its current status. While docket sheets differ somewhat in format, the basic information contained on a docket sheet is consistent from court to court. All docket sheets contain:

- Name of court, including location (division) and the judge assigned;
- Case number and case name;
- Names of all plaintiffs and defendants/debtors;
- Names and addresses of attorneys for the plaintiff or debtor;
- Nature and cause (e.g., statute) of action.

Court Computerization

Most courts are computerized, which means that docket sheet data is entered into a computer system. Within a state or judicial district, the courts *may* be linked together via a single computer system.

Docket sheets from cases closed before the advent of computerization may not be in the computer system. For pre-computer era cases, most courts keep summary case information on microfilm, microfiche, or index cards.

At present, images of actual case documents are not generally available on computer. Courts are still experimenting with electronic filing and imaging of court documents. Generally, documents are only available to be photocopied. You may inquire about where you must go for photocopies by contacting the court where the case records are located.

Author's Tip—

Each state's court system is profiled in Chapter 17 – *State Profiles*. The state court's profile will tell where and what records can be found at the local level. Also, we note which courts offer online access to their records.

Certain Court Records are Reported to the State

Each state has its own rules regarding what records a court must report to that state's central records repository, and when.

It would seem logical that searching the state central repository would be the easy solution when searching for criminal records. However, there are access restrictions and pitfalls, as you will learn in Chapter 6 – *Criminal Record at the State Level.* For quick reference, turn to appendix pages 279-281 where you can read the State Required Data Chart and the State Prohibited Access Chart.

Chapter 6

Criminal Records at the State Level

Facts do not cease to exist because they are ignored.

—Aldous Huxley

The State Central Repository

All states have a central repository of criminal records. Most states make this repository available to the public. The state repository maintains criminal history records of those individuals who have been subject to that state's criminal justice system. A state's record repository will not include records of crimes its citizens committed in other states. The information at the state repository is obtained from local county, parish and municipal courts as well as from law enforcement.

A *Central Repository* is defined as the database (or the agency housing the database) that maintains criminal history records on all offenders in the state. Records include fingerprint files and files containing identification segments, and notations of arrests and dispositions. Although usually housed in the Department of Public Safety, often it is the State Police or other state agency that maintains the central repository.

The central repository is generally responsible for state-level identification of arrestees, and the repository commonly serves as the central control terminal for contact with FBI record systems. Inquiries from local agencies for a national record check—usually for criminal justice purposes or firearm check—are routed to the FBI via the state central repository. It should be noted here that not all states conduct a national FBI check.

In summary, the source of the vast majority of any state's records is from county courts and law enforcement. The crime trail begins when a criminal action is first processed at the local or county level then it is gradually forwarded to the state repository. What information is reported, when it is reported, and how it is reported will all affect the quality and completeness of state data. The charts in the Appendix give information on what is required.

Also, since states are dependent on counties for case information, the state depository may not have the latest information available, e.g., they may have the arrest information, but be lacking the disposition.

Unified Courts

Several states have unified court searches. In these states the administrative office of the courts for the state have joined all the county courts into one searchable system. Unlike the typical state repository, this is not a law enforcement system.

A unified court search can be a particularly useful tool in those states that do not permit a state repository search. However, be aware that the value of a unified court search varies by state. In some states, a few counties may not be included. In other states, there is no uniformity with respect to the length of time criminal activity is archived. For example, one county may have cases dating back for seven years, while another county may have only two years of history.

Examples of some of the states that offer a form of a unified search are:

- Alabama

- Colorado

- North Carolina

It should be noted that some criminal record vendors, through proprietary processes, are able to offer "all county" searches in additional states.

Non-Uniformity of State Systems

As you might expect, state statutes governing dissemination of public criminal history records are as varied as those statutes dealing with non-public information. A few states have no statutory provisions setting statewide policies on access by non-criminal justice agencies; in these states, the Federal Department of Justice regulations control access and use. In a few other states, the statute simply delegates to a designated official the authority to issue rules and regulations on dissemination. In states that do have laws dealing with the subject, the statutory approaches vary. In Florida and other "open record" states, anyone can obtain access to criminal history records for any purpose. In Tennessee, which prohibits access and use except for limited purposes specifically authorized by statute, it is a criminal offense to release criminal history records for unauthorized purposes. The other states fall somewhere in between, and as pointed out earlier, those states with release requirements are hard to categorize.

States that release criminal records to the general public:

• Colorado	• Connecticut
• Florida	• Hawaii
• Iowa	• Idaho
• Kansas	• Maine
• Massachusetts	• Michigan
• Minnesota	• Missouri
• Montana	• Nebraska
• Oregon	• Oklahoma
• Pennsylvania	• South Carolina
• Texas	• Washington
• Wisconsin	

States that release criminal records to the general public—with some form of a release from the subject of the search:

• Alabama	• Arkansas
• Delaware	• District of Columbia
• Illinois	• Maryland
• Nevada	• New Hampshire
• New Mexico	• North Dakota
• Ohio	• South Dakota
• Utah	• West Virginia
• Wyoming	

States that require statutory authority to access their records:

• Alaska	• Arizona
• California	• Georgia
• Indiana	• Kentucky
• Louisiana	• Mississippi
• New Jersey	• New York
• North Carolina	• Rhode Island
• Tennessee	• Vermont
• Virginia	

State Statutory Provisions for Access to FBI Records

Unlike the disparity between state repositories, there are some patterns and similarities among state provisions pertaining to access to FBI records under Department of Justice regulations. To begin with, the Federal regulations do not place restrictions on the dissemination of conviction records or open arrest records (arrest records with no recorded disposition) less than one year old. Non-conviction records may be disseminated for any purpose authorized by statute, ordinance, executive order, or court ruling. This includes favorable dispositions, including decisions not to refer or prosecute charges, indefinite postponements, and open arrest records over a year old and not actively pending. Most of the states have followed this approach of treating conviction records differently from non-conviction records.

Commonly, the states place few or no restrictions on the dissemination of conviction records. Also, a number of states do not restrict the dissemination of open arrest records less than one year old. Non-conviction records are restricted to a greater degree, and in some states non-conviction records may not be disseminated for non-criminal justice purposes, or they may be disseminated *only* for particular purposes, under specified circumstances.

Statutory Provisions by Category of Need

Another similarity among many states is that the statutory provisions do not specifically identify which non-criminal justice agencies or organizations may obtain criminal history records. Instead, these states define classes or types of agencies or organizations that may obtain certain records, or the state may define a specified purpose. So, some states may authorize the use of criminal history records for any occupational licensing or employment purpose, while others authorize such use only for screening applicants for high-risk occupations, such as those involving the public safety, supervision of children, or custody of cash, valuable property, or sensitive personal information. A state's statutes may define permitted purposes in specific terms, or more general terms. Out-of-state or federal agencies may also fall under a state's special rules, having to conform just as in-state, private, and governmental agencies do. Many state-specific rules are explained in that state's profile, found in the Chapter 17 - *State Profiles*.

Need to Know Standards

Many of the laws require that certain agencies or organizations must be able to show specific legal authority under other statutory provisions to obtain criminal records. This helps to prevent those who are not authorized from gaining access to restricted records. Often, the need for the record must be approved by a designated board, council, or official. These statutory provisions that require separate legal authority for certain types of agencies vary considerably from state to state. The requirement may simply provide that the requestor must be "authorized by law" or must have "legal authority," or that the records must be necessary for a "lawful purpose." Such provisions are interpreted in some states as authorizing the dissemination of criminal records for employment and occupational licensing purposes where the employing or licensing agencies are required by law to screen for applicants who are not of "good moral character." Other state criminal record statutes, however, authorize the release of records for non-criminal justice purposes only if the requesting agency is "expressly authorized by some other provision of state or federal law to obtain criminal records for use in the course of official duties." This is a much stricter standard. Still stricter provisions authorize the release of criminal records only pursuant to statutory provisions that expressly refer to criminal conduct or to criminal records. These may contain requirements, exclusions, or limitations based upon such conduct or records.

Where prior approval by a council, board, or designated official is required for the release of criminal records for non-criminal justice purposes, the designated standard for approval varies among the states. For example, to determine who may have access, criminal record laws in New Hampshire and South Dakota delegate general discretion to the director of the criminal history record repository. Massachusetts' law provides that the Criminal History Systems Board must find that the public interest in releasing criminal records to particular non-criminal justice requesters outweighs the security and privacy interests of the record subject.

Several states require that the record subject must consent in writing to any release of his or her criminal history record for non-criminal justice purposes.

State and Interstate Dissemination Policies

On close examination, the criminal history record laws in many states provide only the framework for the state's policies on dissemination of law enforcement records. Specific legal authority for particular agencies or organizations to obtain criminal records may be set out in widely separate statutory provisions, executive orders, or even local ordinances. In addition, the actual policies and practices of particular states may be set out in regulations or may be based upon written or unwritten repository policies. These policies and practices often provide for more restrictive dissemination approaches than the criminal record laws require them to be.

Additionally, concerning interstate dissemination, the fact that most states' dissemination laws are more restrictive than the Federal standard makes it possible for authorized Federal and state non-criminal justice agencies to legally obtain state-contributed records from the FBI for purposes for which they could not, in some cases, obtain the records directly from the states in which the records originated. Georgia's state record repository recently closed a loophole in their system that had allowed access to the national Wants and Warrants lists. For $3.00, requesters received what could be perceived as "criminal information"—often before an arrest, and before a disposition. In most state systems this information is prohibited from the public eye.

Suffice it to say, state statutory provisions for access to FBI records and their dissemination—interstate and otherwise—are complex and filled with nuance.

A New and Controversial California Bill

As of January 1, 2002, a new California bill, AB #655, redefines the act of requesting a criminal record as an "investigative consumer report." On page 136, read details of this controversial new state law and how it affects the use of criminal records in the workplace.

> **Author's Tip—**
>
> For more information, an excellent source for statistics and inter-relationships is the *Compendium of State Privacy and Security Legislation* published by the U.S. Department of Justice Office of Justice Programs, Bureau of Justice Statistics. This compendium, as well as other statistical analyses can be found at http://www.ojp.usdoj.gov/bjs/.

Chapter 7

Criminal Records at the Federal Level

For a nation which has an almost evil reputation for bustle, bustle, bustle, and rush, rush, rush, we spend an enormous amount of time standing around in line in front of windows, just waiting.

—Robert Benchley

This chapter examines two primary and distinctly different locations of federally maintained criminal records—the US District Court System and the FBI.

The *Federal Criminal Records* found at the US District Courts are open to the public (for now). The records maintained by the FBI are primarily non-public records. They are only available to government law enforcement agencies and to those other groups who have been granted statutory authority to access the records.

Federal Criminal Records and the US District Courts

Federal criminal records are a result of an individual committing a federal crime. An example of a federal crime would be kidnapping, hijacking a plane, and increasingly, many crimes involving illegal drugs and the activities facilitating drug trafficking.

Federal criminal records in the United States result from federal district courts and federal appellate courts. There are ninety-four (94) federal judicial districts. A district never crosses state lines, although a state may contain several districts. Likewise, a district may be subdivided into divisions. In fact, there are 296 divisional federal criminal courts that.

Moving up the hierarchy, the ninety-four (94) federal judicial districts are clustered in twelve (12) regional circuits, each of which has a court of appeals that hears criminal appeals from cases in their respective circuits.

How the US District Courts Maintain Records

Case Numbering

When a case is filed with a federal court, a case number is assigned. This is the primary indexing method. Therefore, when searching for case records, you will need to know or find the applicable case number. If you have the number in good form already, your search should be fast and reasonably inexpensive.

You should be aware that case numbering procedures are not consistent throughout the Federal Court System: one judicial district may assign numbers by district while another may assign numbers by location, i.e. the division, within the judicial district, or by judge. Remember that case numbers appearing in legal text citations may not be adequate for searching unless they appear in the proper form for the particular court.

Assignment of Cases

Traditionally, cases were assigned within a district or division by county. Although this is still true in most states, the introduction of computer systems to track dockets has led to a more flexible approach to case assignment, as is the case in Minnesota and Connecticut. Rather than blindly assigning all cases from a county to one judge, their districts are using random numbers and other logical methods to balance caseloads among their judges.

This trend may appear to confuse the case search process. Actually, the only problem that the searcher may face is to figure out where the case records themselves are located. Finding cases has become significantly easier with the wide availability of PACER from remote access and on-site terminals in each court location with the same district-wide information. Note that Chapter 18 – *U.S. District Courts* lists all the Federal District Courts, Divisional Courts, and the counties served.

Computerized Indexes are Available

Computerized courts generally index each case record by the names of some or all the parties to the case—the plaintiffs and defendants (debtors in Bankruptcy Court) as well as by case number. Therefore, when you search by name you will first receive a listing of all cases in which the name appears, both as plaintiff and defendant.

All the basic case information is entered onto docket sheets and into computerized systems like **PACER**. PACER, the acronym for **P**ublic **A**ccess to **E**lectronic **C**ourt **R**ecords, provides docket information online for open cases at most US District courts and all US Bankruptcy courts. Access is via either a commercial dial-up system (user fee of $.60 a minute) or through the Internet (user fee is $.07 per page). Cases for the US Court of Federal Claims are also available.

Four districts offer free Internet access to their court records. They are Arkansas Western District, Idaho District, Indiana Southern District, and Pennsylvania Eastern District.

As each court controls its own computer system and case information database; there are variations among jurisdictions as to how the information is offered.

> **Author's Tip—**
>
> For more information about how to search individual federal courts, including information on the electronic access systems including PACER, RACER, and The National US Party Index, turn to Chapter 18 – *US District Courts*.

Recent Restrictions Imposed to Electronically Accessed Criminal Documents

Established in 1939, the Administrative Office of the US Courts provides service to the federal courts in three essential areas: administrative support, program management, and policy development. It is charged with implementing the policies of the Judicial Conference of the United States and supporting the network of Conference committees.

In September 2001, the Judicial Conference took action regarding Internet and online dial-up systems used to access criminal records. The Conference mandated that **images of documents** filed in a criminal case could no longer be viewed online by the public. However, criminal case documents could still be viewed in-person or ordered by mail. Further, the mandate **did not restrict access to docket sheets.** Docket information is still available in all courts, except the US District Court of South Dakota who has removed all criminal record information from PACER.

The reality is that few PACER courts permit viewing document images—PACER courts primarily offer access to docket sheets. Most of the document images of criminal record filings that are available online appear on the Case Management-Electronic Case Files (CM/ECF) system. This new electronic case management system gives each federal court the option of permitting case documents—pleadings, motions, petitions—to be filed with the court over the Internet. CM/ECF allows courts to maintain case documents in electronic form. Also, CM/ECF allows courts to decide who can view the document, and typically permit attorneys and others involved with cases to do so. Therefore, the Judicial Conference ruling affects the ability of the general public to view the documents. CM/ECF implementation in the bankruptcy courts and district courts has already started; appellate court implementation is scheduled in 2003.

Policy Under Review in 2003

The Judicial Conference made a point of committing to a re-examination of this new policy by September 2003. It is likely that the Judicial Conference will consider ways to insure that certain entities (employers??) are offered the ability to view criminal record image documents, on a permissible need basis. At present, there was no time frame given for compliance with the mandate mentioned above. To date, some courts have fully complied, some have not, and some courts have document images available only for certain years. Most courts are proceeding with implementation of CM/ECF. For more information, visit http://www.uscourts.gov/news.html.

Other Federal Criminal Record Trends

Federal criminal records have long been considered a distant third in value to state and county criminal records. This perception continues, partially due to the inexact matching, partially because of the limited scope and number of records present. The number of records is, however, growing extremely rapidly. Looking at the rate of growth for federal prisoners is instructive.

Under President Reagan, the number of federal prisoners grew from 24,363 to 49,928. Under President Bush, the number increased to 80,259 by 1992. That nearly doubled to 147,126 under President Clinton. This increase is largely a result of new drug laws, many passed during Clinton's administration. Laws setting mandatory prison sentences, coupled with increased spending for new prisons and law enforcement officials, are blamed by most for the increase. While still small compared to the approximately two million Americans incarcerated, federal incarceration is increasing.

About 58 percent of federal prisoners are there for drug offenses. Whether you are for or against the "war on drugs," that is an eye-opening number.

> **Author's Tip—**
>
> Lack of good identifiers—and the time, expense and legal liabilities this lack may cause—as well as the limited number of records present keep federal criminal records from being used by the vast majority of US employers. As a federal court's jurisdiction can include a population of millions, the chance of a name error on a federal record is greater than at the county level. More care must be taken when connecting a name to a federal record.

The FBI NCIC Database

The FBI database's formal name is the *National Crime Information Center (NCIC)* and is an automated database of criminal justice and justice-related records maintained by the FBI.

The database includes the "hot files" of wanted and missing persons, stolen vehicles and identifiable stolen property, including firearms. Two important points about the NCIC are—

- The NCIC is not nearly as complete as portrayed in the movies. Because of the chain of events that must happen in multiple jurisdictions in order for a crime to appear in NCIC, many records of crime do not make it.

- The information the NCIC does have is predominantly solely arrest-related. The disposition of most crimes in NCIC must be obtained by going to the adjudicating jurisdiction. This can be an important issue to employers as will be detailed later in the federal and state legal chapters.

This national database is currently evolving due to the National Crime Prevention and Privacy Compact, which is discussed on the following pages.

Source of the NCIC Data

The sources of the FBI's information are the counties and states that contribute information as well as the federal justice agencies. Public criminal records are found at federal court repositories (for federal crimes), state repositories, and county courthouses. As discussed in a previous chapter, private citizens and businesses, i.e., non-criminal justice agencies, cannot, as a general rule, obtain access to the national FBI database. However, because it is perhaps the most well known repository of criminal records, some discussion is in order.

Access to NCIC files is through central control terminal operators in each state. The operators are connected to NCIC via dedicated telecommunications lines maintained by the FBI. Local agencies and officers on-the-beat can access the state control terminal via the state law enforcement network. Inquiries are based on name and other non-fingerprint identification. Also, most criminal history inquiries of the Interstate Identification Index (usually referred to as "III" or the "Triple I") system are made via the NCIC telecommunications system.

Interstate Identification System

In the discussion of the NCIC above, the term Interstate Identification System (III or "Triple I") was used. The *Interstate Identification Index (III)* is an "index-pointer" system for the interstate exchange of criminal history records. Under III, the FBI maintains an identification index to persons arrested for felonies or serious misdemeanors under state or federal law. The index includes identification information, (such as name, date of birth, race, and sex), FBI Numbers and State Identification Numbers (SID) from each state holding information about an individual. Search inquiries from criminal justice agencies nationwide are transmitted automatically via state telecommunications networks and the FBI's National Crime Information Center (NCIC) telecommunications lines.

Searches are made on the basis of name and other identifiers. The process is entirely automated and takes approximately five seconds to complete. If a hit is made against the Index, record requests are made using the SID or FBI Number, and data are automatically retrieved from each repository holding records on the individual and forwarded to the requesting agency. As of December 2001, forty-one states participated in III. Responses are provided from FBI files when the state originating the record is not a participant in III.

NCIC data may be provided only for criminal justice and other specifically authorized purposes. For criminal history searches, this includes criminal justice employment, employment by federally chartered or insured banking institutions or securities firms, and use by state and local governments for purposes of employment and licensing pursuant to a state statute approved by the U.S. Attorney General. Inquiries regarding presale firearm checks are included as a criminal justice use.

The bold section in the NCIC definition above is significant. Occasionally, an employer happens upon a "good deal." This good deal usually consists of a friend in law enforcement who obtains criminal records from NCIC and provides them free or sells them to the employer. The problem is that this is illegal, and the Feds have been targeting and prosecuting violators. If you want to check criminal records and have a friend in law enforcement (and want to keep the friend) you should not use the friend as a source of criminal records.

National Crime Prevention and Privacy Compact

The entire FBI record system and infrastructure is currently in a state of transition due to the National Crime Prevention and Privacy Compact. The compact became law when passed by Congress and signed by President Clinton in October 1998. It became effective in April 1999, when ratified by the second state. The compact's purpose is to authorize and require participating state criminal history repositories and the FBI to make all unsealed criminal history records available in response to *authorized* non-criminal justice requests.

This compact is changing the functions and relationship between the FBI and state systems. To understand how, it is helpful to look at past system performance and the new, evolving system.

Before the Compact

Before the compact, arrest fingerprint cards were submitted to the FBI by federal, state and local agencies on a voluntary basis. Law enforcement agencies, primarily local police and sheriff's offices, maintained a system of records specific to their state or locality and submitted duplicate prints of arrested and charged persons to the FBI. In exchange, local authorities received information on the individual's prior nationwide criminal history.

The FBI would report its findings back to the state and maintain the new fingerprint and accompanying data in its criminal history files. The FBI began maintaining this duplicate criminal history file in 1924, and by the late 1990's had over 200 million fingerprint cards on file.

After the Compact

The compact provides a decentralized national records system and is intended to facilitate efficient and effective exchange of criminal records. States must ratify their participation in the compact. Once a state has ratified the compact, they are required to forward criminal record information to the FBI. The FBI, rather than actually storing duplicate information, will instead store the "pointer" information. This information will point the inquiring party to the state holding the information. Therefore, there will be far less duplication of information.

When the system is fully operational nationwide, the III index maintained at the national level will contain personal identification data on individuals whose criminal records are maintained in state criminal record repositories (state offenders) and in the criminal files of the FBI (federal offenders), but it will not contain any charge or disposition information. The index will serve as a "pointer" to refer inquiring criminal justice agencies to the state or federal files where the requested criminal history records are maintained. The records will be exchanged directly between the states and between state and federal criminal justice agencies by means of telecommunications lines linking federal, state, and local criminal justice agencies throughout the country. The laws and policies of the receiving jurisdictions will govern dissemination and use of the records obtained by means of the system. Each state will enforce its own laws and policies within its borders; federal law will govern record dissemination and use by federal agencies.

An excellent review of National Crime Prevention and Privacy Compact can be found at http://www.ojp.usdoj.gov/bjs/abstract/ncppcrm.htm.

Access to NCIC for Non-Criminal Justice Purposes

Background

Certain industries or groups have been granted state or federal authority to access NCIC data. It is suspected that more industries will be granted access as a result of the 2001 War on Terrorism. The industries granted access usually obtain the information through their state system, and usually as a result of state law. A majority of the states now permit access to some criminal history records by some types of non-criminal justice agencies and private entities.

For example, special access rights are increasingly accorded to governmental agencies with national security missions, and to licensing boards and some governmental and private employers screening applicants for sensitive positions, such as those involving public safety, supervision of children or the elderly, or custody of valuable property. There is one commonality: this access usually requires the use of fingerprint cards rather than the standard non-biometric identifiers such as name, date of birth, address, social security number, race, etc.

In the 1970s, Congress attempted to enact federal legislation setting nationwide dissemination standards for state criminal history record systems. These efforts failed. This has resulted in the states having a hodge-podge of statutory schemes. It also resulted in a steadily increasing volume of authorized non-criminal justice use. A national survey conducted in 1998 determined that roughly 35 percent of the fingerprint cards submitted by states to the FBI and processed in Fiscal Year 1997 were for non-criminal justice purposes. The survey found that nine "state" jurisdictions—Delaware, the District of Columbia, Florida, Idaho, Massachusetts, Nevada, New Jersey, Oregon, and Washington—submitted more fingerprint cards during that period for non-criminal justice than for criminal justice purposes.

In most states, nearly every session of the legislature now results in new statutory authority for some new non-criminal justice agency or organization to obtain criminal record checks. These new statutes specifically permit record access for such purposes as public and private employment, occupational licensing, and the issuance of various permits, certifications, and clearances. One area of intense activity is health care.

An Example—Health Care

In the 2001 legislative sessions alone, seventeen states had bills introduced that would require the ordering of criminal records for various types of health care workers. These states were Alabama, Arkansas, California, Colorado, Connecticut, Florida, Georgia, Iowa, Kansas, New Hampshire, New York, North Carolina, South Carolina, Tennessee, Texas, Utah, and Virginia.

What's more, in these seventeen states, there were forty-five bills introduced. This is a result of competing bills and narrow bills addressed to just a segment of the health care industry, e.g., nursing home aides, but not registered nurses.

The states are not the only ones getting into the act. The Feds have their own ideas and are targeting segments of various industries. For example, H.R. 453 was introduced to require criminal background checks on drivers providing Medicaid medical assistance transportation services, but on no one else. The bill did not pass.

Chapter 8

Criminal Offender Records

What's in a name? That which we call a rose
By any other name would smell as sweet
> —William Shakespeare

There are several other types of public records that, while not strictly "criminal records" will disclose past criminal activity. While the information may not be particularly germane or useful for employment screening in all cases, the careful researcher may choose to search these various sources to complement their criminal record check.

Following is a short overview of some "non-criminal—criminal records." Please note that additional information on sex offenders and incarcerations records is provided in the Chapter 17 - *State Profiles*.

Incarceration Records

Federal Incarceration Records

These are records of offenders who have been incarcerated in a federal facility after commission of a federal offense. The information is public record, and the value of this search is that you do not have to know the particular federal court that convicted the individual. The federal incarceration search is nationwide in scope.

The downside of this search is that it will not disclose minor offenses or, at least those that did not result in incarceration.

The Federal Bureau of Prisons offers an inmate locator on its website, http://www.bop.gov/. Click "Inmate Info" at left. This "SENTRY" database also contains information about former inmates, dating back to 1982.

The following article, written by Mr. Lawrence C. Lopez, is an interesting overview of this website. Thank you to Mr. Lopez for allowing us to include the article in this book.

About the Federal Bureau of Prisons Web Site

by Lawrence C. Lopez

While this can be a very useful tool, a few words of warning are in order: it is not search-friendly.

I tested it on a couple of names and found the following:

While it provides name, race and age to the nearest year, it does not have middle initials, Jrs., exact DOBs or other details that can help you determine if the inmate Joe Blow is the same Joe Blow that you are researching.

There does not appear to be any standardized data input provisions. For example, I searched for an inmate whose first name is Natel but could not find him that way -- he was only listed as "N." And testing for the last name "Johnson" I found 66 "Joseph Johnson" entries, and 12 "Joe Johnson" entries as well as three "J. Johnson" entries on inmates whose first names may or may not have been Joe.

Don't use "Senior" or "Jr." or the like when you search. In my tests, the database located two "Charles Keating" entries of ages that seem to correspond to the former Arizona S&L chief & his son. But when I searched for "Charles Keating Junior" or "Jr." or "III", the database told me there were no entries.

Overall, this is a great database, but it takes a fair amount of patience to search properly. For those who have serious searching needs, I would recommend cross-searching the names in PACER, which should show the conviction that put the subject into prison in the first place. Of course, many PACER courts don't go back to 1982. But PACER is SO good and cheap that you might as well run it too, unless all you are looking for is where a current inmate is presently imprisoned.

===================

Lawrence C. Lopez is the chairman of Strategic Research and head of its Northeast operations. Strategic Research specializes in complex civil litigation, due diligence and criminal cases, along with research for news organizations. Mr. Lopez has worked previously with the Associated Press as an investigative reporter and has spent four years as a senior investigator at the Investigative Group International. Mr. Lopez can be reached at http://www.srresearch.com.

State Incarceration Records

Most states allow access to incarceration records. As with Federal incarceration records, these records may offer current and past information regarding an individual's incarceration history.

You will read how to access incarceration records from every state as you read the *State Profiles* chapter. These profiles may indicate free access to limited records is available via the Internet.

Here are two recommended websites that have multiple links to state inmate locaters—

- http://www.corrections.com/links/inmate.html
- http://www.crimetime.com/online.htm —click on criminal records

Parole Records

Federal Records

After serving all or part of their sentence, most federal offenders are paroled. These records are a matter of public record and may prove useful in detecting a previous offense.

State Records

There is usually a central state repository for verification of historical parole information. To track or verify current parolees, you must contact the appropriate State Parole Board.

Probation Records

Federal Records

Some federal offenders are not sentenced to prison, but instead are fined and sentenced to probation. Probation means that all or part of the sentence has been reduced in return for a promise of proper conduct. These records are public, but must be obtained by contacting the Federal Chief Probation Officer in the judicial district where the individual was sentenced.

State Records

Most states do not have a central state repository for the records of individuals currently serving probation. However, as you will learn in the *State Profiles* chapter, a number of the incarceration agency web sites that permit searches of inmates online also have limited searching for former inmates on probation. However, these records do not have the utility of other records.

State Sexual Offender Records

On May 17, 1996, President Clinton signed Megan's Law. Megan's Law goals include:

Sex Offender Registration - Each state and the federal government are compelled to register individuals who have been convicted of sex crimes against children.

Community Notification - Each state and the federal government are compelled to make private and personal information on convicted sex offenders available to the public. Community notification is based on the presumption that it will:

- Assist law enforcement in investigations;
- Establish legal grounds to hold known offenders;
- Deter sex offenders from committing new offenses, and;
- Offer citizens information they can use to protect children from victimization.

The criteria for implementing Megan's Law are left up to the states, with the understanding that the state is to follow certain specific guidelines. Despite the guidelines, what has resulted is disparities among the states' rules—and access. For instance, many states make information on registered offenders available on the Internet or by mail, some only the severe offenders either one or by access methods, and some states barely make the information available at all.

Approximately thirty-three state agencies post their sex offender registry via the Internet. In some cases a state agency may not post the information, although a local law enforcement agency may post for offenders within their jurisdiction only. In some cases, the state agency posts the registry and the local agencies post as well.

Here are three recommended websites that maintain multiple links to state sex offender databases—

- http://www.sexoffender.com
- http://www.parentsformeganslaw.com/html/links.lasso
- http://www.publicrecordsources.com

For more information on a particular state, see the *State Profiles* chapter.

More About Megan's Law—

Megan's Law is named for 7-year-old Megan Kanka who was brutally raped and murdered in Monmouth County, NJ.

Megan's Law, which went into effect on October 31, 1994, requires law enforcement agencies to provide information about convicted sex offenders to community organizations and the public. The law provides that sex offenders are required to register with the police, including offenders who were on parole or probation as of October 31, 1994. Also, repeat offenders, regardless of date, are required to register.

Under Megan's Law, sex offenders are classified in one of three levels or "tiers" based on the severity of their crime as follows: high (Tier 3); moderate (Tier 2); or low (Tier 1).

When a registered sex offender moves into a community, there is a notification process. Neighbors are notified of Tier 3 offenders. Registered community organizations involved with children such as schools, day care centers, and camps are notified of Tier 3 and Tier 2 offenders. Local law enforcement agencies are notified of the presence of all sex offenders.

Residents may visit local law enforcement and review all registered sexual offenders in the community or county. The information provided includes the offender's name, description of offense, personal description, photograph, address, place of employment or school, and a description of the offender's vehicle and license plate number.

Typical offenses include aggravated sexual assault, sexual assault, aggravated criminal sexual contact, endangering the welfare of a child by engaging in sexual conduct, kidnapping, and false imprisonment.

Federal Fugitives

The Federal government—through the U.S. Marshal's Service—maintains files on individuals who are wanted fugitives. These wanted individuals—assuming their guilt—have not yet "paid their debt to society," and needless to say, are probably not a good bet as an employee, business partner or as a prospect for a position requiring responsibility.

There is not a readily available database of federal fugitives open to the private sector. However, as you will see in the *State Profiles* chapter, some state agencies will check with the FBI for outstanding federal warrants, and perhaps out-of-state warrants.

Military Criminal Records

Some individuals are naughty in uniform. Court Marshal information, as well as military incarceration information, is available and may prove useful if the individual in question was in the armed forces.

There are a number of great Internet sites that provide valuable information on obtaining military and military personnel records:

www.nara.gov/regional/mpr.html   The National Personnel Records Center (NPRC), maintained by the National Archives and Records Administration. This site is full of useful information and links.

www.army.mil   The official site of the US Army

www.af.mil   The official site of the US Air Force

www.navy.mil   The official site of the US Navy

www.usmc.mil   The official site of the US Marine Corps

www.ngb.dtic.mil   The official site of the National Guard

www.uscg.mil   The official site of the US Coast Guard

Chapter 9

Advice When Obtaining Criminal Records Yourself

I am only one; but still I am one. I cannot do everything, but still I can do something;
I will not refuse to do something I can do.

—Helen Keller

There are several ways you can obtain a criminal record on an individual. First you have to choose between doing it yourself or hiring someone to do it for you.

If you plan to do it yourself, and you will be requesting criminal records from various locales, you will need source materials to tell you where to look and what procedures are there. What county courts will you need to search? What records will the state repository be able to supply you?

If you need criminal records from multiple locales, or have more than an occasional need for criminal records, you will probably decide to hire someone else with expertise in the field—a criminal record vendor. These record retrieval experts offer advantages—they know the territory and have knowledge about such things as costs, turnaround times, and what doors to open. Some have specialized search tools that you are not likely to have. When using a vendor, however, you are getting into an area where there are laws and provisions, of which you should be aware. Chapter 10 evaluates the use of criminal record vendors.

You may not need a vendor. If you are in need of only a single record, or if you have a low *volume* of requests—and the *nature* of the request is simple—it will be easy enough to do it yourself.

Your decision to do it yourself or hire a retriever will, in large part, depend on whether you are doing local searches, i.e., searches in your immediate vicinity, or remote searches, i.e., searches from those locales too distant to conveniently do yourself. Let's look at some of the things you'll need to know.

Know Thy Repositories

The first step in searching criminal records is knowing where to look. If you have read Chapters 5 through 8, you are now aware of the possible record locations—the county, the state repository, online, perhaps even the US District Courts. Deciding which locations to search requires a basic understanding of the differences.

Local Searches

If you are a casual, infrequent user of criminal records and you want to order a criminal record on an individual from your local county, you may elect to go down to the courthouse in person and search the courthouse files.

With over 3,000 local courthouses in the US, the procedures will (literally) vary all over the map. In some locales, a computer terminal in the lobby lets you can do an initial search using name, SSN, DOB or other identifying information. From this computer, you will only be able to determine if that jurisdiction has criminal files of some type on the individual— or an individual with the same or similar name. The attending clerk should be able to tell you if the records from other courts, or other jurisdictions, are also on that computer database. That's helpful. If your search finds there are no files—no hits—that match the subject's name, you can be on your way. However, if you do find a match or potential match, the computer terminal will point you to the actual files, which are usually on paper. From here, turn to the clerk who may allow you to search the actual files, but most likely, the clerk will locate and search the files for you. There may be a fee, there may be a wait. In other jurisdictions, the clerk may have control of the computer and will do all the searching while you wait.

If you are in a state that allows it and you live nearby, you may also choose to search at state repository. Remember, though, how the state agency operates is quite different from the local courthouse. First, the turnaround time will probably be much longer. Even if the state agency permits you to order the record in person, most likely the report will be returned by mail 3 to 10 days later. Second, state agencies do not permit free name searches using a public access computer terminal, as described above. Third, there are likely to be some sort of restrictions, and state people are pretty firm about following the rules.

Searching Several Record Locations

Obtaining a criminal record from your own county or obtaining a state criminal record from your state repository is one thing. You can become familiar with the methods and procedures in your own backyard and perhaps cobble together an efficient process. Obtaining a criminal record from a distant, out-of-state county is often a horse of a different feather. Just because your local county clerk or state agency does things a certain way does not mean you can expect the same process and courtesies elsewhere.

Often, the first obstacle is simply determining what counties should be searched. There are, after all, over 3,000 US counties to choose from. Let's say that you're checking for a criminal record for someone who lists a ZIP Code in Crittenden County, Arkansas. You may not know that directly across the river is a rather large place called Memphis, Tennessee. To complicate matters, a few miles south of Memphis, just past Graceland, is Mississippi. Should you check these areas that border on Crittenden County?

Once the scope of your search is determined, next is the matter of determining the address of the county courts, the identifying information needed, the prices, parties to whom to make out the check (if the search is being conducted through the mail), and the turnaround times that can be expected.

Do-It-Yourself Search Quandary

Here's a typical example: assume an individual applies for a position at an office in Chicago, IL. This individual had previously lived and worked in Mannford, OK. If the Chicago employer decides to order a county criminal record, he must first determine the county where Mannford is located. Through the use of a map, city/county cross directory or other method, the employer determines Mannford is located in Creek County. (A good cross-directory is *The County Locator* book.)

Now, the employer must find out where the county seat or courthouse is located. Assuming the employer eventually determines that the Creek County courthouse is located in Sapulpa, Oklahoma, the employer must now determine how to get access to the records there.

Area code and telephone number to call, address, cost and procedures are all questions that must be answered. At the district court in Sapulpa, the clerk will *not* do a records search for you, so our employer in Chicago will have to hire a public record retriever to go in for him, as this employer obviously cannot do it personally.

Other courts may make the records available over the phone, although this is becoming rare and is not as dependable as an in-person search or even a mailed-in request. Further, most requesters like a written record of the results of their search; a phone search is not particularly reliable. Most jurisdictions, whether they are county or state level, charge a fee for a criminal record. This fee may be a set fee, or it may be based on whether a criminal record exists. The fee may depend on how extensive the record is. Many jurisdictions charge a set fee plus the cost for any copies they make. For mailed-in requests, the court may require a self addressed, stamped envelope. The vast majority of jurisdictions do not take credit cards. They may take checks—business, cashiers, and money order checks over personal checks—and many will wait for the check to clear before mailing your search results. This results in a considerable turnaround time.

The complexity of obtaining records from distant sources, again whether county or state, coupled with the fact that there is usually a cost in time as well as money, is what prompts many employers to use a record retrieval service.

State Versus County Searching

The decision on whether to order a state or a county criminal record requires an understanding of the differences between the two. This is not necessarily an "either/or" decision.

At its most basic, the question can be phrased: "Would you like that search to be a mile wide and an inch deep, or a mile deep and an inch wide?"

A Mile Wide and an Inch Deep

A state search is a wide search, encompassing all counties within the state. As discussed earlier however, state searches are dependant on the counties reporting the information. A state search, while broad, may not have the latest information, or the detail information that might be contained in a county search.

A Mile Deep and an Inch Wide

A county search is a deep search, often containing the latest and most complete information available *from that particular county*. The drawback inherent in a county search is the limited scope of the search. Many US cities have spilled over into several counties. A search in one county—while revealing a great level of detail in that county—may literally miss criminal information that occurred across the street. Consider places like the City of Texarkana, where the state boundary is a main street.

What's an upstanding, conscientious, resourceful criminal record searcher to do? Well, it depends. In those states in which a state repository search is not available, your decision will be fairly easy. You take what you can get.

A strategy that many searchers use is to first order a state record, if access is available. If something comes up that is conclusive, then the process may well end there. A pharmacy that discovers multiple convictions for drug trafficking on a subject's state search probably won't go much farther in the process.

Often, a state search may prove inconclusive, i.e., not contain the disposition. In a case such as this, the results of the state search would point to the county where the latest information could be obtained. The state search might also serve to validate a locale where the searcher had intended to search.

Conversely, if you start with a county search in a locale where there are close, adjoining counties and find something inconclusive—minor arrests or convictions—it may be cause for concern. It may behoove you to order a state search to see if anything else pops up.

The Myth of Public Records and the Internet

Up to this point, readers have probably noted there has been very little mention of accessing criminal records via the Internet. The truth is, very few criminal records are available on the net. To date, there are few counties that offer access to their criminal records via the Internet, and few who offer them for free. Nevertheless, the growing number of court records online shows promise for vendors and the casual searcher. Several states offer online access, but most of these systems are private dial-up commercial systems. Several states that do have Internet access are indicated in the *State Profiles*.

The reality is that for now, obtaining criminal records without hiring a retriever will most likely be a manual, non-online process. It may be a viable alternative if you only need local criminal record searches, but if you will be ordering records from various, distant locales, you should look into outsourcing the job.

It is worth mentioning that the Internet is a good place to find general information about government agencies. Many web sites enable one to download, read and/or print current forms, policies and regulations. A growing number of state departments of corrections web sites are offering access to inmate, parolee, and sex offender registries (see *State Profiles*).

About the Internet and Access to Public Records

Overall, the availability of online public records is not as widespread as one might think. According to studies conducted by the Public Record Research Library, only 20% of public records can be found online.

Keep in mind that the Internet may be a free means to certain agency records, or it may be the conduit to a subscription or commercial site. The commercial online access method to public records is much more prevalent at the state level compared to the county level. Many agencies, such as DMVs, make the information available to pre-approved, high-volume, ongoing accounts. Typically, this access involves fees and a specified, minimum amount of usage. Frequency of usage is a key consideration when purchasing public records online direct from a government agency. Many agencies require a minimum amount of requests per month or per session. Certainly, it does not make economic sense to spend a lot of money for programming and set-up fees if you will be ordering fewer than five records a month. You would be better off to do the search by more conventional methods—in-person, via mail, fax, or by hiring a vendor. Going online direct to the source is not always the least expensive way to go!

However, the trend of agencies posting public record data on the Internet for free is upward. Two examples are Secretary of State offices (whose records include corporation, UCC and tax liens) and county/city tax assessor offices (whose records reveal property ownership). Usually this information is limited to name indexes and summary data, rather than document images. In addition, a growing number of state licensing boards are posting their membership lists on the net, although addresses and phone numbers of the licensed individuals typically are not listed, making identification uncertain. But, when address information is available, such as real estate records, it can point to locales to search for criminal records.

> **Author's Tip—**
>
> There are two premier sources for obtaining the information you need to order criminal records on your own.
>
> The *Sourcebook to Public Record Information,* by BRB Publications, is printed annually and the CD version is updated every six months. This same information is available via the Internet, with weekly updates.
>
> The second source is a book titled *The Guide to Background Investigations.* This stalwart product has been repeatedly updated since its beginning in the mid-1980s and is also available on CD.
>
> Both books contain a city/county cross reference that references cities to counties. Therefore, if you know the city or zip code where your subject lived, worked—or perhaps—ran into trouble, these resources will point you to the county where you need to search. Also, these products list the addresses, availability, identification requirements, prices, and turnaround times for state and local searches.
>
> For more information on these sources, visit:
>
> www.usetheguide.com and
>
> www.brbpub.com

Using the Freedom of Information Act and Other Acts

The Federal Freedom of Information Act (FOIA) has no bearing on state, county or local government agencies because these agencies are subject to that state's individual act. Further, the government agencies that handle criminal records generally already have systems in place to release information, so the FOIA is not needed. However, if you are trying to obtain non-criminal records from agencies, there are many useful Internet sites that give the information you need to complete such a request. We recommend these sites:

www.epic.org/open_gov/rights.html

http://spj.org/foia

Chapter 10

Advice On Using a Criminal Record Vendor

The greatest improvement in the productive powers of labour, and the greater part of the skill, dexterity, and judgment with which it is any where directed, or applied, seem to have been the effects of the division of labour.

—Adam Smith

If you plan on ordering any type of volume from a variety of county or state sources, your best bet will probably be to hire a vendor to perform the searches for you. The service will be faster, more convenient. Many vendors provide in-depth customer services—such as interpreting obscure provincial charges—that court personnel are not equipped to do.

Businesses that provide criminal records may be court retrievers, private detectives or pre-employment screening companies. For purposes of discussion here, they will be referred to as "criminal record vendors."

The Advent of Criminal Record Vendors

The criminal record retrieval business exploded in the 1990s. Sophisticated companies that had a nationwide customer base and provided other types of computerized pre-employment screening information (such as driving records or employment history reports) began setting up nationwide criminal record retrieval networks. As they grew, these national companies hired employees and contracted with multiple local companies that had courthouse retrieval services. Some purchased and absorbed local retrieval firms. Small retrievers, who heretofore serviced one or two local employers, began to branch out into new counties and market to new industries. Some of them became customers of their former peer companies.

Part of the reason for this explosion has been the increase in negligent hiring lawsuits. In the 1970s and even early 1980s, the negligent hiring suit was still a gleam in most plaintiff attorneys' eyes. The idea that an employer would be held responsible for an act of their employee—even when the employee was acting outside the scope of his employment—was for the most part farfetched.

For whatever reasons, workplace violence also became a bigger issue. Historical statistics regarding workplace violence were not tracked as they are today. Our tolerance of violence is less. One theory is that women entering the workplace in greater numbers have caused greater awareness. If a couple of assembly line workers working on Ford "Model Ts" or a couple of roustabouts drilling an oil well went to fisticuffs, often the attitude was "well, boys will be boys." On the other hand, a couple of men going at it in a mixed gender office is somewhat different.

In any event, businesses have increasingly felt compelled to order criminal records on employee applicants. In doing so, they have encountered the morass that is the present state of our criminal record repositories available to employers. The employer's solution is to outsource the criminal record research work, which has led to the proliferation of criminal record vendors.

Types of Vendor Services Offered

There are two broad categories of services provided by criminal record vendors. One category consists of the hands-on court record retrievers and the general search firms who employ any number of record retrievers to "cover" certain geographical areas. These companies obtain the records for other companies that, in turn, sell that information to employers. The general search firms are, in effect, the "wholesalers" of the records.

The other broad type of vendor is the all-encompassing pre-employment screening company that sells to the end user—employers. Pre-employment screening companies are, in effect, the "retailers" of the information.

It is important to note several variations. Many private investigators offer the above-mentioned "record retrieval" or "pre-employment screening" services. There are a number of companies that specialize in compiling proprietary databases of public records. These companies, sometimes known as public record provider companies, may compile state-specific databases of criminal record activity. However, the caveat is that some of these databases may not be compliant with the Fair Credit Reporting Act (FCRA). This issue is discussed in detail in Chapters 13 and 14.

Retrievers and Search Firms

As "wholesalers," retrievers and search firms are probably not "consumer reporting agencies," as defined by the Fair Credit Reporting Act.

"Probably?" There is some debate on this point, but in any event, many wholesalers follow FCRA restrictions because their clients want them to.

Wholesalers frequently use local document retrievers. Local document retrievers use their own personnel to search specific requested categories of public records usually in order to obtain documentation for legal compliance (e.g., incorporations), for lending, and for litigation. They do not usually review or interpret the results or issue reports in the sense that investigators do, but rather return documents—the results of searches. While document retrievers tend to be localized, there are some who offer a national network of retrievers and/or correspondents. The retriever or his/her personnel go directly to the agency to look up the information. A retriever may be relied upon for strong knowledge in a local area, whereas a search generalist has a breadth of knowledge and experience in a wider geographic range.

Companies that provide records to employers

Those companies that provide records to end users, e.g., employers using criminal records as a factor in establishing eligibility for employment, *are* "consumer reporting agencies." They may obtain criminal records directly from the jurisdiction or from a criminal record wholesaler. In turn, they provide these records to employers for a fee. In Chapter 14, the significance of being a consumer reporting agency is discussed at length.

Because criminal records are by no means the only type of pre-employment screening information needed by employers, many of these companies also provide other services. These services may include driving records, also known as motor vehicle reports or MVRs. Other services offered may be employment histories, educational verification, social security number verifications, employment credit reports, worker's compensation history reports along with other industry-specific screening tools.

In the criminal record arena, most of these companies offer statewide records. A few only offer county records. Because of their cost, limited scope and lack of positive identifiers, Federal criminal records are a distant third offering.

Benefits of Service Vendors

Professional criminal record service vendors offer (or should offer) several benefits. These benefits are knowledge and expertise, faster turnaround time, quality control, Fair Credit Reporting Act protections, and ancillary tools that may include automated delivery, email ordering and Internet gateways.

The Knowledge Benefit

The first knowledge aspect is simply having the information on hand to obtain a criminal record from any county in the country. A service provider will have the know-how to obtain criminal records from locales nationwide. They have the databases that can quickly cross-reference the city to the county. They then should be able to immediately ask for the information required by the jurisdiction along with any necessary forms. Earlier in this section, some of the problems inherent in cross-country county searches were detailed.

The Turnaround Benefit

The faster, the better—if accurate. Turnaround advantages are usually directly attributable to having someone "on the ground" who can physically go into a jurisdiction, get the information, get it court certified if need be, and get out. Counties and states are, of course, becoming more computerized, but this does not mean they are allowing outsiders to perform computerized searches of their databases. Any court that is computerized is marginally faster for retrieving records. Those few places that allow online access let the researcher get to the records from afar, so you may expect a speedier turnaround time.

The Expertise and Quality Control Benefit

Many service providers can provide valuable expertise in deciphering reports, knowing what courts will contain what types of offenses. That same service may be able to provide guidance regarding state law. Perhaps more importantly, a service provider worth their salt will "salt" their requests to their field people with known records. "Salting" means that, unknown to the field agent, the provider will occasionally ask the agent to perform a search on an individual that is known to have criminal record in that jurisdiction. If their agent comes back with a "clear" report—a "no record found"—the provider knows they have a problem: the agent isn't doing a thorough job. Most service providers let their court record retrievers know they are salting their records, and a retriever doing thousands of requests for a service provider will not want to gamble the entire book of business to save a few pennies once in awhile with a "lazy search." In this manner, service providers can assert some degree of quality control.

Incidentally, phone searches—especially those performed by a court deputy clerk—are among the least reliable searches. If you absolutely, positively need to know, for the record, an individual's criminal history from a jurisdiction, get it in writing some way or another.

Fair Credit Reporting Act Protections

The Fair Credit Reporting Act is discussed at length in Chapters 13 and 14, but it is appropriate to point out here that this law can be to the record requester's advantage if a vendor is used. While an employer may be sued over a wrongful employment practice, when a company uses a criminal record vendor to obtain criminal records, the company is afforded some legal protections.

For example, if an employer orders a criminal record on their own and bungles the search, e.g., they obtain the wrong record and fire an employee, they're going to have their hands full. If they order the record from a "consumer reporting agency" and take the same action due to the vendor's mistake, the employer will be somewhat shielded from liability.

Ancillary Tools That Criminal Record Vendors Provide

Some criminal record vendors offer ancillary tools that can make the difference between a sub-par and excellent search.

Database Assisted Searches

When a vendor says they offer a database search, two of your primary questions should be "how far back do the records go," and "how current are they?" As detailed in Chapters 13 and 14, the Fair Credit Reporting Act requires additional compliance procedures when public record information is used for employment purposes and the public record information is not the latest available. This fact in no way negates the value of database-assisted searches, as explained below.

There are three main factors that hamper the value of public criminal record searches, particularly for employers ordering criminal records on job applicants.

- Knowing where to look
- Turnaround time
- Cost

A database search can address all three. A database search is one in which a vendor has obtained a database of criminal records from, say, a county or state, or, the vendor has warehoused previously-ordered criminal records. Because the records are databased, the turnaround can be instantaneous—as opposed to the hours or days a physical search of a jurisdiction can take. Because there are fewer costs per item associated with a database search, the price is usually less.

Perhaps the biggest advantage, however, is that the database search can—with the right system—*dramatically* increase the scope of the search and thereby make the difference between finding or not finding a criminal record.

What is the "right" system? Well, there are variations of database searches, some limited and some global. An example of a limited database search would be one in which a vendor purchases a county's database of criminal records. Say, for example, the vendor purchases the Watadoosie criminal record database. (It should be noted that most counties do not make their entire database available, but a few do.) When the vendor's client wants to search Watadoosie County, they may be offered the option of searching just the vendor's Watadoosie database.

This limited database search would address two of the three issues: turnaround and cost. But, dear friends and good neighbors, when you combine databases from multiple sources, the search value rises dramatically.

A global database search differs from a limited database search in that it searches records from various sources and databases. To illustrate, let's go back to the Watadoosie County example. An employer orders a criminal record from Watadoosie County. The vendor employing a global search would—regardless of whether Watadoosie's county data was in their database—perform a search of all the other data in their database. This might mean searching county databases from across the country or across the street—which might happen to be another county.

The global database might also contain previously ordered criminal records. And so, our employer requesting a Watadoosie County record might discover a criminal record that had been ordered by a previous employer six months earlier from a different county. Warehousing previously ordered criminal records can be particularly effective if a vendor has a high concentration of clients in a particular industry.

Database Caveats

As you can see, database searches can be a powerful tool in criminal record searches. However, they are supplemental and not a substitute. The main reasons why are detailed below.

Criminal record vendors should also offer you options and inform you of the type of search they are performing. If you want a current, up-to-the-minute search of Watadoosie County, that should be what you get.

Perhaps the main caveat with database searches—if the information is to be used for employment purposes and is not the latest available—a notice must be sent to the subject of the search. This is a Fair Credit Reporting Act requirement, and is discussed at length in Chapter 14.

The following sidebar is an edited excerpt from a recent article written by Lester S. Rosen. We thank Mr. Rosen for allowing us to edit and reprint.

> ### Shortcomings of Vendor Criminal History Databases
>
> There are a number of public record vendors who advertise they have a "national database of criminal record information." However, a search of a vendor's private or proprietary criminal record database may not contain the latest and most complete data. The fact is, there is no such thing as a truly "national" criminal record database. Perhaps the vendor has purchased some "data" from every state—be it a list of current inmates, or local police records, or unified court records—but no one has all the "data" from all the jurisdictions. Listed below are three major reasons a database search may fail to discover a criminal matter.
>
> **Completeness**—The various databases that vendors purchase or collect may not be the equivalent of a true all-encompassing multi-statewide database. First, the databases purchased by the vendor for resale (or accessed as a

gateway) may not contain complete records from all jurisdictions. For example, not all unified court systems contain all counties. Second, for reporting purposes, the records that are actually reported may be incomplete or lack sufficient detail about the offense or the subject. Third, some databases contain only felonies or contain only offenses where a state corrections unit was involved. Fourth, the database may not carry subsequent information such as a pardon or some other matter that could render an item not reportable under the FCRA.

Name Variations—An electronic search of a vendor's database may not be able to recognize variations in a subject name, which a person would notice if looking at the index. The applicant may have been arrested under a different first name, or some variation of first and middle name. A female applicant may have a record under her maiden name.

Timeliness—There is always the possibility that the records in a vendor database are stale to some extent. The vendor may only enter new data at intervals that may lag behind the timeliness of the available index from the corresponding state or county agency. Generally, this means that the most current offenses are the ones least likely to appear in a search of a vendor database.

Criminal record vendors should make clear what data they are providing when their customers are performing a search of that vendor's database. These searches are ancillary and can be very useful, but proceed with caution. In other words, it cannot be assumed that a search of a proprietary criminal history database solely meets the level of due diligence required to be compliant with the FCRA.

Lester S. Rosen is an attorney at law and President of Employment Screening Resources (ESR), a national background screening company located in California. He is a consultant, writer and frequent presenter on pre-employment screening, safe hiring and the Fair Credit Reporting Act. Visit his web site is www.ESRcheck.com.

Using Credit Headers as Criminal Record Pointers

The major credit bureaus contain files on hundreds of millions of people and credit header reports can be a powerful tool to address the problem of knowing where to look for criminal records.

Credit headers are, at their most basic, credit reports without any credit information. They only contain the "headings" of credit reports, which is primarily identifying information such as name, and current and past addresses.

Some vendors have a program in which a credit header is ordered and the past addresses are used to order criminal records from the locales in which the person has resided. It can be a slick tool, particularly if the header-to-county criminal record jurisdiction is automated. For example, an employer might decide to order a criminal record from every county where their applicant had resided the past three years. The vendor would order a header report, and their system would determine if there were multiple addresses. If so, the vendor would cross-reference the addresses against their county directory and automatically order the requisite criminal records.

Where to Find a Vendor

We listed several good sources below. When you search for a vendor using a search engine on the Internet, you will find a myriad of screening companies. Some of the more professional web sites can indicate their high level of technical expertise and ability to meet fast turnaround times. That is all well and good, but be sure to look, or ask, for their statements on compliance with FCRA. If they respond to your FCRA inquiry with a "of course we have Fine Criminal Record Access," you should suddenly remember you're late for a meeting.

As we have discussed however, many industries have their own specific laws and nuances regarding criminal records. If you are able, talk to others in your industry to determine what vendor they use. What you are looking for is a criminal records vendor who might "specialize" in your industry.

- http://www.publicrecordsources.com Click on the section called *screening firms* and you will be able to search among 200+ of the nation's leading screening companies. Also, this site is an excellent source to find specialty vendors. Click on *sources and search firms*.
- The *National Directory of Public Record Vendors* (BRB Publications, 800-929-3811) has an entire section dedicated to screening companies. This book is also an excellent source for finding specialty vendors.

How to Choose the Best Vendor for You

You won't see the consumer magazines reviewing the different criminal record services and issuing "best buys" any time soon. However, like a consumer magazine, the information here can help to point out a provider's attributes that you should evaluate before making a decision.

The business of criminal record retrieval is more of a service than a product. It probably won't always be so. Someday, you may be able to choose a criminal record service by price and turnaround time. All systems will be computerized, right down to the municipal court level. Criminal records will become a commodity. Today, they are not. It is a service because there are so many variables. Knowledge—operational, legal and otherwise—affects the quality of the service as much as price and turnaround.

The following are some attributes you can use to compare vendors.

Consider Vendor Accuracy

Accuracy can be hard to gauge. You can ask if the vendor "salts" his requests with known criminal records on a random basis. You can do the same to the vendor if you have some known records in a given jurisdiction.

One of the biggest causes of "inaccuracy" in criminal records is actually mis-identification. In fact, the criminal record is accurate—but not accurate for the individual on which it was ordered. This usually happens in instances when a record is ordered on a subject with a common name and the individual's identifying information at the jurisdiction is incomplete. This is discussed in more detail in Chapter 12, but for purposes here, look at an example of the vendor's criminal record report. You should be able to readily distinguish between the information you used to request the search and the information that was actually returned from that jurisdiction. Better is a section on the report that highlights discrepancies between the two.

Consider Vendor Knowledge

The most accurate report in the world is of limited value if you do not fully understand what it means. Most vendors will help you decipher unusual reports and some have a glossary with common terms and charges defined.

A report that includes coding and ambiguous abbreviations may look impressive in your file, but how meaningful is it? For all reports, except those you deal with regularly, interpretation assistance can be very important. Some information vendors offer searches for information they really don't know much about through sources they only use occasionally. Protecting their credibility or their professional pride sometimes prohibits them from disclosing their limitations—until you ask the right questions.

A vendor should also be knowledgeable about laws regarding the use of criminal record information. This includes the FCRA as well as EEOC information discussed later in this book. If you are in an industry with some unique requirements, connecting up with a vendor with knowledge and experience in your industry is an excellent benefit.

Consider The Vendor's Ancillary Services

Database and credit header-assisted searches were discussed earlier. If you believe these services could improve your results, look for a vendor that offers them.

How is Their Turnaround Time?

The faster the better as long as it is not traded for accuracy. The vendor should publish an expected turnaround schedule for each state it serves, and have a standard for most counties.

Consider Price

You get what you pay for? Yeah, this little homily probably has a grain of truth, but on the other hand, there are people who go to different car dealerships and buy identical cars and the price they pay differs by thousands. Buyer beware. One of them made a "best buy," one of them paid more than he should have. The fair price could be somewhere in between.

With that said, there are a lot of hucksters who have opened themselves a little website, bought a phone and gone into the criminal record business. They may be less expensive—until their erroneous report causes you to hire or fire someone you shouldn't, the turnaround isn't what they said it would be, or their lack of knowledge catches up to them (or you) in other ways.

Consider the Locale

"I lost my glasses in the alley, but the light is better out here on the street corner."

This is a punch line to an old joke, but instructive when choosing a vendor. With the Internet and other computerized ordering and delivering systems, the locale of your vendor and proximity to you should not be an issue, but it might be. A vendor in the state capital might offer quicker access to state agency records. A vendor might be able to deliver a hard-copy of a document overnight from the local courthouse.

Summary

All of the above factors are useful to compare vendors. Our best advice when choosing a vendor—talk to the vendor's customers. They have first-hand knowledge of that vendor's accuracy, turnaround and overall knowledge.

If you are a user in a specialized industry, or you have unique requirements, it may also behoove you to determine how many other customers in your industry that vendor has.

Section 3

Employer & Vendor Guidelines to Using Criminal Records

This section defines legal compliance when using criminal records.

It is essential that both the employer and the vendor are aware of and adhere to the criteria mandated by the Fair Credit Reporting Act and Title VII of the Civil Rights Act.

The trident to these federal mandates is compliance with state laws and state restrictions. The ability to obtain criminal records is of minimal value unless you are legally compliant in their use.

Chapter 11

Why Employers Should Use Criminal Records

The only thing necessary for the triumph of evil is for good men to do nothing.
—Edmund Burke

The reason why men enter in society is the preservation of their property.
—John Locke

Watching an employer who does a lot of hiring but neglects to order criminal records is like watching a train wreck unfold. You can see the disaster coming from a long way away, it's inevitable, but you can't do anything to stop it.

While criminal records are legal to use, there are issues to watch. How you obtain them has risks, and costs. Why, then, have most of the larger and progressive employers decided to order criminal records? There are several reasons.

The Negligent Hiring Doctrine

Some employers order criminal records on applicants because the law requires it. Others order criminal records because they are afraid of the harm that may come to them, their business or other employees if they hire someone they shouldn't. Yet another, growing reason why businesses order criminal records is the fear of being sued for negligent hiring.

Created through case law, negligent hiring is a legal doctrine that imposes a duty upon employers to "assess the nature of the employment, its degree of risk to third parties and then perform a reasonable background investigation to insure that the applicant is competent and fit for duty." A closely associated theory is negligent retention. Negligent retention is when the employee, already hired, is retained when the employer knows, or should have known, that the employee was unfit to be retained.

The primary difference between the two is timing. Negligent hiring is a matter of "should have known" before hiring. Negligent retention is a matter of "should have become aware of" after hiring. Employers are most often faulted for failing to order a criminal record check before someone is hired.

There is no consistent, de facto requirement that an employer check applicants for a criminal record, although as discussed earlier, there may be state and federal industry-specific requirements that say a criminal record be obtained. Different courts have come to different conclusions, but the trend is clearly moving in the direction that employers have more obligations depending on the nature of the job.

The "Nature of the Position"

There is a difference in the degree and nature of care that must be used between hiring a daycare worker and a construction worker. Clearly, a daycare worker working unsupervised in close proximity to young children probably presents more of a risk than does someone stomping on a shovel. On the issue of "job relatedness," courts have been extremely liberal in their opinions, a trend that says it's the employer's responsibility not to put the wrong person on the job.

Protections Afforded

It is important to note that ordering criminal records can offer protection to the employer, and especially if no information is found. In many cases, the employer is portrayed as an uncaring entity that was too tight to spend even a nominal amount to insure that someone was not maimed—and it's time to punish them for their greediness. But, what if the employer does order a criminal record and, through no fault of their own, the crime committed in Tupelo, Mississippi by the applicant on vacation does not appear in the Dallas County, Texas search performed by the employer? The point is, the employer tried. The employer assessed the nature of the job, its degree of risk and then conducted a background investigation above that required by law. The fact that this search did not reveal information is another matter.

Florida House Bill H0775—An Example of a Law Creating a Presumption *Against* Negligent Hiring

A statute, approved by Governor J. Bush of Florida on May 26, 1999, which became effective on October 1, 1999, created a presumption against negligent hiring when employers take certain pre-employment screening steps. Employers who follow the steps will be presumed not to have been negligent if the background investigation fails to reveal any information that reasonably demonstrates the unsuitability of the applicant for the particular work to be performed, or for employment in general. One of these steps is ordering a criminal record.

Among the prescribed steps are:

- Ordering a Florida state criminal record.

- Taking reasonable efforts to contact past employers.

- Having the applicant complete an employment application that elicits the following information:

  - Convictions of crimes including type, date and penalty imposed;

  - Whether the applicant was a defendant in a civil action for an intentional tort, including the nature and disposition of the action.

- A driving record must be ordered if it is relevant to the work to be performed.

- The employer must interview the applicant.

Notice that the law does not require that employers find criminal record information if there is any to be obtained. The law only requires that employers make a state inquiry.

Nothing in this legislation requires employers to adopt new procedures. It does afford some protection to those employers who attempt to hire safe, responsible employees.

And for Non-Florida Denizens?

Do you have a similar law in your state? Even if not, the steps prescribed by this Florida law make good sense. While your state may not have codified the protection, a plaintiff would have a tough time proving hiring negligence against you if you had taken the "Florida steps."

In other words, even if you are not in Florida, following the Florida guidelines may provide your company *de facto* protection, if not codified protection.

Workplace Violence

Workplace violence can be related to negligent hiring in that employers have been sued for hiring someone with a propensity for violence, and the employee subsequently harms another employee. A negligent hiring suit does not always follow an act of workplace violence, but courts have increasingly found that employers have at least some duty to provide a safe workplace.

Ronet Bachman, a statistician with the Bureau of Justice Statistics, has reports that "each year, nearly 1 million individuals become victims of violent crime while working or on duty. The victimizations account for 15% of the over 6½ million acts of violence experienced by U.S. residents age twelve or older."

Unfortunately, these statistics do not show the percentage of these victimizations committed by co-workers, but unempirical surveys have shown that co-workers do commit a significant percentage of these victimizations.

Even if an employer does not get sued for an act of workplace violence committed by an employee, workplace violence is, to put it mildly, not conducive to productivity. Among those persons injured by a crime victimization at work, an estimated 876,800 workdays were lost annually, costing employees over $16 million in wages. This does not include the "sick days" and the "annual leave" that the victim might not otherwise take.

The fact is, hiring employees is one of the areas the employer is most able to control. More and more employers are ordering criminal records as a measure that helps thwart workplace violence.

Workplace Theft

It's tough for a business to make a profit when some of its best customers are employees who are not paying for the goods. While John Locke felt men entered into society to preserve their property, many employers are ordering criminal records for the same reason.

Retailers attribute 42.7 percent of their inventory shrinkage—12-*billion* dollars lost annually in missing merchandise, cash, fraud—to employee theft. As a rule, retailers spend approximately $3500 to recruit, screen and hire one employee. The length of time worked by a dishonest employee is 9.4 months. The average cost of hiring and releasing a dishonest employee averages $15,000. In order to thwart the onslaught of shrinkage, retailers hire ten loss prevention employees per $100 million in annual sales…with an average of 1.12 employees per store specifically dedicated to loss prevention.

Considering that 42% of their inventory losses come from employees—and that the total recruiting and screening cost is around $3500—a $20 criminal record makes good sense.

What if Your Employees Must Enter Canada?

Some businesses require their employees go into Canada. Under sections 19(1)(c) and 19(2)(a) of the Canada Immigration Act of 1976, individuals who have been convicted of a "crime or offense" are considered "inadmissible" and precluded from entering in Canada.

Therefore, prior to being permitted to enter into Canada, U.S. workers are subject to random criminal history checks by the Canadian authorities who use information obtained from the NCIC. Using the NCIC database, Canadian authorities are able to determine whether an individual has a "criminal record" and therefore, cannot be admitted without first obtaining a

"Minister's Permit." According to the Canadian Consulate General, a "Minister's Permit" can be issued in a limited number of instances to overcome the inadmissibility rules. This decision to issue or deny a permit is entirely discretionary with the Canadian office before whom the request is pending and will be based on such factors as:

o   The seriousness of the past offense.

o   The number of past offenses committed.

o   The perceived likelihood that the individual will commit another offense.

A Minister's Permit can only be obtained from a Canadian Consulate, are expensive to obtain, and are good for only a limited period of time.

As discussed earlier, the vast majority of US employers do not have access to NCIC, and so many employers who require their employees to travel into Canada order a criminal record from public record sources in the U.S. This decreases problems at the border.

When it is Required by Law

There's many smart reasons to order criminal records on employees, a few dumb ones, and several cases in which the federal or state government has given one of my father's all time favorite reasons: "Because I said so."

In Chapter 7, an example of a Federal 2001 health care initiative was given that would require certain health care providers to order criminal records on certain classes of applicants.

The events surrounding the War on Terrorism in 2001 started a trend toward more criminal record checking requirements on employers.

Several industries already have Federal or state mandates. This book cannot list every one, but two regulations provide examples. One is a requirement. The other includes penalties for hiring someone who doesn't pass the criminal record check.

Federal Aviation Regulations

This first example outlines certain Federal Aviation Administration requirements.

TITLE 14--AERONAUTICS AND SPACE

CHAPTER I--FEDERAL AVIATION ADMINISTRATION, DEPARTMENT OF TRANSPORTATION (Continued)

PART 107--AIRPORT SECURITY--Table of Contents

Sec. 107.31 Employment history, verification and criminal history records checks.

(a) Scope. On or after January 31, 1996, this section applies to all airport operators; airport users; individuals currently having unescorted access to a security identification display area (SIDA) that is identified by Sec. 107.25; all individuals seeking authorization for, or seeking the authority to authorize others to have, unescorted access to the SIDA; and each airport user and air carrier making a certification to an airport operator pursuant to paragraph (n) of this section. An airport user, for the purposes of Sec. 107.31 only, is any person making a certification under this section other than an air carrier subject to Sec. 108.33.

(b) Employment history investigations required. Except as provided in paragraph (m) of this section, each airport operator must ensure that no individual is granted authorization for, or is granted authority to authorize others to have, unescorted access to the SIDA unless the following requirements are met:

(1) The individual has satisfactorily undergone Part 1 of an employment history investigation. Part 1 consists of a review of the previous 10 years of employment history and verification of the 5 employment years preceding the date the appropriate investigation is initiated as provided in paragraph (c) of this section; and

(2) If required by paragraph (c)(5) of this section, the individual has satisfied Part 2 of the employment history investigation. Part 2 is the process to determine if the individual has a criminal record. To satisfy Part 2 of the investigation the criminal record check must not disclose that the individual has been convicted or found not guilty by reason of insanity, in any jurisdiction, during the 10 years ending on the date of such investigation, of any of the crimes listed below:

    (i) Forgery of certificates, false marking of aircraft, and other aircraft registration violation, 49 U.S.C. 46306;

    (ii) Interference with air navigation, 49 U.S.C. 46308;

    (iii) Improper transportation of a hazardous material, 49 U.S.C. 46312;

    (iv) Aircraft piracy, 49 U.S.C. 46502;

    (v) Interference with flightcrew members or flight attendants, 49 U.S.C. 46504;

    (vi) Commission of certain crimes aboard aircraft in flight, 49 U.S.C. 46506;

    (vii) Carrying a weapon or explosive aboard aircraft, 49 U.S.C. 46505;

    (viii) Conveying false information and threats, 49 U.S.C. 46507;

    (ix) Aircraft piracy outside the special aircraft jurisdiction of the United States, 49 U.S.C. 46502(b);

    (x) Lighting violations involving transporting controlled substances, 49 U.S.C. 46315;

(xi) Unlawful entry into an aircraft or airport area that serves air carriers or foreign air carriers contrary to established security requirements, 49 U.S.C. 46314;

(xii) Destruction of an aircraft or aircraft facility, 18 U.S.C. 32;

(xiii) Murder;

(xiv) Assault with intent to murder;

(xv) Espionage;

(xvi) Sedition;

(xvii) Kidnapping or hostage taking;

(xviii) Treason;

(xix) Rape or aggravated sexual abuse;

(xx) Unlawful possession, use, sale, distribution, or manufacture of an explosive or weapon;

(xxi) Extortion;

(xxii) Armed robbery;

(xxiii) Distribution of, or intent to distribute, a controlled substance;

(xxiv) Felony arson; or

(xxv) Conspiracy or attempt to commit any of the aforementioned criminal acts.

Do you think they mean it?

Banking Industry Regulations

Here are excerpts from regulations concerning the banking industry.

Federal Deposit Insurance Act

SEC. 19. PENALTY FOR UNAUTHORIZED PARTICIPATION BY CONVICTED INDIVIDUAL.
  (a) PROHIBITION.--
   (1) IN GENERAL.--Except with the prior written consent of the Corporation--
   (A) any person who has been convicted of any criminal offense involving dishonesty or a breach of trust or money laundering, or has agreed to enter into a pretrial diversion or similar program in connection with a prosecution for such offense, may not--
      (i) become, or continue as, an institution-affiliated party with respect to any insured depository institution;
      (ii) own or control, directly or indirectly, any insured depository institution; or
      (iii) otherwise participate, directly or indirectly, in the conduct of the affairs of any

insured depository institution; and

(B) any insured depository institution may not permit any person referred to in subparagraph (A) to engage in any conduct or continue any relationship prohibited under such subparagraph.

(2) Minimum 10-year prohibition period for certain offenses.--

(A) IN GENERAL.--If the offense referred to in paragraph (1)(A) in connection with any person referred to in such paragraph is--

(i) an offense under--

(I) section 215, 656, 657, 1005, 1006, 1007, 1008, 1014, 1032, 1344, 1517, 1956, or 1957 of title 18, United States Code; or

(II) section 1341 or 1343 of such title which affects any financial institution (as defined in section 20 of such title); or

(ii) the offense of conspiring to commit any such offense,

the Corporation may not consent to any exception to the application of paragraph (1) to such person during the 10-year period beginning on the date the conviction or the agreement of the person becomes final.

Chapter 12

Evaluate Your Record Request Process

I Really Want to Know...Who Are You?

—The Who

Ever wonder if the rock band *The Who* ever ordered criminal records on their roadies? Ah, probably not. In any event, if you've decided to order criminal records on job applicants, you should look at several issues within your criminal record process.

Proper identification—and recognition of improper identification before action is taken—is of primary importance. Two other processes you should examine are the use of misdemeanor records and proper documentation.

Identification Issues

A key issue in using criminal records is evaluating whether the information you have received pertains to the person on whom you inquired. It sounds so simple. Yet, more criminal record legal trouble starts here than anywhere else.

There are two categories of methodology used to identify individuals when ordering criminal records.

- Biometric Identifiers
- Demographics

It is important to understand the strengths and limitations of both.

Biometric Systems

Biometric systems measure an individual's unique physical characteristics. The most common biometric identifiers are fingerprints and retina scans. Of these, fingerprints are far more common and the only biometric identifier in use for criminal record matching. The use of other biometrics—such as DNA and retina scans—are found in the criminal justice field, but their use for matching an individual to past records is novel.

The problem is that existing technology for storing, copying, and matching these great biometric identifiers—fingerprints, photographs and retina scans—makes their use slow and expensive. Nevertheless, the definition of "expensive" has changed since the War on Terrorism began. Fingerprinting applications have been jump-started, and prices for them are expected to decrease. Although rarely used by the general public, fingerprinting will become more common. A short discussion on the fingerprinting process is in order.

Fingerprints

Fingerprint identification is based upon the fact that individuals' fingerprints have unique characteristics. These characteristics are whorls, arches, loops, ridge endings and ridge bifurcations.

Many fingerprints today are still taken the way they were decades ago: with paper and ink. The fingerprints are taken and put on a "ten-print" card. This card is then scanned and digitized for matching purposes.

Finger scan systems can be broadly categorized into two types—verification systems and identification systems. It is important to understand the distinction, and the cost between the two systems varies several hundredfold.

Verification systems capture the flat image of a finger and perform a one-to-one verification. That is, the original print is compared to the subsequent print to determine if it matches. A verification is performed in a few seconds. Applications of this technology have filtered down to the private sector, including personal computer security.

On the other hand, identification systems are used by law enforcement to match one set of fingerprints against millions of other, current prints. To be accurate, this one-to-many task requires that the original fingerprints be of a higher standard of clarity. Currently, a basic fingerprint identification system used simply to capture, digitize and transmit fingerprints costs around $18,000.

As discussed earlier, few employers have been granted statutory authority to access NCIC with fingerprints. As a result, for criminal record searches, most employers will continue to use non-biometric identifiers—name, date of birth, address, etc. In the business, the term used for this type of matching criteria is "demographics."

Demographic Identifiers

Using demographic identifiers means using items such as name, social security number, address, date of birth or other non-physical characteristics in order to identify a person.

Every person's fingerprint is unique. Every person's name is not, even when combined with a date of birth. The Social Security Number should be a unique identifier, but many criminal records don't have a social security number attached to it, and—imagine this—the criminal speaketh with forked tongue when asked for his correct Social Security number. So, the number on this record winds up being the wrong one, maybe even yours.

When using non-biometric identifiers, employers and the record retrievers need all the demographics they can get. Unfortunately there is a misconception on the part of some employers that a key demographic—date of birth—cannot be obtained from job applicants. Because of its importance, it deserves a detailed discussion.

Asking for the Date of Birth

An area that gives many employers pause is asking applicants for their date of birth. But, a correct DOB is very important when ordering a criminal record. Many jurisdictions ask that a DOB be included in a criminal record request. Some may not perform a name search without a DOB attached. The main reason for asking for a date of birth, as discussed earlier, is to have another identifier. Criminal records do not always contain a Social Security Number, and while using the name and DOB is not always conclusive, it is many times better than a name-only search.

The problem arises when employers are afraid to ask applicants their DOB. The reason for their fear? Since the Equal Employment Opportunity Commission (EEOC) prohibits age discrimination, some employers reason that they are much less likely to be accused of age discrimination if they don't know the age of the applicant to begin with.

The fact of the matter is that the EEOC does not prohibit employers from asking applicants for their DOB as long as it is asked for a legitimate, non-discriminatory reason—and not used for an impermissible purpose. In practice, asking for DOB should be done uniformly, not just on select applicants.

In fact, the EEOC has put out an eleven-page guidance document regarding job advertising, and pre-employment inquiries—such as those asked for on printed employment applications—under the Age Discrimination in Employment Act (ADEA). You may be interested to know that the chairman of the EEOC who signed this document into law was Clarence Thomas. Would it be a safe bet that Mr. Thomas may have later wished for a few good hardball age-related inquiries if they would make some other questions go away?

In any event, a copy of the 1989 EEOC guidance document that addresses the subject of asking for the DOB is provided in Chapter 15.

Matching the Date of Birth with the Name

And so, a jurisdiction may be using a name and date of birth from the employer to make a match. Many employers believe that a full first and last name with a date of birth is unique. It's not. As an exercise, pick a first and last name, and date of birth. Assume the chances of there being another person with the same first and last name and a matching DOB are only one in one million. Calculated, there are about 280 of these combinations in the United States. The fact is however, that the chances are much greater than one in one million for most names. There are a lot of common first names—David and John and Debbie and Karen—and a whole lot of Smiths, Jones and other ubiquitous surnames. And, that's not to mention the possibility of identity theft.

The lesson in all this is—

> Look very carefully at any criminal records for identifying information that does **not match** your subject's information.

Do not just assume that the information returned applies to your subject. For example, if you order information on John Doe, 1/1/61 and a record comes back on John Quincy Doe, 1/1/61, be sure to ascertain your subject's middle name. If you order a record on Jane Doe, DOB of 12/12/62, SSN of 123456789 and a record comes back on Jane Doe, 12/12/62, SSN of 12345678, do not automatically assume it is Jane—but don't assume it isn't.

A solution could be as simple as running a check on the social security number, or questioning Jane and speaking with the company or jurisdiction that supplied the record. The solution may come down to this: have your applicant fingerprinted and submit those prints for comparison with those taken at the time of arrest.

Again, simply not reviewing the information they have received is a common area where employers stub their toe when ordering criminal records. They order a report on one person, get back a record on another and, because they've not looked carefully at the record, they mistakenly take some adverse action against their applicant or employee. It is certainly not fair to disqualify an individual for having a name similar to one on a criminal record, or any public record. This mistake should be avoided.

The Importance of Proper Documentation

On the next page is an example of a criminal Background Check Release Form that appears in *25 Essential Lessons for Employee Management* by employment expert Dennis DeMey and published by Facts on Demand Press. You may download copies of employment related forms by going to http://www.brbpub.com/forms.

This form has fields for commonly used demographic data and also includes a place for the applicant to give his permission for your search. (It should be noted that the vast majority of record requests do not require a notary signature and seal.)

Sample Criminal Record Release Form

Criminal Background Check
Release Form

NAME_____
          Last   First   Middle   Maiden

ADDRESS_____
          Street   City   State

ALIASES OR OTHER NAMES USED _____

DATE OF BIRTH _____ AGE _____ RACE _____ SEX _____

SOCIAL SECURITY # _____

DRIVER'S LICENSE # _____ STATE _____

* * *

I hereby authorize _____ of _____
          Name   Name of Company

_____
          Company Address/City/State/Zip

to conduct a criminal background check on myself through the

_____.
          Name of State and Police Agency

X_____
          Applicant Signature

* * *

STATE of:_____   This Instrument was acknowledged before me this _____ day of

COUNTY of:_____   _____, 20 _____, by _____

My commission will expire: _____AS WITNESS.

_____

_____
          Notary Public   No.

Pros and Cons of Using Misdemeanor Records

Perhaps you are thinking you will not hire anyone with a felony conviction, but you will let misdemeanor records slide. Perhaps you will ignore arrest records unless there is more than one in the past year, but a felony conviction—regardless of age—will always disqualify an applicant. Whoops, it's not that easy. Here are some facts to consider before deciding how to evaluate misdemeanor and felony records, as well as convictions and arrests.

Misdemeanor records were defined earlier as "offenses of a minor degree and anything less than a felony." Misdemeanors are often discarded as a factor by some, kind of like "college records" i.e., "if not for the grace of God, there go I" records.

Well, sometimes misdemeanors *are* minor. Let those of you without misdemeanor sin cast the first stone while we duck. Before dismissing them though, consider:

1. A misdemeanor record may be more pertinent than a felony.

How? Imagine you own a construction company and your crew needs some extra hands at an excavation project. One individual who applies for a job looks to be a good prospect, but he has a conviction for felony embezzlement. Should this automatically disqualify the applicant? After all, if while that person is on the job they want to slyly peer around and sneak a dirt clod or two in their pocket to take home, well, no harm is done.

On the other hand, assume you are hiring drivers to haul away the dirt fill that Mr. Sticky Fingers hasn't spirited away in his pockets. One prospect who applies for this position "just" has one misdemeanor on his record: a "Driving While Intoxicated" (DWI) conviction. If you hire this individual and he has an accident that injures someone while drinking, you might as well buy a mirror and start practice saying, "it was just a misdemeanor" without looking dumb. Good Luck.

The point? Consider the severity of the crime in relation to the *job-relatedness* of the crime.

2. Many recorded misdemeanors are for felony crimes.

Sad to say, but the fact that an offense is recorded as a misdemeanor does not mean that the crime committed was a misdemeanor. Plea Bargains—a plea of guilt to a lesser offense in return for a lighter sentence—are common in the legal system. Overloaded court systems, prosecutors with a challenging case to prove, savvy defense attorneys contribute facts are that charges are often downgraded in return for defendant's guilty plea.

> **Author's Tip—**
>
> If you have an applicant with a few "minor" convictions, do some digging to determine what happened in the legal proceeding process. Look at an arrest record—if the law allows—and compare it to the applicant's version of the incident. If this is a key position and the record troubles you, you may wish to call the court or prosecutor to find out what you can.

Chapter 13

Compliance With the Fair Credit Reporting Act

Common sense often makes good law.

—William O. Douglas

As discussed earlier in this book, the vast majority of criminal records used outside of law enforcement are for used for employment purposes. If you are obtaining criminal records from a vendor and using these records to make decisions (e.g., you are not merely reselling the records) a law called the Fair Credit Reporting Act (FCRA) will almost certainly regulate the vendor. As discussed earlier, if a vendor doesn't have a good knowledge of the FCRA, it's a good indicator to choose another vendor.

The FCRA directly affects areas as diverse as what information can be contained on a report, to what notifications to make to the subject prior to the criminal record inquiry.

FCRA and Employers

The first hurdle to understand is that the "Fair Credit Reporting Act" is really misnamed. It should be called the "Fair Credit *and Employment* Reporting Act." The lack of "employment" in the title has contributed to the lack of understanding and knowledge of this law in employment screening. If you are an employer, ordering criminal records on potential employees, you will want to be familiar with this law.

There are three main areas in which the FCRA can affect an employer ordering criminal records—

- **Releases**—What notifications must be made and permissions granted from the subject of the search.
- **Arrest vs. convictions, seven year rule**—What information can appear on the report, and what must be suppressed.
- **Aged public record for employment purposes**—When the vendor databases records, what additional notifications to the subject must be performed.

Before detailing specifics, it is helpful to have a general overview of the act.

Overview of The Fair Credit Reporting Act (FCRA)

In general, the FCRA manages the relationship between the parties who are involved in informational transactions that fall under the Act. Usually, there are at least three affected parties:

- The provider of the information
- The subject of the information
- The user of the information

Before going further, several terms must be defined.

Consumer Reporting Agency

A *Consumer Reporting Agency (CRA)* is "any person which, for monetary fees, dues, or on a cooperative nonprofit basis, regularly engages in whole or in part in the practice of assembling or evaluating consumer credit information or other information on consumers for the purpose of furnishing consumer reports to third parties, and which uses any means or facility of interstate commerce for the purpose of furnishing consumer reports."

Consumer Report

The term consumer report was used in the definition above. A *Consumer Report* is "any written, oral, or other communication of any information by a consumer reporting agency bearing on a consumer's credit worthiness, credit standing, credit capacity, character, general reputation, personal characteristics, or mode of living which is used or expected to be used or collected in whole or in part for the purpose of serving as a factor in establishing the consumer's eligibility for:

- credit or insurance to be used primarily for personal, family, or household purposes;
- employment purposes; or
- any other purpose authorized under section 604 [§ 1681b]."

What are Employment Purposes?

Employment purposes, when used in connection with a consumer report means " a report used for the purpose of evaluating a consumer for employment, promotion, reassignment or retention as an employee."

The purpose of the FCRA is to facilitate the flow of essential information concerning an individual's background, while at the same time protecting that individual's privacy rights. This is accomplished through the imposition of statutory and regulatory safeguards imposed on CRAs and the users and providers of their information. The regulations are designed to ensure the accuracy of the information being provided. A failure to comply with the FCRA's requirements exposes the CRA as well as the CRA customer, to both civil and criminal penalties.

In addition to the federal FCRA, there are state versions of the FCRA. Often, these state versions are more restrictive than the federal FCRA. Their inter-relationship will be detailed in the next chapter.

The Sword and the Shield

The FCRA is both a triple-edged sword *and* a triple-sided shield. The sword imposes obligations on providers, users and consumers. The shield protects.

The Sword Hanging over CRAs

Criminal record vendors must comply with a host of regulatory guidelines, among the most critical being to "use reasonable procedures to insure maximum possible accuracy" of the information they report. Failure to comply with these requirements can expose the CRA to civil penalties. In addition, CRAs must provide to users a notice of their responsibilities. This is shown in Appendix 2. Incidentally, there is another entity regulated by the FTC. These are the *furnishers* of information. This would include creditors reporting credit transaction histories. A copy of the notice to furnishers is shown in the Appendix.

The Shield Protecting CRAs

On the other hand, the FCRA recognizes the need for the free flow of essential information. It recognizes that mistakes will be made and that some information is subjective, i.e., the "truth" of an event can be viewed differently by the consumer and reporting company. The FCRA therefore offers CRAs a shield against defamation and slander lawsuits if they act without malice and a modicum of care.

The Sword Hanging over Users

The sword hanging over users is not very sharp but is does have a little edge to it. Among the more prominent requirements imposed on users is: 1. the duty to inform job applicants before they order information from a CRA; 2. notify the consumer before they "take adverse action," (e.g., not hire the person based in whole or part upon the information received), and; 3. provide the consumer with the Federal Trade Commission-authored "summary of their rights" notice. A copy of this notice is shown in the Appendix.

The Shield Protecting Users

Most of the shield afforded to users is provided by the CRA. If an employment decision is made based on erroneous information, an employer obtaining the information on his own will be defending his data retrieval practices. But, the employer using a CRA is usually able to defer this liability to the CRA, provided they chose their CRA with some due diligence.

The Sword Hanging over Consumers

The consumer's ability to successfully sue CRAs is somewhat constrained by the FCRA. Consumers won't "win the lottery" by suing a CRA even when the CRA has, in fact, reported erroneous information that harmed the individual—provided the CRA has taken reasonable precautions to report accurate information. While the FCRA mandates that CRAs must verify information if disputed by consumers, the FCRA gives them time— about 30 days—to verify and correct the information.

For the most part however, the FCRA does not threaten, but instead protects consumers.

The Shield Protecting Consumers

This is probably the biggest goal of the FCRA. Most of the law deals with consumer protections, from releases that must be provided to the individual, to the information that can be reported, to the procedures in case of disputed accuracy.

Primary Effects of the FCRA on Employers Using a Vendor to Obtain Criminal Records

Criminal records obtained from a vendor and used for employment purposes are "consumer reports" as defined by the FCRA. So are other reports obtained from vendors, such as driving records, credit reports and employment histories. The following discussion on releases and notifications is not exclusive to criminal records.

There are three primary areas where the FCRA will affect employers who obtain criminal records from criminal record vendors. As discussed above, the FCRA affects the entire relationship, and the three areas discussed below pertain to the major considerations of employers using criminal records obtained from a vendor.

Releases and Notifications

Written Notification Before Ordering

Before ordering a criminal record from a vendor that you intend to use as a factor in establishing an individual's eligibility for employment, the FCRA requires that:

(i) a clear and conspicuous disclosure has been made in writing to the consumer at any time before the report is procured or caused to be procured, in a document that consists solely of the disclosure, that a consumer report may be obtained for employment purposes; *(Section 604(b)(2)(A))*

So, "a clear and conspicuous disclosure" must be made to the applicant. In the next paragraph, the FCRA requires the consumer to authorize the company to obtain the report.

(ii) the consumer has authorized in writing (which authorization may be made on the document referred to in clause (i)) the procurement of the report by that person. *(Section 604(b)(2)(B))*

This is a detailed section of the law, in that it goes to the level of mandating what can and cannot be on the written disclosure. CRAs, for their part, must obtain certification from the employer that it has given the required notice and received written authorization from the employee or applicant to obtain the report. So, the FCRA imposes the obligation on the employer to disclose and obtain releases, but it also imposes the obligation on the CRA to obtain certification from the employer that it will be done.

Notices Required Before and After "Adverse Action" is Taken

The FCRA also requires that before taking any "adverse action" based in whole or part on the criminal record, the employer must provide the applicant or employee a copy of the report and a written description of the consumer's rights as written by the Federal Trade Commission. The Federal Trade Commission (FTC) is the primary agency that enforces and interprets FCRA issues. A copy of this notice can be found in the Appendix.

Adverse Action is defined by the FCRA as "a denial of employment or any other decision for employment purposes that adversely affects any current or prospective employee." *{Section 603(k)(1)(B)(ii)}*

Aside from the above requirements *before* taking adverse action, there are other, somewhat redundant, steps that must be taken *after* the adverse action.

(1) provide oral, written, or electronic notice of the adverse action to the consumer;

(2) provide to the consumer orally, in writing, or electronically the name, address, and telephone number of the consumer reporting agency (including a toll-free telephone number established by the agency if the agency compiles and maintains files on consumers on a nationwide basis) that furnished the report to the person; and a statement that the consumer reporting agency did not make the decision to take the adverse action and is unable to provide the consumer the specific reasons why the adverse action was taken; and

(3) provide to the consumer an oral, written, or electronic notice of the consumer's right to obtain, under section 612 [§ 1681j], a free copy of a consumer report on the consumer from the consumer reporting agency referred to in paragraph (2), which

notice shall include an indication of the 60-day period under that section for obtaining such a copy; and to dispute, under section 611 [§ 1681i], with a consumer reporting agency the accuracy or completeness of any information in a consumer report furnished by the agency. {615(a)}

A FCRA Notification Exception

The prior written notice and release, as well as the adverse action requirements have been modified for trucking companies who pre-screen commercial drivers applying for a job remotely.

No doubt about it, the following information detailing the commercial driver limited exemption is dry-as-a-sawpit stuff. If you are not a trucking company hiring drivers by phone, mail or computer, skip it. If you are a trucking company, find a vendor that knows your business.

The government-speak for the disclosure and release waiver in those instances when a trucking company is pre-screening applicants from a remote location is as follows:

(i) the consumer is applying for a position over which the Secretary of Transportation has the power to establish qualifications and maximum hours of service pursuant to the provisions of section 31502 of title 49, or a position subject to safety regulation by a State transportation agency; and

(ii) as of the time at which the person procures the report or causes the report to be procured the only interaction between the consumer and the person in connection with that employment application has been by mail, telephone, computer, or other similar means. {604(b)(2)(B) and (C)}

In addition, the adverse action requirements have been amended, as follows:

(B) Application by mail, telephone, computer, or other similar means.

(i)   If a consumer described in subparagraph (C) applies for employment by mail, telephone, computer, or other similar means, and if a person who has procured a consumer report on the consumer for employment purposes takes adverse action on the employment application based in whole or in part on the report, then the person must provide to the consumer to whom the report relates, in lieu of the notices required under subparagraph (A) of this section and under section 615(a), within 3 business days of taking such action, an oral, written or electronic notification—

    (I)   that adverse action has been taken based in whole or in part on a consumer report received from a consumer reporting agency;

    (II)   of the name, address and telephone number of the consumer reporting agency that furnished the consumer report (including a toll-free telephone number established by the agency if the agency compiles and maintains files on consumers on a nationwide basis);

(III)   that the consumer reporting agency did not make the decision to take the adverse action and is unable to provide to the consumer the specific reasons why the adverse action was taken; and

(IV)   that the consumer may, upon providing proper identification, request a free copy of a report and may dispute with the consumer reporting agency the accuracy or completeness of any information in a report.

(ii)   If, under clause (B)(i)(IV), the consumer requests a copy of a consumer report from the person who procured the report, then, within 3 business days of receiving the consumer's request, together with proper identification, the person must send or provide to the consumer a copy of a report and a copy of the consumer's rights as prescribed by the Federal Trade Commission under section 609(c)(3)

(C) Scope. Subparagraph (B) shall apply to a person procuring a consumer report on a consumer in connection with the consumer's application for employment only if

(i)   the consumer is applying for a position over which the Secretary of Transportation has the power to establish qualifications and maximum hours of service pursuant to the provisions of section 31502 of title 49, or a position subject to safety regulation by a State transportation agency; and

(ii)   (ii) as of the time at which the person procures the report or causes the report to be procured the only interaction between the consumer and the person in connection with that employment application has been by mail, telephone, computer, or other similar means. {604(b)(3)(B) and (C)}

Told you it was dry stuff. Again, this is a narrow exception for trucking companies hiring commercial drivers in certain instances.

FCRA Restrictions on Reporting Arrest Information

The FCRA also affects employers obtaining criminal records from criminal record vendors because it prescribes limits on what information can be provided. Specifically, it limits the amount of time arrest information may be reported. This does not apply to conviction information.

Arrests were defined in Chapter 2 as follows:

An *Arrest* is the taking of an individual into custody by law enforcement personnel (i.e. the person's behavior is arrested) in order to charge them with an illegal act.

Convictions, in contrast to arrests, were defined in Chapter 2 as follows:

A *Conviction* is a finding of guilt after a judicial trial. However, some states have expanded this definition to include such dispositions as a "deferred sentence, adjudication withheld." These are proceedings in which the defendant admits guilt, but if they behave themselves for a specified period of time, the charges are dismissed. With recent changes, these dismissals will still be considered convictions.

The FCRA states that a CRA may not report arrest information that is older than 7 years. In the fed's inimitable legal-speak, it is worded as follows:

(a) *Information excluded from consumer reports.* Except as authorized under subsection (b) of this section, no consumer reporting agency may make any consumer report containing any of the following items of information:

(2) Civil suits, civil judgments, and records of arrest that from date of entry, antedate the report by more than seven years or until the governing statute of limitations has expired, whichever is the longer period. *{605(a)(2)}*

A clear distinction is made for conviction information. Conviction information may be reported without limitation. The FCRA spells it out it in subsection (5). Continuing from part (b) above, they are saying no CRA can report…

(5) Any other adverse item of information, other than records of convictions of crimes which antedates the report by more than seven years. *{605(a)(5)}*

A FCRA Arrest Information Exception

Of course, it really wouldn't be Federal law without an exception would it? Above, in part (a) it says "…except as authorized under subsection (b)…"

Subsection (b) allows arrest information older than 7 years to be reported if the report will be used in connection with a job in which the annual salary is (or is expected to be) $75,000 or more.

(b) *Exempted cases.* The provisions of subsection (a) of this section are not applicable in the case of any consumer credit report to be used in connection with…

(3) the employment of any individual at an annual salary which equals, or which may reasonably be expected to equal $75,000, or more. *{605(b)(3)}*

FCRA Caveat

If the Federal FCRA was the only law pertaining to the use of arrest records, we could be on our merry way. Unfortunately, some states also have laws that restrict the reporting of arrest and conviction information. Some states don't want employers to use *any* arrest information. Some state laws still limit conviction information to seven years. In other words, some state laws are in direct conflict with the Federal FCRA. In Chapter 14, the Federal and state law interrelation will be discussed in detail. The point here is that, while the Federal FCRA guidelines discussed above are the norm, they're not absolute in all states.

Using Aged Public Records for Employment Purposes

Criminal record vendors providing public record information to companies intending to use the information for employment purposes—and the information is likely to have an adverse impact on the individual—must either insure the information they are providing is up-to-date, or, they must notify the subject of the report that a report is being provided along with the name and address of the person to whom it is being reported.

When will this come into play with a criminal record vendor? When a database contains public record information that is not the most complete or up-to-date available from actual public record sources, **and** the record contains derogatory information, i.e., a record of arrest or conviction.

An Example—

Assume a criminal record vendor has obtained Watadoosie County's entire database and the database contains less than up-to-date info. ACME Employer requests a criminal record on an individual and the vendor reports a record containing an arrest and conviction. The subject of the search must be notified by the vendor that a report has been provided to ACME, along with ACME's address.

Now assume the criminal record vendor warehouses criminal records previously ordered by other clients. ACME requests a criminal record on an individual. The vendor searches its database and informs ACME that a criminal record was ordered on the subject by another employer two months previously. Offered the choice, ACME elects to obtain the two month-old record instead of ordering a fresh record. If the two-month-old record is clear, i.e., it does not contain a record of arrest or conviction, the notice must not be sent by the vendor, as there is nothing on the report "likely to have an adverse effect upon the consumer."

Using Records from Vendor Databases

In previous chapters, database searches were discussed and it was noted that they could assist users by addressing three aspects of criminal record searching:

- Knowing where to look
- Turnaround time
- Cost

Database searches can be dynamite—but if you avail yourself of a vendor who uses them, insure that they are complying with the following FCRA requirement.

This requirement regarding aged public record for employment purposes is found in section 613 of the FCRA. The FCRA text is as follows:

Public record information for employment purposes

(a) *In general.* A consumer reporting agency which furnishes a consumer report for employment purposes and which for that purpose compiles and reports items of information on consumers which are matters of public record and are likely to have an adverse effect upon a consumer's ability to obtain employment shall

1. at the time such public record information is reported to the user of such consumer report, notify the consumer of the fact that public record information is being reported by the consumer reporting agency, together with the name and address of the person to whom such information is being reported; or

2. maintain strict procedures designed to insure that whenever public record information which is likely to have an adverse effect on a consumer's ability to obtain employment is reported it is complete and up to date. For purposes of this paragraph, items of public record relating to arrests, indictments, convictions, suits, tax liens, and outstanding judgments shall be considered up to date if the current public record status of the item at the time of the report is reported.

Oh, one more thing. The feds do grant themselves an exemption:

(b) *Exemption for national security investigations.* Subsection (a) does not apply in the case of an agency or department of the United States Government that seeks to obtain and use a consumer report for employment purposes, if the head of the agency or department makes a written finding as prescribed under section 604(b)(4)(A).

It's really a shame they couldn't have stopped here, with a federal law that governed all transactions of this type across the country. Unfortunately, there are state laws in direct conflict with the federal FCRA, and you must follow the state law in some instances. The next chapter details these instances.

Chapter 14

The Federal FCRA Interrelation with State FCRAs

Laws are like sausages. It's better not to see them being made.

—Otto von Bismarck

When the German statesman Otto Von Bismarck said the public should not watch sausage or laws being made, he was making a couple of points.

Explicit in the comment was that watching either of the processes was not a pretty sight. When making "law," unwritten deals are cut between incongruous allies that are interdependent on secret deals later denied.

Implicit was the thought that after the process, the laws and sausages wouldn't look too bad. The finished law would be a blend of the various constituencies and while not perfect, perhaps a pretty good compromise.

The Federal Fair Credit Reporting Act and its relationship with the various state Fair Credit Reporting Acts is different. The laws in and of themselves are kind of pretty, but when you take the finished product, i.e., how the Federal and state FCRAs interrelate, it gets ugly.

By most accounts, the original Federal FCRA was a thoughtful, forward-looking piece of legislation. It certainly stood the test of time well, protecting users, consumers and providers. The original law was enacted in October 1970, and while amended several times over the years, the amendments were, until the late 1990's, minor. The September 30, 1996 "amendment" was really a re-write of the law. It was after this re-write that the inter-relation between the federal and state FCRA's got ugly. The ugliness is seen, in great part, in our efforts to unravel the complexity and figure out—on a state-by-state basis—which law (federal or state) we should be trying to follow.

What Do Federal and State Interrelations Have To Do with Ordering Criminal Records?

As we saw in the previous chapter, Section 605 of the federal Fair Credit Reporting Act (FCRA) allows criminal record *conviction* information to be reported through *a consumer reporting agency* in perpetuity. Non-conviction information must be, ahem, arrested after seven years i.e., suppressed or hidden. So far, so easy. The rub comes when you have a state with their own version of the FCRA in conflict with the federal version. Now you find yourself in a position where an interpretation based on the inter-relation of the state and federal law will dictate what information you can receive from a criminal record provider.

Why is it so darn complicated?

Prior to the 1996 FCRA amendment, federal and state law (when a state law was present) was consistent. Furthermore, when there was a difference, the federal FCRA pre-empted the state law. Prior to the 1996 amendment, there was no distinction made between arrests and convictions. The FCRA simply stated that there were to be no:

> " Records of arrest, indictment, or conviction of crime which, for the date of disposition, release or parole, antedate the report by more than 7 years."

Unless

> The report was to be used in connection with

- "(1) a credit transaction involving, or which may reasonably be expected to involve, a principal amount of **$50,000** or more;

- (2) the underwriting of life insurance involving, or which may reasonably be expected to involve, a face amount of **$50,000** or more; or

- (3) the employment of any individual at an annual salary which equals, or which may reasonably be expected to equal **$20,000** or more."

That's was simple enough. The 1996 FCRA Amendment changed the exceptions to:

> " The report was to be used in connection with

- (1) a credit transaction involving, or which may reasonably be expected to involve, a principal amount of **$150,000** or more;

- (2) the underwriting of life insurance involving, or which may reasonably be expected to involve, a face amount of **$150,000** or more; or

- (3) the employment of any individual at an annual salary which equals, or which may reasonably be expected to equal **$75,000** or more."

Okay, no need to call in a rocket scientist yet. One problem is that not all the states changed their state FCRAs to mirror the federal amounts. So, what amount do you use—the federal amount or your state's amount.

Problem two is that exactly one year after the 1996 amendment was implemented there was another amendment titled (you gotta love this) "The Consumer Reporting Employment Clarification Act of 1998." This clarification changed the *type* of information that could be reported to today's federal standard. It also created an FCRA distinction between arrest information and conviction information.

Today, the FCRA allows conviction information to be reported by a CRA regardless of the record's age. Non-conviction records must be suppressed if they did not happen within the past seven years and do not meet the exceptions as outlined above. Again, however, not all states have changed their laws to fit this new national standard. Some states still limit the release of *records with convictions* to seven years, no more.

In summary, there is a stew of federal law and state laws dealing with exceptions to rules for the types of information that may be reported.

When in Conflict, Which Law—Federal or State— Pre-empts the Other?

The Federal FCRA provides the answer...if you can decipher it.

Thank heaven the federal FCRA clears all this up with section 624, *Relation to State Laws.* It says this:

> Except as provided in subsections (b) and (c), this title does not annul, alter, affect, or exempt any person subject to the provisions of this title from complying with the laws of any State with respect to the collection, distribution, or use of any information on consumers, except to the extent that those laws are inconsistent with any provision of this title, and then only to the extent of the inconsistency. *{§624(a)}*

Okay, this is saying that the federal law does not overrule a state law unless they differ, and if they do, only the differing parts of the state law are overruled. There was that first sentence, though, about "except as provided in subsections (b) and (c)." Section (c) we can skip. However, Subsection (b) says:

> *General exceptions.* No requirement or prohibition may be imposed under the laws of any State
>
> (1) with respect to any subject matter regulated under
>
>> (E) section 605, relating to information in consumer reports, except that this subparagraph shall not apply to any State law in effect on the date of

enactment of the Consumer Credit Reporting Reform Act of 1996. *{§624(b)(1)(E)})*

I dunno about you, but my head is starting to hurt. Once this has been read about forty times however, it can easily be determined that this says that the federal law prevails over the state law unless the state law was in effect on or before September 30th, 1996. It is bad enough that the *General Exceptions* stopped here, but it tries to get worse. The pertinent parts in Subsection (d) read as follows:

Limitations. Subsections (b) and (c)

(2) do not apply to any provision of State law (including any provision of a State constitution) that

- is enacted after January 1, 2004;
- states explicitly that the provision is intended to supplement this title; and
- gives greater protection to consumers than is provided under this title.

Now I'm looking around for Werner Von Braun's pager number. The sum of all this is that federal law does not supercede any state law enacted before September 30, 1996 or, any state law passed after January 1, 2004 if the future law states explicitly that the provision is intended to supplement the federal FCRA, and gives greater protection to the consumer than the federal FCRA. "Greater protection" in our criminal record context means fewer years reported or convictions only, or higher money exceptions.

The question for CRAs to answer is: what states had more restrictive laws (offered more protection to the consumer) before September 30, 1996 and have not, as we draw nearer to 2004, passed less restrictive legislation that mirrors the federal FCRA?

> **Examples—**
>
> State A has a 7-year restriction in 1992. They have not updated their law to date. State law prevails.
>
> State B had no law in 1996, but its legislature passed one that was more restrictive than the federal law in 1998. The federal law applies.

Summary of FCRA and State Law Interrelations— Good News for Users

It's a devilishly complex task to determine what information should be reported, but if you are a user of criminal records—say, as part of your duties as an employer—*there is good news.* You don't have to understand and monitor the intricacies of compliance, because you're not at risk. Why? Because, *in regard to reporting information*, the FCRA and the state equivalents do not apply to you. They apply to the CRAs. CRAs are prohibited from reporting the information. As a recipient or user of the information, you are not prohibited by the FCRA from using the information.

What you do have to concern yourself with is the **use** of criminal record information—both arrest and conviction information. For employers, there are federal guidelines and there are also several states that prohibit employers from using arrest information if the arrest information does not have a resulting conviction, (or the disposition is pending).

The following chapter deals with federal considerations when using criminal records for employment purposes. Following the federal chapter, state guidelines are detailed.

Chapter 15

Title VII and Criminal Records

Injustice anywhere is a threat to justice everywhere. We are caught in an inescapable network of mutuality, tied in a single garment of destiny. Whatever affects one directly, affects all indirectly.

—Martin Luther King Jr.

Determining how you feel about the issue as a moral or political matter is one thing. However, when you are an employer, many issues have already been decided for you. It is your responsibility to be aware of what is legal and what isn't. When it is your business, you are considered accountable. And, when considering minorities, the main Federal law dealing with the legality of criminal records is Title VII of the Civil Rights Act.

Criminal Records and Bias Employment Practices

What is "fair?" Title VII of the Civil Rights Act prohibits apparently neutral or "color blind" employment practices if these practices have a disparate impact against minorities or other protected groups.

Why this prohibition exists requires some explaining. Let's consider this scenario. Assume you were to receive employment applications by mail and had an independent third party delete any references to race. In addition, names, all addresses and any other clues that someone might use to infer an individual's race were suppressed. Now, assume that criminal records checks were ordered and those found to have a criminal record of any severity were automatically disqualified. You might think that because you didn't even know the race of the person being disqualified, you couldn't possibly be discriminating against minorities. You would be wrong.

The Use of Statistics

The Equal Employment Opportunity Commission (EEOC) enforces title VII. It is their position that "an employer's policy or practice of excluding individuals from employment on the basis of their conviction records has an adverse impact on Blacks and Hispanics in light of statistics showing that they are convicted at a rate disproportionately greater than their representation in the population." (Policy Statement on the Issue of Conviction Records Under Title VII [February 4,1987]).

The leading Title VII case on the issue of conviction records is Green v. Missouri Pacific Railroad Company. (523 F.2d 1290, 10 EPD ¶ 10, 314 (8th Cir. 1975). In this case, the court held that the defendant's policy of refusing employment to any person convicted of a crime other than a minor traffic offense had an adverse impact on Black applicants and was not justified by business necessity. In a second appeal following remand, the court upheld the district court's injunctive order prohibiting the defendant from using an applicant's conviction record as an absolute bar to employment, but allowed it to consider a prior criminal record as long as it constituted a "business necessity." The EEOC later expanded on "business necessity," and this subject will be addressed later.

The main point here however, is that an employer's policy or practice of excluding individuals from employment on the basis of their conviction records may have an adverse impact on Black and Hispanics in light of statistics showing that they are convicted at a rate disproportionately greater than their representation in the population.

"May have" an adverse impact? Yes, statistics can also be used by the employer for defense. The EEOC has stated that "when the employer can present more narrowly drawn statistics showing either that Blacks and Hispanics are not convicted at a disproportionately greater rate or that there is no adverse impact in its own hiring process resulting from the convictions policy, then a no cause determination would be appropriate." By "more narrowly drawn statistics," the EEOC means that "local, regional or applicant flow data" may be different than the national statistics, and more appropriate. So, if an employer could prove that Whites in their town were evenly convicted in relation to their population with minority groups, the "blind" exclusion policy would probably cause no EEOC problems.

Granted, few employers have a statistician on staff who is monitoring local and national rates of conviction, so it would be a task to turn around the "adverse impact" position with statistics. The key point for an employer to take away from all this is that the EEOC does presume that employers using criminal records as an absolute bar to employment has a disparate impact. So, this aspect of Title VII is something for the employer to be aware of when using criminal records *even though* their employment procedures may seem neutral. A "cookie cutter" or blanket policy of exclusion based on a criminal conviction is not the intelligent way for an employer to operate.

What are the EEOC's Guidelines?

Thus far, the EEOC and *conviction* records have been discussed. The EEOC also differentiates between arrest and conviction records.

EEOC Policy on the Use of Arrest Records

In short, the EEOC summarizes their policy regarding the use of arrest records by saying that

> "the use of arrest records as an absolute bar to employment has a disparate impact on some protected groups and arrest records cannot be used to routinely exclude persons from employment. However, conduct which indicates unsuitability for a particular position is a basis for exclusion. Where it appears that the applicant or employee engaged in the conduct for which he was arrested and that the conduct is job-related and relatively recent, exclusion is justified."

Obviously, there are some subjective factors here. First, notice that the EEOC notes that Blacks and Hispanics are not only convicted of crimes at a disparate rate than non-protected groups, but that they are also arrested at a disparate rate.

Again, with the use of arrest records, no blanket exclusions—no matter how color blind—should be adopted.

Second (provided that you haven't hired a statistician to disprove a disparate impact in your area using local statistics) there must be a "business justification" for using the arrest records as a factor in your decision making.

There must be a "Business Justification" for your use of arrest records.

Business justification revolves around two issues—

1. Job relatedness. Does the conduct for which the person is accused render them unsuitable for the particular position for which they are being considered?

2. Credibility. Did the individual actually commit the action for which he was arrested?

The Job Relatedness Issue

The EEOC has ruled that "an employer may deny employment opportunities to persons based on any prior conduct which indicates that they would be unfit for the position in question, whether that conduct is evidenced by an arrest, conviction or other information provided to the employer. It is the conduct, not the arrest or conviction per se, which the employer may consider in relation to the position sought."

So, if you believe that the individual committed the conduct, even if you know the individual committed the conduct because you watched him do it, there's another consideration: job relatedness.

Sometimes this is easy. A convicted pedophile's prior conduct would make them unfit to work in a Daycare profession. The individual applying for a job digging a ditch should probably not have his past bad check charge exclude him. Sometimes "job-related-ness" is not easy to determine, and, the problem is, you can not just impose a strict standard, i.e., "I will hire anyone with a criminal record unless it directly relates to the position being sought" because the courts, through the negligent hiring doctrine have sometimes been extremely liberal in what they consider "job-related." Consider what an appeals court found "job related."

The Case of Malorney vs. B & L Motor Freight, Inc

In this case a hitchhiker sued the employer of an over-the-road truck driver for sexual assault committed by the truck driver.

Here is the case summery. A man named Edward Harbour applied for a position of over-the-road driver with defendant, B & L. On the employment application, Harbour was questioned as to whether he had any vehicular offenses or other criminal convictions. His response to the vehicular question was verified by B & L, but Harbour's negative reply to the criminal conviction question was not checked by B & L. It turns out that Harbour did have a history of convictions for sex-related crimes. Harbour had been arrested just the previous year for aggravated sodomy of two teenage hitchhikers while driving an over-the-road truck for another employer. Upon being hired by B & L, Harbour was given the company's written instructions, which included a prohibition against picking up hitchhikers in a B & L truck.

Later, Harbour picked up the plaintiff, a 17-year-old hitchhiker. In the sleeping compartment of the truck, he repeatedly raped, assaulted and viciously beat her. After being released, the plaintiff notified police and Harbour was arrested, convicted and sentenced to fifty years with no parole. The plaintiff sued B & L for negligent hiring.

B & L contended that they could not foresee that one of its drivers would rape and assault a hitchhiker, that sexual assault isn't job-related to driving a truck anyway. The Circuit Court denied B & L's motion for summary judgment. B & L appealed. The Appellate Court agreed with the circuit court (did not rule for B & L), and stated:

> "…it is clear that B & L has a duty to entrust its truck to a competent employee fit to driver an over-the-road truck *equipped with a sleeping compartment*. Lack of forethought may exist where one remains in voluntary ignorance of facts concerning the danger in a particular act or instrumentality, where a reasonably prudent person would become advised on the theory that such ignorance is the equivalent of negligence. B & L gave Harbour an over-the-road vehicle *with a sleeping compartment*

and B & L knew, or should have known, that *truckers are prone to give rides to hitchhikers despite rules against such actions* and so the question now becomes one of fact—whether B & L breached its duty to hire a competent driver who was to be entrusted with a B & L over-the-road truck." (*Italics added*).

As talk-show host Johnny Carson would have said, "that's wild, weird, wacky stuff." Virtually all trucks employed in interstate commerce, many in intrastate commerce and some in intra-city commerce, are equipped with a sleeping berth for the driver. How this fact was used as a justification or "business necessity" to order a criminal record is instructive to the careful employer who has to consider job relatedness.

Before you dismiss a criminal offense as unrelated to the job, give this case a quick remembrance if only in your subconscious. The courts have caused many employers grief by making some interesting determinations.

Four Important EEOC Notices

The Appendix contains copies of four important notices written by the EEOC. These notices have set the bar so to speak on what an employer and cannot do with criminal records.

- Evaluation of employer's policy of refusing to hire individuals with conviction records

- Commission's procedure for determining whether arrest records may be considered in employment decisions

- Job advertising and pre-employment inquiries

- A business justifying the exclusion of an individual from employment on the basis of a conviction record

For more information about the EEOC, visit their web site at www.eeoc.gov.

Chapter 16

State Restrictions on Criminal Record Use by Employers

Crime wouldn't pay if the government ran it.

—Anon

So, as an employer, you have learned the EEOC guidelines and now know all the legal precautions you must take, right? Not so fast there. Some states have their own regulations on what information employers may use. These restrictions can be more restrictive than the federal EEOC guidelines.

Okay, here comes the obligatory legal caveat. Ready? The following information is true to the best of our knowledge and research. However, these restrictions can change in the blink of a legislator's eye on the last day of the session. Some of the information is a matter of interpretation. In addition, there's always the chance—however slight—that a mistake has been made. So, before treating the following information as gospel, seek legal advice.

States That Prohibit the Use of Arrest Records (i.e., non-conviction records)

Several states have made a legislative decision that certain arrest records are irrelevant and should not be considered by employers when making employment decisions. They are addressing the credibility issue, i.e., did the individual actually commit the action he's being accused of? This issue was discussed in the EEOC section.

At the time of this writing, thirteen states prohibit employers from reviewing arrest records without a resulting conviction unless the charge is pending. So, if an arrest has been made and the individual is not convicted, the information should not be reviewed by an employer. If an arrest has been made and there is no disposition yet, the arrest may be reviewed because the result is pending. Please note that even here there are shades of prohibition.

Some states' laws clearly prohibit the practice, while others pre-employment Inquiry Guides note that it is "improper."

The states that have some type of prohibition against employers reviewing arrest records not connected to a conviction and without a pending charge are—

- California

  There is an exception for certain arrests when the applicant will be employed at a health facility and have access to patients, drugs or medication.

- Hawaii
- Illinois
- Massachusetts

  However, facilities caring for the elderly and disabled, and long-term care facilities must obtain all available criminal offender information concerning an individual before hiring.

- Michigan

  This prohibition in Michigan only applies to misdemeanor arrests.

- Nevada
- New York
- Pennsylvania
- Rhode Island

  Unless the applicant is applying for a job in law enforcement

- Utah
- Virginia
- Washington
- Wisconsin

  Unless the applicant is applying for a bondable position

State That Prohibit the Use of Misdemeanor Convictions

Several states also restrict the use by employers of misdemeanor convictions.

If the arrest prohibition is an attempt by some states to address the credibility issue, the misdemeanor prohibition is an attempt to address the "job related" issue. These states have decided that in some cases, misdemeanor infractions should not be considered by employers—that they are never "job related."

The states that to some degree limit employers from reviewing misdemeanor records are—

- California

  In those cases in which probation has been successfully completed or otherwise discharged and the case has been judicially dismissed.

- Hawaii

  Employers cannot consider misdemeanor convictions for which a jail sentence cannot be imposed. (They are restrictive on felony convictions too.)

- Massachusetts

  Employers cannot inquire into or maintain records regarding any misdemeanor conviction where the date of such conviction or completion of incarceration, whichever date is later, occurred five or more years prior to the date of application for employment, unless such person has been convicted of any offense within the five years immediately preceding the date of such application for employment.

- Minnesota

  Employers cannot consider misdemeanor convictions for which a jail sentence cannot be imposed.

- New York

  Employers may not consider misdemeanor convictions older than 5 years unless the person has also been convicted of some other crime within the past 5 years.

States That Prohibit the Use of Expunged or Sealed Records

An expunged or sealed criminal record is one that a court has ordered to be kept a secret. When ordering a criminal record on an individual, some locales will report that that they may not report the criminal record because it has been sealed or expunged.

This absurdity is along the lines of "they made me promise not to tell you that your dog got ran over by a car, so I won't."

Sealed or expunged criminal records are controversial, but reporting that an individual's criminal record is not available because it has been sealed or expunged seems one tick disingenuous. Especially ludicrous are those records I have seen that report that there is no criminal record by stating "Record Expunged." Crazy…and yet it happens. As a result, ten states explicitly prohibit the consideration of expunged or sealed records. These states are:

- California
- Colorado
- Hawaii

- Illinois
- Ohio

    Employers are prohibited from inquiring about job applicants' juvenile arrest records that have been expunged.

- Oklahoma
- Oregon

    Employers cannot refuse to hire based upon a juvenile record that have been expunged.

- Rhode Island
- Texas
- Virginia

A few more states, while not explicitly prohibiting employers from reviewing the records do all allow job applicants to "lawfully deny or fail to acknowledge" sealed or expunged records. Frankly, it is probably unwise to put too fine a point on the legalities of using a sealed or expunged record. An employer using a legally sealed or expunged record to deny employment will probably be challenged, if the reason for the denial is known. Incidentally, if you are using a criminal record vendor, the vendor will probably suppress notations regarding sealed or expunged records.

States that Limit the Use of First Offense Records

Two states give first offenders a mulligan.

- Georgia

    Certain first offender crimes in which the offender has been discharged without court adjudication of guilt are not reportable under Georgia law and a notification of discharge and exoneration is to be placed upon the record by the court. The discharge is not considered a conviction of a crime and may not be used to disqualify a person in any application for employment.

- Massachusetts

    Employers may not inquire or maintain records related to a first conviction for any of the following misdemeanors: drunkenness, simple assault, speeding, minor traffic violations, affray, or disturbance of the peace.

States That Restrict the Use of Records Based on Time Periods

Two states restrict the use of criminal records based on their age.

- Hawaii

  Employers may not examine conviction records older than 10 years.

- Massachusetts

  Certain misdemeanors (as detailed in the misdemeanor section above) older than five years.

State Reporting Restrictions

There is a big difference in a state law that restricts the *use* of a criminal record by *employers* and a state law that restricts what a *vendor* can *report*. Several states restrict what a vendor can report, i.e., they have different limitations than the federal FCRA based on time periods. However, there are many exceptions and many of the states are changing their laws to mirror the federal guidelines. (For more information on this complex interrelation, see Chapter 14.) States that recently still restricted vendor reporting of criminal conviction information to 7 years were California, Kansas, Maryland, Massachusetts, Montana, New Hampshire, New Mexico, New York and Washington. However, Kansas, Maryland Massachusetts, New Hampshire and Washington waive the time limit if the applicant is reasonably expected to make $20,000 or more annually. In New York, the exception is $25,000.

Is it any wonder that many employers and vendors concentrate on complying with the federal FCRA?

States That Limit Record Access to Employers Only Within Certain Industries

Finally, in some states, they have tried to do your thinking for you. If you are in an industry they have deemed to be critical (or the industry had good lobbyists,) you are privileged for criminal record access and use from the state repository. These states permit access, by statute, to certain industries, such as childcare, nurseries, etc.

If, on the other hand, you're some poor soul trying to eek out a living by running a business in some "non-critical" industry, you may be up a river for state repository access.

However, as discussed earlier, criminal records from the counties will almost certainly be available and the fact that the state prohibits access to its repository should not prove a deterrent to getting the information you need. In fact, as was discussed earlier, county records are superior to statewide records in some respects.

Legal Concerns Versus Gut Reactions

Employers will find times when their legal concerns conflict with their gut feelings.

I won't tell you what to do if you are the owner of a laundromat hiring an employee to collect the change from your equipment and you find a misdemeanor conviction for theft. I won't even give advice to you if you are running a daycare or hiring a nanny to watch your children, and your state prohibits your use of all available arrest information.

I will tell you to weigh your options and give it some thought. Here's an example.

> **Example—**
>
> I once knew an old, no-nonsense safety director at a huge trucking company. He was a "law and order" man, not given to (or accepting of) most any illegal dalliance you'd care to name. He was in charge of screening and hiring the truck drivers. They had terminals in a state that restricted the use of misdemeanor records. We discussed the issue of finding a misdemeanor DWI (driving while intoxicated) on a potential driver.
>
> I educated him on the law. He educated me on what he thought about the law. He ended with this thought that has stuck with me. "Son, I'd much rather be sitting there in the witness box explaining why I didn't hire that driver than be sitting there explaining to the jury why I did hire him after he's killed somebody."

Food for thought.

If You Get Into Trouble

Here in the Land of the Free and Home of the Brave, anyone can sue most anyone for anything.

If you are an employer and order criminal records, chances are, they will keep you out of court one heck of a lot more than they will bring you to court. However, there is always the chance that a prospective or current employee will sue you in relation to ordering a criminal record. If you've ordered a criminal record and taken an "adverse action" against the subject of the report for something you've found on the report, there is a slim chance you will get sued (or more likely, threaten to get sued). There are several reasons criminal record lawsuits are rare.

Consider first that most people do not have criminal records. The percentage of records you will find that contain a criminal record will vary greatly depending on your applicant pool. (You could expect differing percentages for Nuns and pro football players for instance.) A good average to use for illustrative purposes is 13%.

This means that 87% of the time a criminal record is ordered, it will come back with no criminal record activity. We're litigious, but not yet so much so that the 87% will cause any trouble.

That leaves 13%. As we have discussed, you will not take adverse action on all 13% of these individuals. Some of the criminal activity will be minor, non-job-related activity. Let's say you've ordered 1000 criminal records. Of this amount 130 will have criminal records. You may take "adverse action " against 100 of the 130 applicants.

Of the 100 individuals, most who are turned down for employment will apply elsewhere. Whether the applicant goes down the street or gets ticked at you depends on how many other roughly equal opportunities to yours exist. The attorney-folk would ask if the position being applied for is "fungible." The position, and how many similar others there are will influence the applicant's reaction. In my experience, far fewer than 1 in 100 applicants turned down by a job for a criminal record sue or threaten to sue. You can see, though, that even if it *were* 1 in 100 refused applicants, that is only 1 in 1000 criminal records ordered.

Compare this to the damage that could have been caused by even one of the 100 in 1000 applicants you turned away. Truly, the fear of being sued is far greater than the chance of being sued.

If You Do Get Hit by (Legal) Lightning

When you didn't use a vendor

The first advice I can give if you get sued is to procure an attorney who specializes in your trouble. Due, at least in part, to the litigious society in which we live, specialties have come about in law. Just as would not go to your general practitioner Doctor to perform a triple bypass on your heart, I would advise you not to hire your tax attorney to handle your criminal record employment case. Find an attorney well versed in employment law.

If you obtained the record from a vendor

If there is a dispute as to the accuracy of the record or a question as to whether the report you received pertains to your applicant (the most two most common reasons for disputes) and you used a vendor, call your vendor. They should be able to direct you to an attorney well versed in Fair Credit Reporting Act (FCRA) protections.

Many attorneys specializing in employment law are not aware of the provisions of the FCRA, and you need to find one who is.

One benefit of this advice is that you are more likely to win your case if it goes to trial. The huge benefit of this advice is that an attorney who knows his stuff in this area will likely short circuit the case long before it goes to trial. Even if you have an in-house employment attorney, or one on retainer, I recommend a consultation with an attorney who knows the FCRA.

Author Tip—

I've spent a lot of time on employment FCRA cases, sat in many depositions and worked with many attorneys—of the plaintiff and defense varieties. My unsolicited opinion is that the premier attorney on this subject, with over 20 years experience is:

Larry Henry of the firm Boone, Smith, Davis Hurst & Dickman.

Email: Lhenry@Boonesmith.com

Firm Website: www.Boonesmith.com

Telephone: (918) 587-0000.

Section 4

Government Agency Profiles

This section has two chapters.

Chapter 17 - State Profiles - consists of detail pages on each state. Here you will find information about a state's criminal record agency, the sexual offender registry, central state incarceration records agency, and state court system.
The agencies are examined for the following information: access requirements, restrictions, fees, online modes, policies and procedures. Special attention is given to employer needs.

Chapter 18 - US District Courts - presents an overview of criminal record access at the federal court level. Each District and Division Court is listed, along with the specific counties served.

Editor's note: The data in Section 4 is provided by BRB Publications, Inc. (www.brbpub.com)

Alaska

State Criminal Records Agency

Department of Public Safety
Records and Identification
5700 E Tudor Rd
Anchorage, AK 99507

Phone: 907-269-5765.
Fax: 907-269-5091

Web: http://www.dps.state.ak.us/

Total Records: 251,100

Who Can Access: There are two record types released. A requester can provide verification of status as an "Interested Person" defined as person who employs, appoints or permits the subject to have supervisory power over others, usually related to child care. Otherwise, an "Any Person" report is processed. In-state employers may also request an FBI check for an additional fee.

Search Requirements: Include the following: set of fingerprints, full name. If an FBI check is ordered, include a second set of prints (available only to in-state requesters).

What Is Released: For "Interested Person" reports, all records are released, including those without dispositions, except sealed records. "Any Person" reports include only those records with dispositions. Records are available for 10 years from the unconditional discharge date of the incident.

Indexing & Storage: 86% of arrests in database have final dispositions recorded; 85% for those arrests in last 5 years. Approximately 62% of records are fingerprint-supported. Arrest records without dispositions are not purged from the state's database.

Access By: Mail, in person.

Mail Search: Results of search are also sent to the subject.

In Person Search: Results are usually mailed.

Fee & Payment: The fee is $35.00 per search. The subject may, in person, request a search for $20.00, without fingerprints. This also applies to government agencies. If authorized, a requester may also request a national check by the FBI for an additional $24.00. Fee payee: State of Alaska. Prepayment required. No credit cards accepted.

Sexual Offender Registry

Sex offender data is available online at www.dps.state.ak.us/nSorcr/asp/, and by mail or in person from the Permits and Licensing Unit at the address listed above. Call 907-269-0396 for more information.

State Incarceration Records Agency

Alaska Department of Corrections   **Phone:** 907-269-7390

DOC Classification Office   **Fax:**   907-269-7426

4500 Diplomacy Drive, Suite 270   **Web:**   www.correct.state.ak.us

Anchorage, AK 99508-5918

Access by:	Phone and mail. For a search, you must provide full name, DOB and SSN helpful.
What is released:	Information on current and former inmates is available. Location, physical identifiers, charges, bail data, conviction and sentencing data are released.
Search Notes:	No fee for search.

State Court System

Court Structure:	Alaska is not organized into counties, but rather into 15 boroughs and 12 home rule cities, which do not directly coincide with the 4 Judicial Districts, that is, judicial boundaries cross borough boundaries. You should search through the city court location names to determine the correct court to search. S.E. Alaska is the 1st District with five trial courts: Ketchikan, Wrangell, Petersburg, Sitka and Juneau. District Magistrate Courts are Haines, Skagway, Yakutat, Angoon, Kake, Hoona, Craig.
Find Felony Records:	Superior Courts
Misdemeanor Records:	District Courts, Magistrate Courts
Online Access:	There is no internal or external online statewide judicial computer system available.
Searching Hints:	The fees established by court rules for Alaska courts are: search fee–$15.00 per hour or fraction thereof; certification fee–$5.00 per document and $2.00 per add'l copy of the document; copy fee–$.25 per page. Magistrate Courts vary widely in how records are maintained and in operating hours (some are open only a few hours per week).
Court Administrator:	For add'l questions about the state's court system, visit the web site at http://www.state.ak.us/courts/ or contact: Office of the Administrative Director, 303 K St, Anchorage, AK 99501, Phone: 907-264-0547.

Alabama

State Criminal Records Agency

Alabama Department of Public Safety
A.B.I., Identification Unit
PO Box 1511
Montgomery, AL 36102-1511

Phone: 334-395-4340.
Fax: 334-395-4350
Web: http://www.dps.state.al.us/

Total Records: 1,077,000

Who Can Access: Records are available to the general public with written consent of subject.

Search Requirements: The request must be on a state form (call to have copy sent). Include the following in your request: notarized release from subject, date of birth, Social Security Number, full name, race, sex. Fingerprints optional. 100% of the record files have fingerprints.

What Is Released: All records or arrests (except juvenile records) are released, including those without dispositions. Records are available from 1942 on.

Indexing & Storage: It takes about 7 days before new records are available for inquiry. 40% of arrests in database have final dispositions recorded, 65% for those arrests in last 5 years.

Access By: Mail, in person. This agency does not provide online access, but the State Court Administration provides records over its State Judicial Online System (SJIS) at www.alacourt.org. See the next page for details.

Mail Search: Turnaround time is 7 days. No self addressed stamped envelope is required.

In Person Search: You may bring in the required release and request form.

Fee & Payment: The fee is $25.00 per name. For a fingerprint search of both the state and FBI records, the fee is $49.00 per name. Prepayment is required. Fee payee: Alabama Bureau of Investigation. Cashier checks and money orders accepted. No personal checks accepted. No credit cards accepted.

Sexual Offender Registry

Sex offender data is maintained by the Alabama Bureau of Investigations who can be reached at 334-260-1100. Free searching of records is available online at www.gsiweb.net/so_doc/so_index_new.html

State Incarceration Records Agency

Alabama Department of Corrections   **Phone:** 334-240-9501

Central Records Office

1400 Lloyd St., P.O. Box 301501   **Web:**   www.agencies.state.al.us/doc

Montgomery, Al 36130

Access by:	Online and mail. For a search, you must provide first and last name, AIS number.
What is released:	Only current inmate information is available online at this time. Location, AIS number, physical identifiers, projected release date are released.
Search Notes:	No fee for search.

State Court System

Court Structure:	Jefferson (Birmingham), Madison (Huntsville), Marshall, and Tuscaloosa Counties have separate criminal divisions for Circuit and/or District Courts. Misdemeanors committed with felonies are tried with the felony. The Circuit Courts serve as appeals courts for misdemeanors. District Courts can receive guilty pleas in felony cases.
Find Felony Records:	Circuit Courts
Misdemeanor Records:	District Courts, Municipal Courts
Online Access:	A commercial online system is available over the Internet or through the Remote Access system of the State Judicial Information System (SJIS). Users can retrieve basic case information and have access to any criminal, civil, or traffic record in the state. $150 setup fee and monthly charge of $50 for unlimited access. Call Ms. Lenoir at 334-242-0300 for add'l information. The Alabama legal information web site offers commercial access to appellate opinions. For information, see http://alacourt.org.
Searching Hints:	Although in most counties Circuit and District courts are combined, each index may be separate. Therefore, when you request a search of both courts, be sure to state that the search is to cover "both the Circuit and District Court records." Several courts do not perform searches. Most courts have public access computer terminals.
Court Administrator:	Director of Courts, 300 Dexter Ave, Montgomery, AL 36104-3741, Phone: 334-242-0300. www.alacourt.org

Arizona

If You Are an Employer—

If you are an employer located outside of Arizona and wish a criminal records check from the Department of Public Safety, it is strongly recommended to use the services of a pre-employment screening firm.

State Criminal Records Agency

Department of Public Safety   **Phone:**   602-223-2223.
Applicant Team One
PO Box 18430//Mail Code 2250
Phoenix, AZ 85005-8430   **Web:**   http://www.dps.state.az.us/

Total Records:	915,100
Who Can Access:	Record access is limited to agencies that have specific authorization by law which includes employers or pre-employment search firms located in AZ.
Search Requirements:	Fingerprints are required for a search. Include the following in your request: full set of fingerprints plus demographic information on the applicant. Be sure to address requests to Applicant Team One.
What Is Released:	All records are released, including those without dispositions. Records are available from 1988.
Indexing & Storage:	It takes about 14 days before new records are available for inquiry. 50% of arrests in database have final dispositions recorded. Records are indexed on computer back to 1983; non-automated records may go back as far as 1960's, depending on charge.
Access By:	Mail.
Mail Search:	Turnaround time is 2 to 3 days. Arizona employers may call 602-223-2223 to request fingerprint cards and forms. No self addressed stamped envelope is required.
Fee & Payment:	The fee is $6.00 per name. Fee payee: Department of Public Safety. Only cashier's checks and money orders accepted. No credit cards accepted.

Sexual Offender Registry

Sex offender data is maintained by the Department of Public Safety's Sex Offender Cummunity Notification Unit. Free online searching is available at www.azsexoffender.com or call 602-255-0611.

State Incarceration Records Agency

Arizona Department of Corrections

Records Department

1601 West Jefferson

Phoenix, AZ 85007

Phone: 602-542-5586

Fax: 602-545-1638

Web: www.adc.state.az.us

Access by: Fax, online. For online search, you must provide last name, first initial or ADC number. Fax requires full name, the DOB and SSN are helpful.

What is released: Information on current and former inmates is available. Location, ADC number, physical Identifiers and sentencing information are released. Inmates admitted and released from 1972 to 1985 are not searchable on the web.

Search Notes: No fee for search.

State Court System

Court Structure: The Superior Court is the court of general jurisdiction. Justice, and Municipal Courts generally have separate jurisdiction over case types as indicated in the text. Most courts will search their records by plaintiff or defendant. Estate cases are handled by Superior Court.

Find Felony Records: Superior Courts

Misdemeanor Records: Justice of the Peace, Municipal Courts

Online Access: A non-public system called ACAP (Arizona Court Automation Project) is implemented in over 100 courts. When fully implemented ACAP will provide all participating courts access to all records on the system. Plans call for public availability over the Internet sometime in the near future. For more information, call Tim Lawler at 602-542-9614.

The Maricopa and Pima county courts maintain their own systems, but will also, under current planning, be part of ACAP. These two counties provide ever-increasing online access to the public.

Searching Hints: Public access to all Maricopa County court case indexes is available at a central location - 1 W Madison Ave in Phoenix. Copies, however, must be obtained from the court where the case is heard.

Many offices do not perform searches due to personnel and/or budget constraints. As computerization of record offices increases across the state, more record offices are providing public access computer terminals.

Fees across all jurisdictions, as established by the Arizona Supreme Court and State Legislature, are as follows as of August 9, 2001: search at Superior Court is $18.00 per name; at lower courts is $17.00 per name; certification at Superior Court is $18.00 per document; at lower courts is $17.00 per document. Copies are $.50 per page for all courts. Courts may choose to charge no fees. Fees are the same as for civil and criminal case searching.

Court Administrator: For add'l questions aboutP the state's court system, visit the web site at www.supreme.state.az.us/aoc, or contact: Administrative Offices of the Courts, Arizona Supreme Court Bldg, 1501 W Washington, Phoenix, AZ 85007-3231, Phone: 602-542-9301.

Arkansas

State Criminal Records Agency

Arkansas State Police
Identification Bureau
#1 State Police Plaza Dr
Little Rock, AR 72209

Phone: 501-618-8500.
Fax: 501-618-8404
Web: http://www.asp.state.ar.us

Total Records:	499,800
Who Can Access:	Records are available with consent; a notarized release of subject is required.
Search Requirements:	You must use the Bureau's request form. Include the following in your request: notarized release from subject, name, date of birth, sex, Social Security Number, driver's license number. Fingerprints are not required, but may be included. 100% of the arrest records are fingerprint-supported.
What Is Released:	Records without dispositions are not released. Records are available for the past 25 years. Older records are located in the off-site State Archives.
Indexing & Storage:	It takes 2-3 weeks before new records are available for inquiry. 58% of arrests in database have final dispositions recorded, 77% for those arrests in last 5 years. Records are indexed on fingerprint cards.
Access By:	Mail, in person.
Mail Search:	Turnaround time is 3 to 4 weeks. A self addressed stamped envelope is requested.
In Person Search:	Bring in signed release. If applicant is subject, record is released immediately, otherwise it is mailed back.
Fee & Payment:	The fee is $15.00 per record. Fee payee: Arkansas State Police. Prepayment required. Personal checks accepted, credit cards are not.

Sexual Offender Registry

The sexual offender registrant list is maintained by the Arkansas Crime Information Center at 501-682-2222. Records are not available from this agency, but local law enforcement will do searches for employers. The web site is www.acic.org/registration, but records are not available online.

State Incarceration Records Agency

Arkansas Department of Corrections   **Phone:** 870-267-6424

Records Supervisor

7500 Collections Circle   **Web:**   www.accessarkansas.org/doc/

Pine Bluff, AR 71603

Access by:	Mail, online. For a search, you must provide first and last name or ADC number. The online access has many search criteria capabilites.
What is released:	Information on current and former inmates is available; however, the online access is limited to current inmates. Location, ADC number, physical Identifiers and sentencing information, release dates are released.
Search Notes:	No fee for search. A mail search must be directed through the Attorney General's office; phone 510-682-2007.

State Court System

Court Structure:	Circuit Courts are the courts of general jurisdiction and are arranged in 25 circuits. County Courts are, fundamentally, administrative courts dealing with county fiscal issues. Circuit and County Courts can be combined. Chancery and Circuit Courts may be combined under the same judge. As of 7/1/2001, Municipal Courts are known as District Courts.
Find Felony Records:	Circuit Courts
Misdemeanor Records:	District, City, Justice of the Peace and Police Courts
Online Access:	There is a very limited internal online computer system at the Administrative Office of Courts. Benton County provides an online name search of docket information.
Searching Hints:	Most courts that allow written search requests require an SASE. Fees vary widely across jurisdictions as do prepayment requirements.
Court Administrator:	For add'l questions about the state's court system, visit the web site at http://courts.state.ar.us/courts/aoc.html, or contact: Administrative Office of Courts, 625 Marshall Street, 1100 Justice Bldg, Little Rock, AR 72201-1078, Phone: 501-682-9400.

California

> **If You Are an Employer—**
>
> Be aware of three nuances:
>
> 1. By state statute, employers may not use arrest records (records without dispositions) when making employment decisions. There is an exception for certain arrests when the applicant is applying for work at a health care facility and would have access to patients, drugs or medication.
>
> 2. Pre-employment screening firms are restricted from reporting criminal conviction information more than seven years old.
>
> 3. When making employment decisions, employers may not review misdemeanor records in cases where probation has been successfully completed or otherwise discharged and the case has been judicially dismissed.

State Criminal Records Agency

Department of Justice

Records Search Section

PO Box 903417

Sacramento, CA 94203-4170

Phone: 916-227-3460

Web: http://www.caag.state.ca.us

Access to Records is Restricted

Note: Penal Code Sec. 11105 permits access by law enforcement officers acting in their capacity and certain entities authorized by law including county agencies, adoption agencies, and public schools. The subject of the report can obtain their own copy.

Total Records: 6,166,000

Search Requirements: Those entities permitted to obtain records must submit a completed fingerprint card, a letter explaining why the record is needed, and address of the authorized agency where record will be sent. Include the following in your request: fingerprints, full name, DOB, and SSN of subject.

What Is Released: If for a statutorily-required employment check, only records with dispositions are released. However, certain social service agencies may be eligible for all arrest records.

Sexual Offender Registry

The database is maintained by the Sexual Offender Program of the Department of Justice. Their web site is http://caag.state.ca.us/megan/info.htm A search of the database is available for free at local law enforcement agencies, or for $10.00 per search via phone at 900-448-3000.

State Incarceration Records Agency

California Department of Corrections   **Phone:** 916-557-5933

Communications Office   **Fax:**   916-327-1988

P.O. Box 942883   **Web:**   www.cdc.state.ca.us

Sacramento, CA 94283-0001

Access by: Phone, fax, mail. For a search, you must provide full name, DOB and CDC number helpful.

What is released: Information on current and former inmates is available. Location, conviction and sentencing information, and county of conviction are released.

Search Notes: No fee for search. Past prison record information may be searched through the mail or by faxing a request to: 916-327-1988.

State Court System

Court Structure: In July, 1998, the judges in individual counties were given the opportunity to vote on unification of Superior and Municipal Courts within their respective counties. By late 2000, all counties had voted to unify these courts. Courts that were formally Municipal Courts are now known as Limited Jurisdiction Superior Courts. In some counties, Superior and Municipal Courts were combined into one Superior Court.

It is important to note that Limited or Municipal Courts may try minor felonies not included under our felony definition.

Find Felony Records: Superior Court

Misdemeanor Records: Superior Court and Limited Jurisdiction Superior Court

Online Access: There is no statewide online computer access available, internal or external. However, a number of counties have developed their own online access sytems and provide Internet access at no fee. Also, www.courtinfo.ca.gov contains very useful information about the state court system.

Searching Hints: Some courts now require signed releases from the subjects in order to perform criminal searches and will no longer allow the public to conduct such searches.

Although fees are set by statute, courts interpret them differently. For example, the search fee is supposed to be $5.00 per name per year searched, but many courts charge only $5.00 per name. Generally, certification is $6.00 per document and copies are $.50 per page, in some counties $.75 each, and in Los Angeles county, $.57 each. Personal checks are acceptable by state law.

Court Administrator: For add'l questions about the state's court system, visit the web site at www.courtinfo.ca.gov, or contact: Administration Office of Courts, 455 Golden Gate Ave, San Francisco, CA 94102-3660, Phone: 415-865-4200.

A New and Controversial Bill—

In January, 2002, a new and controversial bill passed in California. AB #655 changes the definition of the standard federal "consumer report" to an "investigative consumer report." Under this new law, the employer must provide the subject with a copy of the investigative consumer report.

What is of interest here is that criminal records obtained from public record sources are not "investigative consumer reports" under the federal definition, but they are under California's new law.

The California law states:.". . . (2) If, at any time, an investigative consumer report is sought for employment purposes other than suspicion of wrongdoing by the subject of the investigation, the person procuring or causing the report to be made shall, not later than three days after the date on which the report was first requested, notify the consumer in writing that an investigative consumer report regarding the consumer's character, general reputation, personal characteristics, and mode of living will be made. This notification shall include the name and address of the investigative consumer reporting agency conducting the investigation, the nature and scope of the investigation requested, and a summary of the provisions of Section 1786.22."

This re-definition of "investigative consumer report" is unprecedented, and it remains to be seen if this law will remain in effect for the long term.

Colorado

State Criminal Records Agency

Bureau of Investigation, State Repository   **Phone:**   303-239-4208.

Identification Unit   **Fax:**   303-239-5858

690 Kipling St, Suite 3000   **Web:**   http://cbi.state.co.us/

Denver, CO 80215

Total Records:	970,000
Who Can Access:	Records are available to the general public, but purpose is monitored.
Search Requirements:	The requester must sign a disclaimer stating "This record shall not be used for the direct solicitation of business for pecuniary gain." Include the following in your request: full name, date of birth, sex, race, and disclaimer. The SSN is optional, but suggested. Fingerprints are optional unless statutorily-required. Records are 100% fingerprint supported. If charged after fingerprinted, the practice of notifying the state is becoming more common, though this not yet statewide.
What Is Released:	All records or arrests are released, including those without dispositions, except for sealed records, juvenile records and pending mental comps. Records are available from 1967 on. Records prior to 1967 are in on-site computer archives.
Indexing & Storage:	It takes less than 72 hours before new records are available for inquiry. 12% of all arrests in database have final dispositions recorded, a higher percentage exists those arrests within last 5 years. Records are indexed on inhouse computer, fingerprint cards.
Access By:	Mail, in person, online.
Mail Search:	Turnaround time is 3 days. No self addressed stamped envelope is required.
In Person Search:	You may request information in person.
Online Search:	There is a remote access system available called the Electronic Clearance System (ECS). This is an overnight batch system, open M-F from 7AM to 4PM. The fee is $5.50 per record. There is no set-up fee, but requesters must register and meet quotas. Billing is monthly. For more information, call 303-239-4233.
Fee & Payment:	Name check is $10.00 per name; fingerprint search is$13.00 per fingerprint. A state mandated fingerprint search plus notification of subsequent arrest in CO is $14.00; or nationwide fingerprint search is $22.00. Possible fee changes take place in July each year. Fee payee: Colorado Bureau of Investigations

(CBI). Prepayment required. No personal checks accepted. Credit cards accepted: MasterCard, Visa.

Sexual Offender Registry

Records are maintained by the Sex Offender Registry of the Colorado Bureau of Invesitgation, 303-239-4222. A state-wide sex offender search is not available to the public. It is suggested to search through local law-enforcement agencies.

State Incarceration Records Agency

Colorado Department of Corrections

Offender Records Customer Support

2862 South Cricle Dr., Suite 400

Colorado Springs, CO 80906-4195

Phone: 719-226-4884

Fax: 719-226-4899

Web: www.doc.state.co.us/index.html

Access by: Phone, fax, mail. For a search, you must provide full name. The DOB, SSN, and DLC number are helpful.

What is released: Information on current and former inmates is available. Location, release date, conviction and sentencing information, and DLC number are released.

Search Notes: No fee for search. Computer records go back to 1977.

State Court System

Court Structure: District and County Courts are combined in most counties. Combined Courts usually search both criminal indexes for a single fee. Municipal Courts only have jurisdiction over traffic, parking, and ordinance violations.

Find Felony Records: District Courts

Misdemeanor Records: County Courts

Online Access: There is no official government system, but there is a unique commercial system. All district court and all county court records, except Denver County Court, are available on the Internet at www.cocourts. There is a fee for this subscription Internet access, generally $5.00 per search and there are discounts for volume users.

Searching Hints: All state agencies require a self-addressed, stamped envelope (SASE) for return of information.

Court Administrator: For add'l questions about the state's court system, visit the web site at www.courts.state.co.us, or contact: State Court Administrator, 1301 Pennsylvania St, Suite 300, Denver, CO 80203, Phone: 303-861-1111.

Connecticut

State Criminal Records Agency

Department of Public Safety
Bureau of Identification
PO Box 2794
Middletown, CT 06757-9294

Phone: 860-685-8480.
Fax: 860-685-8361
Web: http://www.state.ct.us/dps

Total Records: 825,600

Who Can Access: In general, records are available to the general public.

Search Requirements: Records are open to the public using a name search. Fingerprint searches are not available to the public. Include the date of birth fo subject in your request. Request forms may be downloaded from the web site. Approximately 90% of the records on file are fingerprint supported.

What Is Released: The records released to the public only contain convictions. Nolles are usually released if in conjunction with a conviction. Records are available from the 1950's on. Records were first computerized in 1983. The following data is not released: pending cases, dismissals or juvenile records.

Indexing & Storage: It takes about 30 days before new records are available for inquiry. 90% of all arrests in database have final dispositions recorded, 90% for those arrests within last 5 years.

Access By: Mail, in person.

Mail Search: Turnaround time is 7 to 10 days. Records can only be requested by mail. If you come in-person, the results are still mailed.

In Person Search: Request must be on agency form; results are returned only by mail.

Fee & Payment: The fee is $25.00 per request. The copy fee is $.25 per page. Fee payee: Commissioner of Public Safety. Prepayment required. Personal checks accepted. No credit cards accepted.

Sexual Offender Registry

The sexual offender data is maintained by the same agency mentioned above. However, due to court order, sex offender data is currently not available to the public.

State Incarceration Records Agency

Connecticut Department of Corrections   **Phone:** 860-692-7780

Office of Public Information

24 Wolcott Hill Road   **Web:**   www.state.ct.us/doc

Wethersfield, CT 06109

Access by:	Phone, mail. For a search, you must provide first and last name, DOB and SSN helpful.
What is released:	Information on current and former inmates is available. Location, conviction and sentencing information, bond, and release dates are released.
Search Notes:	No fee for search. Computer records go back to 1980.

State Court System

Court Structure:	The Superior Court is the sole court of original jurisdiction for all causes of action, except for matters over which the probate courts have jurisdiction as provided by statute. The state is divided into 13 Judicial Districts, 22 Geographic Area Courts, and 14 Juvenile Districts. The Superior Court—comprised primarily of the Judicial District Courts and the Geographical Area Courts—has five divisions: Criminal, Civil, Family, Juvenile, and Administrative Appeals. When not combined, the Judicial District Courts handle felony and civil cases while the Geographic Area Courts handle misdemeanors and small claims.
Find Felony Records:	Judicial District Court
Misdemeanor Records:	Geographic Area Courts
Online Access:	There is currently no online access to criminal records; however, criminal and motor vehicle traffic ticket data is available for purchase in database format.
Searching Hints:	Mail requests to perform criminal searches should be made to the Department of Public Safety, 1111 Country Club Rd, PO Box 2794, Middletown, CT 06457, 860-685-8480. The search fee is $25.00.
	A second source of older records is the State Record Center in Enfield, CT. This is the repository for criminal and some civil records sent to the Record Center some three months to 5 years after disposition by the courts. These records are then maintained 10 years for misdemeanors and 20+ years for felonies. If a requester is certain that the record is at the Record Center, it is quicker to direct the request there rather than to the original court of record. Only written requests are accepted. Search requirements: full defendant name, docket number, disposition date, and court action. Fee is $5.00 for

each docket. Fee payee is Treasurer-State of Connecticut. Direct Requests to: Connecticut Record Center, 111 Phoenix Avenue, Enfield CT 06082, 860-741-3714.

Personal checks must have name and address printed on the check; if requesting in person, check must have same address as drivers' license.

Court Administrator: For add'l questions about the state's court system, visit the web site at www.jud.state.ct.us or contact: Chief Court Administrator, 231 Capitol Ave, Hartford, CT 06106, Phone: 860-757-2100.

Delaware

State Criminal Records Agency

Delaware State Police   **Phone:**   302-739-5880.
State Bureau of Identification   **Fax:**   302-739-5888
PO Box 430   **Web:**   http://www.state.de.us/dsp/
Dover, DE 19903-0430

Total Records: 490,000

Who Can Access: Records are only available with the consent of the subject.

Search Requirements: Requester must have a signed release form, it is not necessary to use the state's forms. Include the following in your request: fingerprints, full name, signed release.

What Is Released: If the disposition is not known by this agency, the record will say "disposition not known." Pre-employment screeners only receive records with dispositions. Records are available from 1935.

Indexing & Storage: It takes up to 3 days before new records are available for inquiry. 81% of all arrests in database have final dispositions recorded, 92% for those arrests within last 5 years.

Access By: Mail, in person.

Mail Search: Turnaround time is 14 days.

In Person Search: It can take up to 14 days before records are ready for pickup.

Fee & Payment: The search fee is $25.00 per request and increases to $30.00 after 7/1/2002. Prepayment is required. Fee payee: Delaware State Police. Funds must be certified or money order. No credit cards accepted.

Sexual Offender Registry

The State Bureau of Investigations also oversees the sexual offender records. Free public access is available online at www.state.de.us/dsp/sexoff/search.htm

State Incarceration Records Agency

Delaware Department of Corrections

Probation and Parole

Central Records

511 Maple Parkway, Dover, DE 19901

Phone: 302-739-2091

Web: www.state.de.us/correct/index.htm

What is released: The Department of Correction does not have an automated database of offender information. The public may receive basic information about an offender, including whether the individual is incarcerated in Delaware, where the individual is incarcerated and, how to contact an offender, by contacting the Department's Office of Community Relations at 302-739-5601 Ext. 246.

State Court System

Court Structure: Superior Court and Court of Chancery are the courts of general jurisdiction, with one court per county. Superior Courts have jurisdiction over felonies and all drug offenses, the Court of Common Pleas has jurisdiction over all misdemeanors. Court of Chancery handles corporation and equity matters, as well as probate and estates. Guardianships are handled by the Register of Wills, corporate matters such as equity disputes and injunctions are handled by the Clerk of Chancery.

Find Felony Records: Superior Court

Misdemeanor Records: Court of Common Pleas

Online Access: Supreme   Court   Final   Orders   and   opinions   are   available   at http://courts.state.de.us/supreme/opinions.htm.

An online system called CLAD, developed by Mead Data Central and the New Castle Superior Court, is currently available in Delaware. CLAD contains only toxic waste, asbestos, and class action cases; however, based on CLAD's success, Delaware may pursue development of online availability of other public records by working in conjunction with private information resource enterprises.

Searching Hints: The Superior Courts will not perform criminal record searches, but permit visitors to search records via public access terminals. Courts suggest to contact the Delaware State Police Headquarters, Criminal Records Section in Dover.

Court Administrator: For add'l questions about the state's court system, visit the web site at http://courts.state.de.us/supreme/index.htm,   or   contact: Administrative Office of the Courts, Supreme Court of Delaware, 820 N French, 11th Fl, Wilmington, DE 19801, Phone: 302-577-2480.

District of Columbia

State Criminal Records Agency

Metropolitan Police Department
Identification and Records Section
300 Indiana Ave NW, Rm 3055
Washington, DC 20001

Phone: 202-727-4245
Fax:
Web: http://www.mpdc.dc.gov/main.shtm

Note: The Superior Court, Criminal Division, is located at 500 Indiana NW, same zip as above. They do not charge a fee for a search and they will indicate over the phone if there is an existing record.

Total Records: 532,000

Who Can Access: Records are available to the general public, but only with consent of subject.

Search Requirements: Include the following in your request: signed, notorized release from subject, full name (middle initial), date and place of birth, year. The SSN, race, curent address and case number, if known, are helpful. Fingerprints searches are not available.

What Is Released: No records are released without dispositions. Police Dept. keeps felony records back to '92, misdemeanors to '97.

Indexing & Storage: It takes 1 day before new records are available for inquiry. 46% of all arrests in database have final dispositions recorded, 84% for those arrests within last 5 years.

Access By: Mail, fax, in person.

Mail Search: Turnaround time is 2 to 4 weeks. A self addressed stamped envelope is required. The Search fee is $5.00 per page.

Fax Search: Records are available by fax.

In Person Search: Records are returned by mail.

Fee & Payment: The fee is $5.00 per page. Fee payee: Metropolitan Police. Personal checks accepted, credit cards are not.

Sexual Offender Registry

The Sex Offender Registry is maintained by the Police Department. Records are available for searching at http://www.mpdc.org/Registry/default.htm.

State Incarceration Records Agency

District of Columbia Department of Corrections   **Phone:** 202-673-8270

DC Detention Facility, Office of Records

1901 D. Street, S.E.

Washington, DC 20003

Access by:	Mail. For a search, you must provide first and last name, DOB and PVID number helpful.
What is released:	Information on current and former inmates is available. Type of data released varies depending on request.
Search Notes:	No fee for search. The reason for the search must be stated in your request.

State Court System

Court Structure:	The Superior Court in DC is divided into 17 divisions, one of which is criminal.
Find Felony Records:	Superior Court
Misdemeanor Records:	Superior Court
Online Access:	The Court of Appeals maintains a bulletin board system for various court notices, and can be dialed from computer at 202-626-8863. Additionally, opinions from 1/1997 to 5/2001 are listed, also memorandum opinions and judgments from 9/1999 to 5/2001. The Court of Appeals has their own web site at www.dcca.state.state.dc.us. The Superior Court at www.dcsc.gov lists Administrative Orders from 1/16/2001 to 5/25/2001.
Searching Hints:	Records at the Superior Court are indexed in microfilm from 1974 on, index cards from 1970 on, in house computer from 1978 on and District Archives from 1962 on. There is no search fee. Call 202-879-1373 for further details.
Court Administrator:	For add'l questions about the court system, visit the web site at www.dcsc.gov, or contact: Executive Office, 500 Indiana Ave NW, Room 1500, Washington, DC 20001, Phone: 202-879-1700.

Florida

State Criminal Records Agency

Florida Department of Law Enforcement   **Phone:**   850-410-8109.

User Services Bureau   **Fax:**   850-410-8201

PO Box 1489

Tallahassee, FL 32302   **Web:**   http://www.fdle.state.fl.us/index.asp

Total Records:	4,187,200
Who Can Access:	Records are available to the general public.
Search Requirements:	Include the following in your request: date of birth, race, sex, name. You can submit fingerprints, for the same fee, but it is not required. 100% of the arrest records are fingerprint-supported.
What Is Released:	All records are released, including those without dispositions. Records are available from the early 1930's. The following data is not released: sealed or expunged records, juvenile records prior to 10/94.
Indexing & Storage:	It takes 1 day before new records are available for inquiry. 70% of all felony arrests in database have final dispositions recorded; 63% of misdemeanors. 68% of all records within last 5 years include dispositions. Records are indexed on microfilm, NIST Archive inhouse computer.
Access By:	Mail, in person, online.
Mail Search:	Turnaround time is 5 working days, 2 days if pre-paid account.
In Person Search:	Turnaround time is same as mail searches, records not released immediately.
Online Search:	Criminal history information from 1967 forward may be ordered over the Department Program Internet site at www2.fdle.state.fl.us. A $15.00 fee applies. Juvenile records from 10/1994 forward are also available. Credit card ordering will return records to your screen or via e-mail.
Fee & Payment:	The fee is $15.00 per individual. Fee payee: Department of Law Enforcement. Prepayment required. Personal checks accepted. Credit cards accepted only for online requests.

Sexual Offender Registry

The Florida Department of Law Enforcement maintains a Sexual Offender/Predator Search System for access to sexual offenders and predators. The public may call 888-357-7332 to request information. Also, sex offender data is available online at www.fdle.state.fl.us/sexual_predators.

State Incarceration Records Agency

Florida Department of Corrections   **Phone:** 850-413-9359

Central Records Office   **Fax:**   850-413-8302

2601 Blair Stone Road   **Web:**   www.dc.state.fl.us

Tallahassee, FL 32399-2500

Access by: Phone, fax, mail, and online at the web site. For a search, you must provide first and last name and DOB. The SSN, DOC number are helpful.

What is released: Information on current and former inmates is available. Location, DOC number, physical identifiers, conviction information, and release dates are released.

Search Notes: No fee for search.

State Court System

Court Structure: There are 20 circuits with 104 courts. The Circuit Court is the court of general jurisdiction. All counties have combined Circuit and County Courts.

Find Felony Records: Circuit Court

Misdemeanor Records: County Court

Online Access: There is a statewide, online computer system for internal use only; there is no external access available nor planned currently. However, a number of courts do offer online access to the public.

Searching Hints: All courts have one address and switchboard; however, the divisions within the court(s) are completely separate. Requesters should specify which court and which division the request is directed to, even though some counties will automatically check both with one request.

Fees are set by statute and are as follows: Search Fee - $1.00 per name per year; Certification Fee - $1.00 per document plus copy fee; Copy Fee - $1.00 per certified page, $.15 per non-certified page.

Court Administrator: For add'l questions about the state's court system, visit the web site at www.flcourts.org, or contact: Office of State Courts Administrator, Supreme Court Bldg, 500 S Duval, Tallahassee, FL 32399-1900, Phone: 850-922-5082.

Georgia

If You Are an Employer—

Be aware that some first-time offenders are given a "mulligan." Certain first offender crimes in which the offender has been discharged without court adjudication of guilt are not reportable under Georgia law and a notification of discharge and exoneration is to be placed upon the record by the court. The discharge is not considered a conviction of a crime and may not be used to disqualify a person in any application for employment.

State Criminal Records Agency

Georgia Bureau of Investigations
Attn: GCIC
PO Box 370748
Decatur, GA 30037-0748

Phone: 404-244-2590.
Fax: 404-244-2878

Web: http://www.ganet.org/gbi

Total Records: 2,323,874

Who Can Access: Records are available to employers, government agencies including licensing agencies, and adoption and foster care providers.

Search Requirements: Include the following in your request: name, set of fingerprints, date of birth, sex, race, Social Security Number. Certain law enforcement agencies, who are online, and local agencies may perform record searches for investigative & background purposes. These agencies have the option of requesting a signed release from subject or including a set of fingerprints.

What Is Released: Information released includes arrest, disposition, and custodial information for offenses designated as fingerprintable by the State AG. Records without dispositions are released. Records are available from 1972 forward. The following data is not released: juvenile records, traffic ticket information or out-of-state or federal charges.

Indexing & Storage: It takes 1-3 days before new records are available for inquiry. 70% of all arrests in database have final dispositions recorded, 81% for those arrests within last 5 years. Records are indexed on fingerprint cards.

Access By: Mail, in person.

Mail Search: Turnaround time is 7 to 10 days.

In Person Search: In-person requests are returned by mail in about 14 days.

Fee & Payment: The fee is $15.00 per name. If statutues require a FBI check, submit 2 sets of fingerprints and a total search fee of $24.00 per name. A $3.00 fee is charged for an "Inspection Challenge" of your own personal record. Agencies may establish an account. Fee payee: Georgia Bureau of Investigations. Prepayment required. Money orders are accepted. No credit cards accepted.

Sexual Offender Registry

The state sexual offender data is available from GCIC as well. Records may be requested in person or at www.state.ga.us/gbi/disclaim.html. There is no fee.

State Incarceration Records Agency

Georiga Department of Corrections   **Phone:** 404-656-4593

Inmate Records Office, Eastern Tower

2 Martin Luther King, Jr. Drive, S.E.   **Web:**   www.dcor.state.ga.us

Atlanta, GA 30334-4900

Access by: Mail or online via the web site. For a search, you must provide first and last name. The DOB, SSN are helpful.

What is released: Information on current and former inmates is available, including the web search. Location, physical identifiers, conviction information, release dates, and inmate number are released. The web site has an extensive array of search capabilities.

Search Notes: No fee for search. Requests in writing must be on letterhead paper.

State Court System

Court Structure: Georgia's Superior Courts are arranged in 48 circuits of general jurisdiction, and these assume the role of a State Court if the county does not have one. The 69 State Courts, like Superior Courts, can conduct jury trials, but are limited jurisidiction. Each county has a Probate, a Juvenile, and a Magistrate Court. Magistrate Courts handle bad check cases, also issue arrest warrants and set bond on all felonies. Probate courts can, in certain cases, issue search and arrest warrants, and hear miscellaneous misdemeanors.

Find Felony Records: Superior Court

Misdemeanor Records: Superior, State, Magistrate, and Municipal Courts

Online Access: Cobb County has Internet access to records, but there is no online access available statewide, although one is being planned.

Searching Hints: In most Georgia counties, the courts will not perform criminal record searches. Use of in person search or hiring a record retriever is required. Courts suggest utilizing the Georgia Crime Information Center (GCIC), the state felony criminal history repository.

Court Administrator: For add'l questions about the state's court system, visit the web site at www.georgiacourts.org/aoc/index.html, or contact: Administrative Office of the Courts, 244 Washington St SW, Suite 300, Atlanta, GA 30334, Phone: 404-656-5171.

Hawaii

> **If You Are an Employer—**
>
> By state statute, employers making employment decisions may only use criminal records without dispositions and no more than 10 years old. Further, employers cannot consider misdemeanor convictions for which a jail sentence cannot be imposed.

State Criminal Records Agency

Hawaii Criminal Justice Data Center   **Phone:**   808-587-3106.

Liane Moriyama, Administrator

465 S King St, Room 101   **Web:**   http://www.state.hi.us/hcjdc/

Honolulu, HI 96813

Total Records:	393,000
Who Can Access:	Records are available to the general public.
Search Requirements:	Include the following in your request: any aliases, date of birth, Social Security Number. Submission of fingerprints is an option. 99% of the records are fingerpirnt-supported.
What Is Released:	Arrest records which have resulted in non-convictions or are still pending are considered confidential and not available to the general public.
Indexing & Storage:	It takes 1 to 20 days before new records are available for inquiry. 89% of all arrests in database have final dispositions recorded, 81% for those arrests within last 5 years. Records are available from the 1930's.
Access By:	Mail, in person.
Mail Search:	Turnaround time is 7 to 10 days. A self addressed stamped envelope is requested.
In Person Search:	The public may access conviction information by computer on-site. Name, SSN, and gender are required. Date of birth is optional. If SSN is unavailable, the staff will do the search.
Fee & Payment:	The search fee for a name-based criminal record search is $15.00 or $25.00 for a fingerprint-based search. A public access (convictions only) printout, available only in-person at this office or at main police stations, is $10.00. Certification fee: $10.00. Fee payee: Director of Finance, State of Hawaii. Prepayment required. Money orders and cashiers' checks are the only acceptable methods of payment. No credit cards accepted.

Sexual Offender Registry

The Criminal Justice Data Center maintains the sexual offender registration. This information is no longer available to the public.

State Incarceration Records Agency

Hawaii Department of Public Safety   **Phone:** 808-587-3100

Hawaii Criminal Justice Data Center

465 South King Street, Room 101   **Web:**   www.state.hi.us/icsd/psd/psd.html

Honolulu, HI 96813

Access by: Mail. For a search, you must provide full name, DOB, SSN helpful.

What is released: Conviction information is available on current and former inmates.

Search Notes: Fee for search is $15. Fee must be a paid by money order.

State Court System

Court Structure: Hawaii's trial level is comprised of Circuit Courts (with Family Courts) and District Courts. These trial courts function in four judicial circuits: First (Honolulu City/County), Second (Maui/Molokai/Lanai), Third (Hawaii County), and Fifth (Kauai/Niihau). The Fourth Circuit was merged with the Third in 1943. Circuit Courts are general jurisdiction and handle all jury trials, felony cases, and civil over $20,000, also probate and guardianship. The exception to to jury trial rule is DUI jury trial cases, which can be conducted in District Court. The District Court handles "minor felonies" (less then 1-yr sentence) and some civil cases up to $20,000, also landlord/tenant and DUI cases.

Find Felony Records: Circuit Court

Misdemeanor Records: District Court

Online Access: Online access to Circuit Court (and family court) records is available at http://www.state.hi.us/jud/. Search by name or case number.

Searching Hints: Most Hawaii state courts offer a public access terminal to search records at the courthouse.

Court Administrator: For add'l questions about the state's court system, visit the web site at www.state.hi.us/jud, or contact: Administrative Director of Courts, 417 S. King St, Honolulu, HI 96813, Phone: 808-539-4900.

Idaho

State Criminal Records Agency

State Repository   **Phone:** 208-884-7130.
Bureau of Criminal Identification   **Fax:**   208-884-7193
PO Box 700
Meridian, ID 83680-0700   **Web:**   http://www.isp.state.id.us

Total Records:	188,700
Who Can Access:	Records are available to the general public.
Search Requirements:	A signed release is not required, but suggested; see below. Include the name and DOB. The SSN and alias will aid in identification. Fingerprints are optional but may be required to establish positive identification. Fingerprint searches take 5-7 days. 100% of records are fingerprint-supported.
What Is Released:	A record of an arrest without disposition after 12 months from date of arrest will only be given if signed release presented. Requests without release will receive only records with dispositions. Records are available from 1960 on.
Indexing & Storage:	It takes about 3 days before new records are available for inquiry. 61% of all arrests in database have final dispositions recorded, 56% for those arrests within last 5 years.
Access By:	Mail, in person.
Mail Search:	Turnaround time is 5 to 7 days.
In Person Search:	You may request information in person, but results are still mailed.
Fee & Payment:	The $10.00 fee per person is applicable for either a name search or a fingerprint search. Fee payee: BCI. Prepayment required. Cashier check or money order is preferred form of payment. No credit cards accepted.

Sexual Offender Registry

The Bureau of Identification restricts access to the online Sex Offender Registry to those authorized by law. Registration and password is required at www.isp.state.id.us/. This service is provided to those agencies qualifying under Idaho Code 18-8283 (c) for special lists; schools and non-profit organizations. The public may submit a written request to this agency or county sheriff on the appropriate form for a $5.00 fee. Call 208-884-7305 for more information.

State Incarceration Records Agency

Idaho Department of Corrections   **Phone:** 208-658-2000

Records Bureau

2444 Old Penitentiary Road   **Web:**   www.corr.state.id.us

Boise, ID 83712

Access by:	Phone, mail. For a search, you must provide first and last name, DOB, SSN, DOC number are helpful.
What is released:	Information on current and former inmates is available. Information released varies depending on request.
Search Notes:	No fee for search. Requests in writing must be specific about information requested.

State Court System

Court Structure:	The District Court oversees felony and most civil cases. Small claims are handled by the Magistrate Division of the District Court (44 courts in the state combined the courts). Probate is handled by the Magistrate Division of the District Court.
Find Felony Records:	District Court
Misdemeanor Records:	District Court
Online Access:	There is no statewide computer system offering external access to the public. All courts provide public access terminals on-site.
Searching Hints:	A statewide court administrative rule states that record custodians do not have a duty to "compile or summarize information contained in a record, nor to create new records for the requesting party." Under this rule, some courts will not perform searches.
	Many courts require a signed release for employment record searches.
	The following fees are mandated statewide: Search Fee - none; Certification Fee - $1.00 per document plus copy fee; Copy Fee - $1.00 per page. Not all jurisdictions currently follow these guidelines.
Court Administrator:	For add'l questions about the state's court system, visit the web site at http://www2.state.id.us/judicial, or contact: Administrative Director of the Courts, 451 W State St, Supreme Court Bldg, Boise, ID 83720, Phone: 208-334-2246.

Illinois

If You Are an Employer—

By state statute, employers making employment decisions may only use criminal records with dispositions. The good news is that the central state agency only releases records with dispositions.

State Criminal Records Agency

Illinois State Police   **Phone:** 815-740-5164.
Bureau of Identification
260 N Chicago St
Joliet, IL 60432-4075   **Web:** http://www.state.il.us/isp/isphpage.htm

Total Records: 3,280,000

Who Can Access: Records are available only with consent of the subject.

Search Requirements: Requester must use the state's Uniform Conviction Information Form ISP6-405B signed by person of record. Personal requests are honored per Illinois statute. Include the following in your request: the signed release, name, date of birth, sex, race. Fingerprint cards are an option; a fingerprint search using Form ISP6-404B is recommended in order to assure proper identification.

What Is Released: No records are released without a disposition of conviction. Records are available from 1930's on.

Indexing & Storage: It takes 1 to 5 days before new records are available for inquiry. 61% of all arrests in database have final dispositions recorded, 67% for those arrests within last 5 years. Records are indexed on microfilm, index cards, inhouse computer.

Access By: Mail, in person, online.

Mail Search: Turnaround time is 6 to 12 weeks. No self addressed stamped envelope is required.

In Person Search: An in person search saves mailing time only.

Online Search: Online access costs $7.00 per name. Upon signing an interagency agreement with ISP and establishing a $200 escrow account, users can submit inquiries over modem. Replies with convictions are returned by mail. Clear records can be returned via e-mail, by request. Modem access is available from 7AM-

4PM M-F, excluding holidays. Users must utilize LAPLINK version 6.0 or later. For more information on the Modem Porgram, call 815-740-5164.

Fee & Payment: The search fee is $12.00 per form. A fingerprint search is $14.00. Forms are available online at http://www.isp.state.il.us/ucia0002.html. Fee payee: Illinois State Police. Prepayment required. Modem users and ongoing UCIA requesters must prepay for records in groups of 35 at a time. Personal checks accepted. No credit cards accepted.

Sexual Offender Registry

The state police also maintain the sex offender data for the state. The information may be searched online for no charge at http://samnet.isp.state.il.us/ispso2/sex_offenders/index.asp   and also at http://12.17.79.4.

State Incarceration Records Agency

Illinois Department of Corrections   **Phone:** 217-522-2666

Public Information Office

1301 Concordia Court, P.O. Box 19277   **Web:**   www.idoc.state.il.us

Springfield, IL 62794-9277

Access by: Phone, mail, online. For a phone or mail search, you must provide full name and DOB, SSN, gender, race helpful. For a online search, you can provide name or DOB or IDOC #, there is no fee.

What is released: Information on current and former inmates is available, except online is current only. Location, conviction information, physical identifiers, and release dates are reported.

State Court System

Court Structure: Illinois is divided into 22 judicial circuits; 3 are single countys: Cook, Du Page (18th Circuit) and Will (12th Circuit). The other 19 circuits consist of 2 or more contiguous counties. The Circuit Court of Cook County is the largest unified court system in the world. Its 2300-person staff handles approximately 2.4 million cases each year. The civil part of the various Circuit Courts in Cook County is divided as follows: under $30,000 are "civil cases" and over $30,000 are "civil law division cases." Probate is handled by the Circuit Court in all counties.

Find Felony Records: Circuit Court

Misdemeanor Records: Circuit Court

Online Access: While there is no statewide public online system available, a number of Illinois Circuit Courts offer online access.

Searching Hints: In most Illinois courts the search fee is charged on a per name, per year basis. The search fees are set by statute and have three levels based on the county population. The higher the population, the larger the fee.

In most courts, both civil and criminal data are on computer from the same starting date.

Court Administrator: For add'l questions about the state's court system, contact: Administrative Office of Courts, 222 N. Lasalle - 13th Floor, Chicago, IL 60601, Phone: 312-793-3250.

Indiana

State Criminal Records Agency

Indiana State Police
Central Records
IGCN - 100 N Senate Ave Room 302
Indianapolis, IN 46204-2259

Phone: 317-232-8266.

Web: http://www.IN.gov/isp/

Total Records: 998,068

Who Can Access: The release of records is governed by IC 5-2-5. A "Limited Criminal History" is available to designated entites including employers, licensing agencies, schools, and certain other designates.

Search Requirements: Use State Form 8053. Include the following in your request: full name, date of birth, sex, race. Submitting fingerprints is an option. 100% of the records are fingerprint-supported.

What Is Released: Record will show all activity, including arrests, dismissals, and convictions. But, if a charge is over a year old with no disposition, then the record will not be released. Records are available from 1935.

Indexing & Storage: It takes 10 days before new records are available for inquiry. Approximately 10% of all arrests in database have final dispositions recorded, over 50% for those arrests within last 5 years. This agency now is notified when charges are made after fingerprints are submitted. Records are indexed on inhouse computer.

Access By: Mail, in person, online.

Mail Search: Turnaround time: 5 to 10 working days. Use State Form 8053.

In Person Search: Requester must have picture ID, turnaround time is 30 minutes.

Online Search: Subcribers to accessIndiana can obtain limited records for $22.50 per search. Go to http://www.in.gov/isp/lch/centralsearch.html.

Fee & Payment: The fee for employers is $7.00 per name if no fingerprints used. The fee for a fingerprint search is $10.00. If subject requests own record, fee is $10.00, and this is for a FULL record. Fee is $20.00 for online searches by non-government agencies. Fee payee: State of Indiana. Prepayment required. Cash, money orders, and certified checks are accepted. Ongoing requesters may open a monthly billing account. No credit cards accepted.

Sexual Offender Registry

Sex offender data is available online at www.state.in.us/serv/cji_sor, and maintained by the Indiana Department of Corrections. Phone requests can be made to 317-232-1233.

State Incarceration Records Agency

Indiana Department of Corrections, IGCS   **Phone**: 317-232-5765

Indiana Supervisor of Records, Room E-334

302 W. Washington Street   **Web:**   www.in.gov/indcorrection

Indianapolis, IN 46204

Access by:	Phone, mail, online. For a search, you must provide first and last name; the DOB and SSN helpful. To search online provide either full name or inmate number.
What is released:	Information on current and former inmates is available. Location, DOC number, physical identifiers, sentencing and conviction information, and release dates are released.
Search Notes:	No fee for search. Computer records go back to 1989.

State Court System

Court Structure:	There are 92 judicial circuits with Circuit Courts, or Combined Circuit and Superior Courts. In addition, there are 47 City Courts and 25 Town Courts. County Courts are gradually being restructured into divisions of the Superior Courts.
Find Felony Records:	Circuit or Superior or County Court
Misdemeanor Records:	Circuit, Superior, County, City, and Town Courts
Online Access:	No online access computer system, internal or external, is available, except for Marion County through CivicNet/Access Indiana Information Network, which is available on the Internet at www.civicnet.net. Account and password are required. Fees range from $2.00 to $5.00 for civil case summaries, civil justice name searches, criminal case summaries, and party booking details. There is no charge for civil court name searches
Searching Hints:	The Circuit Court Clerk/County Clerk in every county is the same individual and is responsible for keeping all county judicial records. However, it is recommended that, when requesting a record, the request indicate which court heard the case (Circuit, Superior, or County).

Many courts are no longer performing searches, especially criminal searches, based on a 7/8/96 statement by the State Board of Accounts.

Certification and copy fees are set by statute as $1.00 per document plus copy fee for certification and $1.00 per page for copies.

Court Administrator: For add'l questions about the state's court system, visit the web site at www.in.gov/judiciary/admin/, or contact: State Court Administrator, 115 W Washington St, #1080, Indianapolis, IN 46204-3417, Phone: 317-232-2542.

Iowa

State Criminal Records Agency

Division of Criminal Investigations
Bureau of Identification
Wallace State Office Bldg
Des Moines, IA 50319

Phone: 515-281-4776.
Fax: 515-242-6297

Web:
http://www.state.ia.us/government/dps/dci/crimhist.htm

Total Records:	411,000
Who Can Access:	Records are available to the general public.
Search Requirements:	A signed release or waiver is not required, nor are fingerprints. Include the following in your request: date of birth, sex, Social Security Number. A signed release is an option (see below). Be sure to give the full name. Request Form A is required for each surname. This form can be obtained from the web site, by fax, mail, or in person.
What Is Released:	A signed release by subject entitles requester to all records including those without dispositions (up to 4 years old). If the subject's signed release is not presented, then no arrest records over 18 months old without dispositions are released. Records are available until the person is 80 years old or passes away, then records are deleted.
Indexing & Storage:	It takes up to 10 days before new records are available for inquiry. 91% of all arrests in database have final dispositions recorded, 91% for those arrests within last 5 years. Records are indexed on in house computer (100%). There is a computerized index going back to 1935. File records are normally destroyed after 4 years if there is no disposition.
Access By:	Mail, fax, in person.
Mail Search:	Turnaround time: 1 to 2 days. No self addressed stamped envelope is required.
Fax Search:	Only those requesters who have opened a pre-paid account may fax.
In Person Search:	Only the subject or their attorney will receive the record while they wait, within 15 minutes. Otherwise, results are mailed or can be picked up later.
Fee & Payment:	The fee for a record search is $13.00 per surname checked. If married and maiden names are checked, the fee would be $26.00. Iowa law requires employers to pay the fee for potential employees' record checks. Fee payee: Iowa Division of Criminal Investigation. Payment is required unless pre-arranged billing has been arranged. Ongoing requesters can set up an account

with a $500 deposit. Personal checks accepted. Credit cards accepted: MasterCard, Visa.

Sexual Offender Registry

The Iowa Sex Offender Registry, maintained by the Division of Criminal Investigations, can be searched at http://www.state.ia.us/government/dps/dci/isor/ and at http://www.iowasexoffender.com/default.asp. Only high-risk offenders are listed. The entire database may be searched at a local police or sheriff's department.

State Incarceration Records Agency

Iowa Department of Corrections   **Phone:** 515-242-5707

420 Watson Powell Jr. Way   **Fax:**   515-281-7345

Des Moines, IA 50309-1639   **Web:**   www.doc.state.ia.us.

Access by:	Phone, fax, mail. For a search, you must provide full name, DOB and SSN helpful.
What is released:	Information on current and former inmates is available. Location, physical identifiers, county of conviction, and conviction information details are released.
Search Notes:	No fee for search. Computer records go back to 1986.

State Court System

Court Structure:	The District Court is the court of general jurisdiction and handles all court matters. There are no limited jurisdiction courts.
Find Felony Records:	District Court
Misdemeanor Records:	District Court
Online Access:	There is a statewide online computer system called the Iowa Court Information System (ICIS), which is for internal use only. There is no public access system. The web site below provides access to previous day opinons form the Court of Appeals and the Supreme Court.
Searching Hints:	In most courts, the Certification Fee is $10.00 plus copy fee. Copy Fee is $.50 per page. Most courts do not do searches and recommend either in person searches or use of a record retriever.
Court Administrator:	For add'l questions about the state's court system, visit the web site at www.judicial.state.ia.us/courtadmin, or contact: State Court Administrator, State Capitol, Des Moines, IA 50319, Phone: 515-281-5241.

Kansas

If You Are an Employer—

By state statute, vendors may only report 7 years of criminal conviction information to employers. However, this time limit is waived if the applicant is reasonably expected to make $20,000 or more annually.

State Criminal Records Agency

Kansas Bureau of Investigation
Criminal Records Division
1620 SW Tyler, Crim. History Record Sec.
Topeka, KS 66612-1837

Phone: 785-296-8200.
Fax: 785-296-6781

Web: http://www.kbi.state.ks.us

Total Records:	821,000
Who Can Access:	Records are available to the general public. Non-criminal justice agencies, organizations, individuals and commercial companies are entitled to receive recorded conviction information.
Search Requirements:	First time requesters must complete a user's agreement. Include the following in your request: full name, sex, race, date of birth, Social Security Number. Each request must be on a separate "Records Check Request Form." Fingerprints are optional. Approximately 85% of records are fingerprint supported. Turnaround time may be several weeks if the record is not currently automated; approximately 46% of records are automated.
What Is Released:	Arrests with no convictions over 12 months old are not shown; are shown if arrest is less than 12 months old. The following data is not released: expunged records, non-convictions or juvenile records except to criminal justice agencies and agencies required by law.
Indexing & Storage:	It takes up to 4 days before new records are available for inquiry. 46% of all arrests in database have final dispositions recorded, 57% for those arrests within last 5 years. Records are indexed on Kansas Central Repository database, which is synchronized with the automated fingerprint ID system db.
Access By:	Mail, fax.
Mail Search:	Turnaround time is 2 to 4 weeks. A self addressed stamped envelope is requested.
Fax Search:	Prior arrangement is required, same criteria as mail.

Fee & Payment: Fees: $10.00 for a name check; $17.00 for fingerprint search. All requests are allowed one additional alias name per person. However, add $5.00 per third and each additional alias name. Fee payee: KBI Records Fees Fund. Prepayment required. Personal checks accepted. No credit cards accepted.

Sexual Offender Registry

Sex offender data maintained by the Kansas Bureau of Investigation at the address listed above. Offender data is available online at http://www.ink.org/public/kbi/kbiregoffpage.html. Phone look-ups are available at 785-296-6656. Most sheriffs' offices will process requests. Note that the data contains only information from 04/14/94 forward.

State Incarceration Records Agency

Kansas Department of Corrections

Public Information Officer

900 SW Jackson, 4th floor

Topeka, KS 66612-1284.

Phone: 785-296-5873

Fax: 785-296-0014

Web: http://docnet.dc.state.ks.us

Access by: Phone, fax, mail. For a search, you must provide full name, DOB and SSN helpful.

What is released: Information on current and former inmates is available. Location, KDOC number, physical identifiers, sentencing and conviction information, disciplinary record, and custody or supervision level are released.

Search Notes: No fee for search.

State Court System

Court Structure: The District Court is the court of general jurisdiction. There are 110 courts in 31 districts in 105 counties. The Municipal Courts handle DUIs and local matters.

Find Felony Records: District Court

Misdemeanor Records: District Court

Online Access: Commercial online access is available for District Court Records in 4 counties - Johnson, Sedgwick, Shawnee, and Wyandotte - through Access Kansas (http://www.accesskansas.org/). Franklin and Finney counties may be available later in 2002. A user can access records their Internet site at www.accesskansas.org/ or via a dial-up system. There is a $75.00 subscription fee and an annual renewal fee is $60.00. There is no per minute connect charge, but there is a transaction fee. Other information from this site includes Drivers License, Title, Registration, Lien, and UCC searches. For additional information or a registration packet, call 800-4-KANSAS (800-452-6727).

Searching Hints:

Five counties - Cowley, Crawford, Labette, Montgomery and Neosho - have two hearing locations, but only one record center.

Many Kansas courts do not do criminal record searches and will refer any criminal requests to the Kansas Bureau of Investigation. The Kansas Legislature's Administrative Order 156 (Fall, 2000) allows Courts to charge up to $12.00 per hour for search services, though courts may set their own search fees, if any.

Court Administrator:

For add'l questions about the state's court system, visit the web site at www.kscourts.org, or contact: Judicial Administrator, Kansas Judicial Center, 301 SW 10th St, Topeka, KS 66612-1507, Phone: 785-296-4873.

Kentucky

If You Are an Employer—

Note that local Kentucky courts will not do criminal searches. They refer all requesters to the Administrative Office of Courts in Frankfort, KY. This office has a statewide database of records. Access details are described on the next page.

The central state agency only will process criminal record requests for those entities permitted by state statute, which does not include general employers.

State Criminal Records Agency

Kentucky State Police
Records Branch
1250 Louisville Rd
Frankfort, KY 40601

Phone: 502-227-8713.
Fax: 502-227-8734

Web:
Http://www.state.ky.us/agencies/ksp/ksphome.htm

Total Records:	856,857
Who Can Access:	Per statute, requests are accepted for employment purposes connected to nursing, schools, lottery, EMT, YMCA, daycare, and adoptive/foster parent background searches. Other requesters are advised to submit requests through the court system.
Search Requirements:	Include the following in your request: signed release from subject, full name, date of birth, Social Security Number, reason for information request. Fingerprints are not requested.
What Is Released:	Records without dispositions, including pending and dismissed cases, are not released. Records are available from 1952 on for criminal records. The following data is not released: juvenile records.
Indexing & Storage:	It takes a minimum of 30 days before new records are available for inquiry. 69% of all arrests in database have final dispositions recorded, 59% for those arrests within last 5 years. Records are indexed on inhouse computer, fingerprint cards. Nearly 75% of records are automated. Statistical information about criminal offenses and accidents is available from 1971 on.
Access By:	Mail, in person.

Mail Search: Turnaround time is 2 to 3 weeks. A self addressed stamped envelope is requested.

In Person Search: Turnaround time is while you wait. There is a limit of 5 searches.

Fee & Payment: The fee is $10.00 per name. Fee payee: Kentucky State Treasurer. Prepayment required. Personal checks accepted. No credit cards accepted.

Sexual Offender Registry

The state sexual offender list is available online at at http://kspsor.state.ky.us/. The database is maintained by the Kentucky State Police. They will not release information by phone or mail, only online.

State Incarceration Records Agency

Kentucky Department of Corrections   **Phone:** 502-564-2433

Offender Information Services   **Fax:**   502-564-1471

Health Service Building, Room 619   **Web:**   www.cor.state.ky.us

275 E. Main, P.O. Box 2400

Frankfort, KY 40602-2400

Access by: Phone, fax, mail, online at web site. For a search, you must provide first and last name. The DOB and SSN are helpful.

What is released: Information on current and former inmates is available. Location, physical identifiers, conviction and sentencing information, and release dates are reported.

Search Notes: No fee for search. Computer records go back to 1979.

State Court System

Court Structure: The Circuit Court is the court of general jurisdiction and the District Court is the limited jurisdiction court. Most of Kentucky's counties combined the courts into one location and records are co-mingled.

Find Felony Records: Circuit

Misdemeanor Records: District

Online Access: There are statewide, online computer systems called "SUSTAIN" and "KyCourts" available for internal judicial/state agency use only. No courts offer online access.

Searching Hints: Until 1978, county judges handled all cases; therefore, in many cases, District and Circuit Court records go back only to 1978. Records prior to that time are archived.

Many courts refer requests for criminal searches to the Administrative Office of Courts (AOC - 502-573-2350 or 800-928-6381) due to lack of personnel for searching at the court level. AOC maintains records on an internal system called COURTNET, which contains information on opening, closing, proceedings, disposition, and parties to including individual defendants.

Felony convictions are accessible back to 1978, and Misdemeanors back five years. This is a statewide search. The required Release Form is available from the AOC at the numbers above. A check or money order for the Search Fee of $10.00 per requested individual ($5.00 fee if non-profit or if requester is the subject) is payable to the State Treasurer of Kentucky. A SASE and a second postage-attached envelope must accompany the request.

Court Administrator: For add'l questions about the state's court system, visit the web site at www.kycourts.net, or contact: Administrative Office of Courts, 100 Mill Creek Park, Frankfort, KY 40601, Phone: 502-573-2350.

Louisiana

State Criminal Records Agency

State Police
Bureau of Criminal Identification
265 S Foster
Baton Rouge, LA 70806

Phone: 225-925-6095.
Fax: 225-925-7005
Web: http://www.lsp.org

Access to Records is Restricted

Total Records: 1,850,000

Who Can Access: Records are not available to the public in general. Records are available for employment screening purposes only if the employment statutorily requires a criminal record check (such as childcare or schools).

Search Requirements: Include the following in your request: set of fingerprints, signed release. 100% of the records are fingerprint-supported.

What Is Released: Only records with convictions are released. The following data is not released: pending records or juvenile records.

Indexing & Storage: Records are available from the early 1900's. Records are indexed by name on computer from 1974 to present.

Sexual Offender Registry

Sex offender and child predator data is maintained by the State Police. Records are open to the public and available online at http://www.lasocpr.lsp.org/Static/Search.htm. Names searches are available by mail, or phone at 800-858-0551.

State Incarceration Records Agency

Department of Public Safety and Corrections
P.O. Box 94304
Baton Rouge, LA 70804-9304

Phone: 225-342-6642

Web: www.corrections.state.la.us.

Access by: Phone. For a search, you must provide full name, DOC number helpful.

What is released: Information on current and former inmates is available. Location, conviction and sentencing information is released.

Search Notes: No fee for search. Computer records go back to 1975.

State Court System

Court Structure: The District Court is the court of general jurisdiction. Limited jurisdiction courts include City, Parish, and the New Orleans City Court. In addiction there are over 640 Municipal Courts known as Justice of the Peace and Mayor's Courts. Each Parish has its own clerk and courthouse.

Find Felony Records: District Court

Misdemeanor Records: City and Parish Courts, and the New Orleans City Courts

Online Access: The online computer system, Case Management Information System (CMIS), is operating and development is continuing. It is for internal use only; there is no plan to permit online access to the public. However, Supreme Court opinions are currently available.

There are a number of Parishes that do offer a means of remote online access of criminal records to the public.

Court Administrator: For add'l questions about the state's court system, visit the web site at www.lajao.org, or contact: Judicial Administrator, Judicial Council of the Supreme Court, 1555 Poydras Street, Suite 1540, New Orleans, LA 70112-1814, Phone: 504-568-5747.

Maine

State Criminal Records Agency

Maine State Police   **Phone:** 207-624-7009.
State Bureau of Identification   **Fax:**   207-624-7088
42 State House Station
Augusta, ME 04333   **Web:**   http://www.state.me.us/dps/

Total Records: 359,500

Who Can Access: Records are available to the general public.

Search Requirements: Requests must be in writing. Submit one name per page (otherwise list could be held or sent back). Include the following in your request: name, date of birth, any aliases. Include maiden name for females. Also include purpose of the inquiry and name and address of requester. Submitting fingerprints is optional. 35% of the records are fingerprint-supported. Fingerprints are not submitted with arrest information to this agency by the courts or police.

What Is Released: All convictions and all pending cases less than 1 year old are reported, or if the case has not yet been adjudicated in court. Records are available from 1937 on. The following data is not released: juvenile records.

Indexing & Storage: It takes 1 to 2 days before new records are available for inquiry. 90% of all arrests in database have final dispositions recorded, 90% for those arrests within last 5 years. Records are indexed on computer (43%) and court index cards. Records are normally destroyed after 99 years, if no activity within last five years.

Access By: Mail, in person.

Mail Search: Normal turnaround time is less than one week, those records with "hits" may take slightly longer to process. A self addressed stamped envelope is requested. Search costs $8.00 per individual.

In Person Search: This only saves mail-in time; records are returned by mail.

Fee & Payment: The search fee is $8.00 per individual. Fee payee: Treasurer, State of Maine. Personal checks accepted. No credit cards accepted.

Sexual Offender Registry

The sex offender registry can be requested by phone or fax from the Maine State Police, call 207-624-7009. No fee is required. The registry should be available electonically in mid-2002.

State Incarceration Records Agency

Maine Department of Corrections   **Phone:** 207-287-4360

111 State House Station   **Fax:**   207-287-4370

Augusta, ME 04333   **Web:**   www.state.me.us/corrections.

Access by: Phone, fax, mail. For a search, you must provide full name, DOB and SSN helpful.

What is released: Information on current and former inmates is available. Location, conviction and sentencing information, and release dates are reported.

Search Notes: No fee for search.

State Court System

Court Structure: The Superior Court is the court of general jurisdiction, the District Court is the court of limited Jurisdiction. In 16 counties, there are 17 Superior Courts and 31 District Courts.

Both Superior and District Courts handle "misdemeanor" and "felony" cases, with jury trials being held in Superior Court only. Superior Court has exclusive jurisdiction over pleas or trials for murder cases.

Prior to year 2001, District Courts accepted civil cases involving claims less than $30,000. Now, District Courts have jurisdiction concurrent with that of the Superior Court for all civil actions except those cases vested in the Superior Court by statute.

Find Felony Records: Superior Court, District Court

Misdemeanor Records: Superior Court, District Court

Online Access: Development of a judicial computer system is in use statewide for all criminal and certain civil case types. The remainder of civil case types will be available statewide in the near future. The system is initially for judicial and law enforcement agencies and will not include public access in the near term.

Searching Hints: In most courts, mail requests for full criminal history record information are returned to the sender, referring them to the State Bureau of Investigation or the Bureau of Motor Vehicles. Mail requests that make a specific inquiry related to an identified case are responded to in writing, with appropriate copy and attestation fees.

Telephone requests for information will only be provided to parties to the case and criminal justice agencies.

Court Administrator: For add'l questions about the state's court system, visit the web site at www.courts.state.me.us, or contact: State Court Administrator, PO Box 4820, Portland, ME 04112, Phone: 207-822-0792.

Maryland

> **If You Are an Employer—**
>
> By state statute, vendors may only report 7 years of criminal conviction information to employers. However, this time limit is waived if the applicant is reasonably expected to make $20,000 or more annually.

State Criminal Records Agency

Criminal Justice Information System
Public Safety & Correctional Records
PO Box 5743
Pikeville, MD 21282-5743

Phone: 410-764-4501

Web: www.dpscs.state.md.us

Total Records:	1,503,700
Who Can Access:	Records are available to the general public, but with certain stipulations.
Search Requirements:	Release of criminal records is somewhat restricted. All private parties must first write to this office and receive a "petition package," then apply for a petition number. Employers and investigative firms are eligible to apply for this petition number. Include the following in your request: signed release, set of fingerprints, photo ID of requester. 100% of the records are fingerprint-supported.
What Is Released:	All records are released to law enforcement; public receives records with dispositions only. Records are available from 1978.
Indexing & Storage:	It takes a week before new records are available for inquiry, if not submitted electornically. Approximately 80% of all arrests in database have final dispositions recorded. Records are indexed on in-house computer (90+%).
Access By:	Mail.
Mail Search:	Turnaround time is 2 to 4 weeks.
Fee & Payment:	The fee is $18.00 per request. If a statutorily-required FBI fingerpint check is required, add $24.00. Fee payee: CJIS. Prepayment required. Money orders and cashier's checks are preferred. Personal checks accepted. No credit cards accepted.

Sexual Offender Registry

The Sexual Offender Registry is maintained by the Department of Public Safety. Names searches can be done by mail or e-mail, sor@dpscs.state.md.us. Be sure to provide your full name, address, and reason for the request. Visit http://www.dpscs.state.md.us/sor/ for instructions. Also, many local law enforcement agencies offer access to the registry.

State Incarceration Records Agency

Dept of Public Safety and Correctional Services	**Phone:** 410-585-3351
Maryland Division of Corrections	**Fax:** 410-764-4182
6766 Reistertown Road, Suite 310	**Web:** www.dpscs.state.md.us/doc
Baltimore, MD 21215-2342	

Access by: Phone, fax, mail. For a search, you must provide full name, DOB.

What is released: Information on current and former inmates is available. Location and DOC number are released.

Search Notes: No fee for search. Computer records go back to 1980. To obtain any other information than DOC number you must contact individual institutions.

State Court System

Court Structure: The Circuit Court is the highest court of record. Effective 10/1/98, the civil judgment limit increased from $20,000 to $25,000 at the District Court level.

Certain categories of minor felonies are handled by the District Courts. However, all misdemeanors and felonies that require a jury trial are handled by Circuit Courts.

Find Felony Records: Circuit Court, District Court (minor)

Misdemeanor Records: Circuit Court, District Court

Online Access: An online computer system called the Judicial Information System (JIS) or (SJIS) provides access to civil and criminal case information from the following:

- All District Courts - All civil and all misdemeanors
- Circuit Courts Criminal - Three courts are on JIS - Anne Arundel, Carroll County, and Baltimore City Court

- Circuit Courts Civil - All Circuit Courts are online through JIS except Montgomery and Prince George who have their own systems.

Inquiries may be made to: the District Court traffic system for case information data, calendar information data, court schedule data, or officer schedule data; the District Court criminal system for case information data or calendar caseload data; the District Court civil system for case information data, attorney name and address data; the land records system for land and plat records. The one-time fee for JIS access is $50.00, which must be included with the application, and there is a charge of $5.00 per hour for access time, with a $10.00 minimum per month. For additional information or to receive a registration packet, write or call Judicial Information Systems, Security Administrator, 2661 Riva Rd., Suite 900, Annapolis, MD 21401, 410-260-1031.

Court Administrator: For add'l questions about the state's court system, visit the web site at www.courts.state.md.us, or contact: Administrative Office of the Courts, 580 Taylor Ave, Annapolis, MD 21401, Phone: 410-260-1400.

Massachusetts

If You Are an Employer—

By state statute, vendors may only report 7 years of criminal conviction information to employers. However, this time limit is waived if the applicant is reasonably expected to make $20,000 or more annually.

Employers may not inquire or maintain records related to a first conviction for any of the following misdemeanors: drunkenness, simple assault, speeding, minor traffic violations, affray, or disturbance of the peace.

Further restrictions apply to misdemeanor records. Employers cannot inquire into or maintain records regarding any misdemeanor conviction where the date of such conviction or completion of incarceration, whichever date is later, occurred five or more years prior to the date of application for employment, unless such person has been convicted of any offense within the five years immediately preceding the date of such application for employment.

State Criminal Records Agency

Criminal History Systems Board   **Phone:** 617-660-4600.
200 Arlington Street, #2200   **Fax:** 617-660-4613
Chelsea, MA 02150
                                     Web: http://www.state.ma.us/chsb/

Note: Three types of searches are offered: Personal, Certified Agency, and Publicly Accessible (PUBAC). Certified Agency requests are pre-approved via statute or by the Board. PUBAC is open to the public; information is limited.

Total Records: 2,530,000

Who Can Access: Records are available to the general public.

                         PUBAC requesters are limited to adult records; the crime must include a sentence of 5 years or more OR sentenced and convicted for any term if, at the time of request, the subject is on probation or has been released within 2 years of felony conviction.

                         "Certified Agency" searchers (see below) may include youth organizations, child care providers, and others approved by CHSB.

Search Requirements: Include the following in your request: name, date of birth. The Personal Request (on one's self) requires a notarized signature. This agency does not conduct FBI fingerprint searches.

What Is Released: A Certified Agency record includes all conviction and all open or pending actions. A PUBAC record contains only convictions. Records are available for at least 50 years. The following data is not released: pending cases; misdemeanor convictions or incarcerations beyond five years old.

Indexing & Storage: It takes 1 day before new records are available for inquiry. 100% of PUBAC records have final dispositions recorded. Records are indexed on inhouse computer, file folders.

Access By: Mail.

Mail Search: Turnaround time is 2 weeks. A self addressed stamped envelope is required.

Fee & Payment: The Personal request is free. The Certified Agency request is $10.00. The PUBAC request is $25.00. No fingerprint requests are permitted, thus no fingerprint fees. In fact, 0% of the records are fingerprint-supported. Fee payee: The Commonwealth of Massachusetts. Prepayment required. Personal checks accepted. No credit cards accepted.

Sexual Offender Registry

The Sex Offender Registry Board, PO Box 4547 Salem, MA 01970, 978-740-6400 maintains the state's sexual offender records. Name searches can be ordered from this agency or from most local law enforcement agencies. Requesters must submit their name, address, and reason for the request.

State Incarceration Records Agency

Massachusetts Executive Office of Public Safety   **Phone:** 617-660-4600

Criminal History Systems Board

200 Arlington, Suite 2200   **Web:**   www.state.ma.us/doc

Chelse, MA 02150

Access by: Phone, mail. For a search, you must provide first and last name, DOC and SSN. Call 8770421-8463.

What is released: Information on current and former inmates is available. Location, conviction and sentencing information, and release dates are reported.

Search Notes: No fee for search. Requests in writing must be on letterhead paper.

State Court System

Court Structure:

There are 19 Superior Courts and 68 District Courts in 14 counties. The various court sections are called "Departments." Both Superior and District Courts can hear felony cases. While Superior and District Courts have concurrent jurisdiction in civil cases, the practice is to assign cases less than $25,000 to the District Court and those over $25,000 to Superior Court.

In addition to misdemeanors, the District Courts and the Boston Municipal Court have jurisdiction over certain minor felonies.

Find Felony Records:

Superior Court, District Court

Misdemeanor Records:

District Court, Boston Municipal Court, Housing Court

Online Access:

Online access to records on the statewide Trial Courts Information Center web site is available to attorneys and law firms (but not to employers or screening firms) at www.ma-trialcourts.org. Contact Peter Nylin by e-mail at nylin_p@jud.state.ma.us. Site is updated daily.

Court Administrator:

For add'l questions about the state's court system, visit the web site at www.state.ma.us/courts/admin/index.html, or contact: Chief Justice for Administration & Management, 2 Center Plaza, Room 540, Boston, MA 02108, Phone: 617-742-8575.

Michigan

If You Are an Employer—

For pre-employment inquiry, Michigan prohibits employers from reviewing misdemeanor arrest records that are not connected to a conviction and without a pending charge.

State Criminal Records Agency

Michigan State Police, Ident. Section
Criminal Justice Information Center
7150 Harris Dr
Lansing, MI 48913

Phone: 517-322-5531.
Fax: 517-322-0635
Web: http://www.msp.state.mi.us

Total Records:	1,259,500
Who Can Access:	Records are available to the general public.
Search Requirements:	Include the following in your request: full name, sex, race, date of birth. A SSN or maiden name/previous name is very helpful. Records can be searched with or without a fingerprint card.
What Is Released:	Records without dispositions are not released. Records are available until the subject's DOB indicates 99 years or a death is reported.
Indexing & Storage:	It takes up to 30 days before new records are available for inquiry. 76% of all arrests in database have final dispositions recorded. Records are indexed on inhouse computer.
Access By:	Mail, fax, online.
Mail Search:	Turnaround time: 2 to 4 weeks.
Fax Search:	The state will permit ongoing requesters to set up a pre-paid account and submit requests by fax, but this may be discontinued.
Online Search:	Online access is limited to businesses that are ongoing requesters. Access is via the Internet, credit cards are required. To set up an account, call 517-322-5546.
Fee & Payment:	The search fee is $5.00 per name without a fingerprint card, $15.00 with a fingerprint card, and $39.00 with state and FBI fingerprint cards. Registered users may be eligible for a fee waiver. Non-profit organizations may submit a copy of Federal Form 501C3 in lieu of payment for a name search. Fee payee: State of Michigan. Prepayment required. Payment required in advance unless a prepaid account has been arranged with Division cashier. Personal checks accepted. Credit cards will be accepted for online access.

Sexual Offender Registry

The State Police maintain the state sex offender data. One may search online by name or ZIP Code at at www.mipsor.state.mi.us. Local law enforcement agencies also provide access to the database.

State Incarceration Records Agency

Michigan Department of Corrections   **Phone:** 517-373-0284

Central Records Office   **Fax:**   517-373-2628

P.O. Box 30003   **Web:**   www.state.mi.us/mdoc

Lansing, MI 48909

Access by: Phone, fax, mail, online. For a search, you must provide full name or MDOC number. The DOB and SSN are helpful. The online search has an extensive array of searching criteria.

What is released: Information on current and former inmates is available. Location, MDOC number, conviction and sentencing information, physical identifiers, and release dates are provided.

Search Notes: No fee for search. Computer records go back to 1979.

State Court System

Court Structure: The Circuit Court is the court of general jurisdiction. District, Municipal and Probate Courts are limited jurisdiction.

There is a Court of Claims in Lansing that is a function of the 30th Circuit Court with jurisdiction over claims against the state of Michigan.

A Recorder's Court in Detroit was abolished as of October 1, 1997.

As of January 1, 1998, the Family Division of the Circuit Court was created. Domestic relations actions and juvenile cases, including criminal and abuse/neglect, formerly adjudicated in the Probate Court, were transferred to the Family Division of the Circuit Court. Mental health and estate cases continue to be handled by the Probate Courts.

Find Felony Records: Circuit Court

Misdemeanor Records: District Court, Municipal Court

Online Access: There is a wide range of online computerization of the judicial system from "none" to "fairly complete," but there is no statewide court records network. Some Michigan courts provide public access terminals in clerk's offices, and some courts are developing off-site electronic filing and searching capability. A few offer remote online to the public.

Searching Hints: Court records are considered public unless spcifically made non-public by statute, court rules, caseload, or court order. Courts will, however, affirm that cases exist and provide case numbers.

Some courts will not perform criminal searches. Rather, they refer requests to the State Police.

Note that costs, search requirements, and procedures vary widely because each jurisdiction is permitted to create its own administrative orders.

Court Administrator: For add'l questions about the state's court system, visit the web site at www.supremecourt.state.mi.us, or contact: State Court Administrator, 309 N Washington Sq, Lansing, MI 48909, Phone: 517-373-2222.

Minnesota

If You Are an Employer—

For pre-employment inquiry, Minnesota prohibits employers from considering misdemeanor convictions for which a jail sentence cannot be imposed.

State Criminal Records Agency

Bureau of Criminal Apprehension
Criminal Justice Information Systems
1246 University Ave
St Paul, MN 55104

Phone: 651-642-0670.

Web: http://www.dps.state.mn.us/bca

Total Records:	428,607
Who Can Access:	For most requesters, to obtain the entire adult history, including all arrests, you must have a notarized release form signed by person of record. To get a 15-year record of convictions only, a consent form is not required.
Search Requirements:	Include the following in your request: name, date of birth, and sex. Fingerprint searches are not permitted. However, 100% of records are fingerprint-supported.
What Is Released:	With consent, all records, including those without dispositions, are released. If no consent, then only conviction records released. Targeted misdemeanors (violent, DV, DUI, etc., where a jail sentence may be imposed) are released; other misdemeanors are not. Records are available from 1924. The following data is not released: juvenile records.
Indexing & Storage:	It takes 1 day before new records are available for inquiry. 72% of all arrests in database have final dispositions recorded, 63% for those arrests within last 5 years. Records are indexed on inhouse computer, microfilm and digital disc.
Access By:	Mail, in person.
Mail Search:	Turnaround time: 1 to 2 weeks. A self addressed stamped envelope is requested.
In Person Search:	Turnaround time is 2 days, unless you are the person of record, then it is immediate. Public access (15-year search) is also immediate.
Fee & Payment:	The fee for the full adult history is $15.00, for non-profits the fee is $8.00. The fee for the 15-year public record is $4.00. Non-profits have a reduced fee, call first. Fee payee: BCA. Prepayment required. Business checks, personal

checks, money orders and certified funds are accepted. No credit cards accepted.

Sexual Offender Registry

The Predatory Offender Registry Unit of the Bureau of Criminal Apprehension maintains the state database of sexual offenders. Search by city or county the Level 3 sexual offenders registry at http://www.doc.state.mn.us/level3/countysearch.htm

State Incarceration Records Agency

Minnesota Department of Corrections

Records Management Unit

450 Energy Park Drive, Suite 200

St. Paul, MN 55108

Phone: 651-642-0200

Fax: 651-643-3588

Web: www.corr.state.mn.us

Access by:	Phone, fax, mail, online. For a search, you must provide first and last name and DOB or by OID number. Online is via the web site.
What is released:	Information on current and former inmates is available; however, the online search is limited to those either still in prison or under probation. Location, OID number, physical identifiers, conviction and sentencing information, and release dates are provided.
Search Notes:	No fee for search. Computer records go back to 1978.

State Court System

Court Structure:	There are 97 District Courts comprising 10 Judicial Districts in the state.
Find Felony Records:	District Court
Misdemeanor Records:	District Court
Online Access:	There is an online system in place that allows internal and external access, but is not open to the general public.
Searching Hints:	Statewide certification and copy fees are as follows: Certification Fee: $10.00 per document, Copy Fee: $5.00 per document (not per page).
	The 3rd, 5th, 8th and 10th Judicial Districts no longer will perform criminal record searches for the public.
	An exact name is required to search, e.g., a request for "Robert Smith" will not result in finding "Bob Smith." The requester must request both names and pay two search and copy fees.

When a search is permitted by "plaintiff or defendant," most jurisdictions stated that a case is indexed by only the 1st plaintiff or defendant, and a 2nd or 3rd party would not be sufficient to search.

Court Administrator: For add'l questions about the state's court system, visit the web site at www.courts.state.mn.us, or contact: State Court Administrator, 135 Minnesota Judicial Center, 25 Constitution Ave, St Paul, MN 55155, Phone: 651-296-2474.

Missouri

State Criminal Records Agency

Missouri State Highway Patrol   **Phone:**   573-526-6153.
Criminal Record & Identification Division   **Fax:**   573-751-9382
PO Box 568
Jefferson City, MO 65102-0568   **Web:**   http://www.mshp.state.mo.us/

Total Records: 1.070,650

Who Can Access: Records are available to the general public, but youth service providers must have signature of the subject.

Search Requirements: Include the following in your request: full name, date of birth, sex, race, Social Security Number. Fingerprints are an option. A request form can be downloaded from the web site. Records are 100% fingerprint-supported.

What Is Released: Open records are accessible by the public. These are convictions, or arrests less than 30 days old unless charges are sought, or suspended imposition of sentence during probation period. Certain entites may access closed record files in accordance with state statute, with the submission of fingerprints and required fee. Records are available from 1970 on.

Indexing & Storage: It takes 5 weeks before new records are available for inquiry. 64% of all arrests in database have final dispositions recorded, 62% for those arrests within last 5 years. Records are indexed on inhouse computer (84%) including images. Records are normally maintained indefinitely.

Access By: Mail, in person.

Mail Search: Turnaround time: 3-4 weeks. No self addressed stamped envelope is required.

In Person Search: Turnaround time is while you wait for one search only.

Fee & Payment: The search fee is $5.00 per individual for a name search. Searches by fingerprint cost $14.00 each, $22.00 if the fingerprint search includes an FBI fingerprint check. Fee payee: State of Missouri. Prepayment required. Personal checks accepted. No credit cards accepted.

Sexual Offender Registry

The Missouri State Highway Patrol maintains the state sex offender registry. However, this database is not searchable online, and mail or phone search requests are not honored. It is suggested to visit local law enforcement agencies, keeping in mind they can only report on their corresponding area.

State Incarceration Records Agency

Missouri Department of Corporations   **Phone:** 573-751-2389

Legal Section   **Fax:**   573-751-4099

P.O. Box 236   **Web:**   www.corrections.state.mo.us

Jefferson City, MO 65102.

Access by: Mail, fax. For a search, you must provide full name, DOB; SSN helpful.

What is released: Information on current and former inmates is available. Location, conviction and sentencing information.

Search Notes: No fee for search. Record requests must include reason for request.

State Court System

Court Structure: The Circuit Court is the court of general jurisdiction. There are 45 circuits comprised of 114 County Circuit Courts and one independent city court. There are also Associate Circuit Courts with limited jurisdiction and some counties have Combined Courts. Municipal Courts only have jurisdiction over traffic and ordinance violations.

Find Felony Records: Circuit Court

Misdemeanor Records: Associate Circuit Court

Online Access: Missouri Case.net, a limited but growing online system, is available at http://casenet.osca.state.mo.us/casenet. This system includes records from over 30 counties (with 16 more projected) as well as the Eastern, Western, and Southern Appellate Courts, the Supreme Court, and Fine Collection Center. Cases can be searched case number, filing date, or litigant name.

Court Administrator: For add'l questions about the state's court system, visit the web site at www.osca.state.mo.us, or contact: Court Administrator, 2112 Industrial Drive - PO Box 104480, Jefferson City, MO 65110, Phone: 573-751-4377.

Mississippi

State Criminal Records Agency

Criminal Information Center   **Phone:**   601-933-2600.
Dept. of Public Safety
PO Box 958
Jackson, MS 39205

Access to Records is Restricted

Note: Mississippi does not permit the public to access their central state repository of criminal records, except for pre-approved entities with purposes provided for by state statute such as health care, banking/finance, military, childcare and schools.

Total Records: 250,000
Search Requirements: They suggest that you obtain information at the county level. The records on file are 100% fingerprint supported. 40% of the records contain dispositions.

Sexual Offender Registry

The Department of Public Safety maintians the state Sex Offender Registry. Name and location searching is available at access at http://www.sor.mdps.state.ms.us/. The agency will, also, process mail and phone requests. Call 601-368-1740 or write to the address listed above.

State Incarceration Records Agency

Mississippi Department of Corrections   **Phone:** 601-359-5000

Records Department

P.O. Box 880   **Web:**   www.mdoc.state.ms.us

Parchman, MS 38738

Access by: Phone, e-mail. To search, you must provide full name. The inmate #, county of crime and DOB are helpful. You can e-mail your request to: alee@mdoc.state.ms.us

What is released: Information on current and former inmates is available. Location, MDOC number.

Search Notes: No fee for search. Computer records go back to 1978.

State Court System

Court Structure: The court of general jurisdiction is the Circuit Court with 70 courts in 22 districts. Justice Courts were first created in 1984, replacing the Justice of the Peace. Prior to 1984, records were kept separately by each Justice of the Peace, so the location of such records today is often unknown. Probate is handled by the Chancery Courts, as are property matters.

Find Felony Records: Circuit Court

Misdemeanor Records: County Court, Justice Court, Municipal Court

Online Access: A statewide online computer system is in use internally for court personnel. There are plans underway to make this system available to the public. For further details, call Susan Anthony at 601-354-7449. The web site allows the public to search the Mississippi Supreme Court and Court of Appeals Decisions

Searching Hints: A number of Mississippi counties have two Circuit Court Districts. A search of either court in such a county will include the index from the other court.

Full Name is a search requirement for all courts. DOB and SSN are very helpful for differentiating between like-named individuals.

Court Administrator: For add'l questions about the state's court system, visit the web site at www.mssc.state.ms.us, or contact: Court Administrator, Supreme Court, Box 117, Jackson, MS 39205, Phone: 601-354-7406.

Montana

State Criminal Records Agency

Department of Justice
Criminal Records
PO Box 201403
Helena, MT 59620-1403

Phone: 406-444-3625.
Fax: 406-444-0689
Web: http://www.doj.state.mt.us/

Total Records: 141,800

Who Can Access: Records are available to the general public.

Search Requirments: Include the following in your request: name, date of birth, Social Security Number, any aliases. Place on request letterhead. Fingerprint searches are optional. 100% of records are fingerprint-supported.

What Is Released: All felonies and misdemeanors (except traffic violations, unless felony driving under the influence) are released. Records without dispositions are released; the agency attempts to locate the disposition prior to public release. Records are available from 1950's on and are 100% computerized.

Indexing & Storage: It takes 1 week to 1 month before new records are available for inquiry. 85% of all arrests in database have final dispositions recorded. Records are normally destroyed after misdemeanor traffic and DUI records are purged; see MVR Dept. for these records.

Access By: Mail, in person.

Mail Search: Turnaround time is 5-10 days. A self addressed stamped envelope is requested.

In Person Search: Turnaround time is usually immediate, unless there is a record or "hit."

Fee & Payment: The fee is $5.00 per individual for a name check, or $8.00 per individual for a fingerprint check; $32 for a fingerprint check plus FBI fingerprint check, when required by statute for child care or schools. Account status available to approved screening firms. Fee payee: Montana Criminal Records. Prepayment required. Personal checks accepted. No credit cards accepted.

Sexual Offender Registry

The state sexual offender list is maintained by the agency listed above and is open to the public. Online access is available at http://svor2.doj.state.mt.us:8010/index.htm. Phone requests are available 406-444-9479. Community seaches are available for local law enforcement agencies.

State Incarceration Records Agency

Montana Department of Corrections   **Phone:** 406-444-3910

Directors Office   **Fax:**   406-444-4920

P.O. Box 201301   **Web:**   www.cor.state.mt.us/css/default.asp

Helena, MT 59620-1301.

Access by: Phone, mail. For a search, you must provide first and last name; DOB and SSN helpful.

What is released: Information on current and former inmates is available. Location, physical identifiers, conviction and sentencing information, and release dates are provided.

Search Notes: No fee for search. Computer records go back to 1978.

State Court System

Court Structure: The District Court is the court of general jurisdiction, with 57 courts in 21 districts. There are 64 Limited Jurisdiction Courts (also known as Justice Courts), 83 City Courts and 1 Municipal Court.

Many Montana Justices of the Peace maintain case record indexes on their personal PCs, which does speed the retrieval process.

Find Felony Records: District Court

Misdemeanor Records: Limited Jurisdiction Court, City Court, Municipal Court

Online Access: There is no statewide internal or external online computer system available. Those courts with computer systems use them for internal purposes only.

Searching Hints: Most courts charge $.50 per name per year to search, with a maximum fee of $25.00.

Court Administrator: For add'l questions about the state's court system, visit the web site at www.lawlibrary.state.mt.us, or contact: Court Administrator, PO Box 203002, Helena, MT 59620-3002, Phone: 406-444-2621.

Nebraska

State Criminal Records Agency

Nebraska State Patrol
CID
PO Box 94907
Lincoln, NE 68509-4907

Phone: 402-479-4924.

Web:
http://www.nebraska-state-patrol.org/

Total Records: 197,600

Who Can Access: Records are available to the general public.

Search Requirements: Include the following in your request: full name, disposition, date of birth, Social Security Number, sex, race. Fingerprints required for certain state occupation checks; this includes an FBI fingerprint search. State keeps record of requesters and will inform the person of record if asked. 100% of records are fingerprint-supported. Felonies are required to be submitted this agency, though not all misdemeanors are. Agency will refer you to the proper county.

What Is Released: Records without dispositions are not released, except if an arrest without disposition is less than one year old. Records are available from 1937 to present. The following data is not released: juvenile records.

Indexing & Storage: It takes 15 to 60 days before new records are available for inquiry. 64% of all arrests in database have final dispositions recorded. Records are indexed on inhouse computer, fingerprint cards.

Access By: Mail, in person.

Mail Search: Turnaround time is 15 days. No self addressed stamped envelope is required.

In Person Search: They accept requests in person and turnaround is 15 minutes, but they will mail back the report if it is lengthy or incomplete (unless it is the requester's own report).

Fee & Payment: The search fee is $10.00 per name. A fingerprint search including FBI fingerprint check is $33.00. Fee payee: Nebraska State Patrol. Prepayment required. Personal checks accepted. No credit cards accepted.

Sexual Offender Registry

The Nebraska State Patrol maintains the sexual offender database for the state. A Level 3 sexual offender registry search is available at http://www.nsp.state.ne.us/sor/find.cfm. For more information call the CIB Record Check Unit at 608/266-5764, call 402-471-4545.

State Incarceration Records Agency

Nebraska Department of Correctional Services   **Phone:** 402-479-5765

Central Records Office   **Fax:**   402-479-5913

P.O. Box 94661   **Web:**   www.corrections.state.ne.us

Lincoln, NE 68509-4661

Access by: Phone, fax, mail, online. For a search, you must provide full name or DOC. The DOB and SSN number helpful. To serach online, only the name is needed.

What is released: Information on current and former inmates is available. Location, DOC number, physical identifiers, conviction and sentencing information, and release dates are provided.

Search Notes: No fee for search. Computer records go back to 1977.

State Court System

Court Structure: The District Court is the court of general jurisdiction, the County Court is the court of limited jurisdiction, each with 93 court locations.

Find Felony Records: District Court

Misdemeanor Records: County Court

Online Access: Online access to District and County courts is being tested. For more information, call John Cariotto at 402-471-2643. Currently, Douglas County's County Court offers remote online access.

Searching Hints: Most Nebraska courts require the public to do their own in-person searches and will not respond to written search requests. The State Attorney General has recommended that courts not perform searches because of the time involved and concerns over possible legal liability.

Court Administrator: For add'l questions about the state's court system, visit the web site at http://court.nol.org/AOC, or contact: Court Administrator, PO Box 98910, Lincoln, NE 68509-8910, phone: 402-471-3730.

Nevada

> **If You Are an Employer—**
>
> By state statute, employers making employment decisions may only use criminal records with dispositions. The good news is that the central state agency only releases records with dispositions.

State Criminal Records Agency

Nevada Highway Patrol
Record & ID Services
808 W Nye Lane
Carson City, NV 89703

Phone: 775-687-1600.
Fax: 775-687-1843
Web: http://nhp.state.nv.us/

Total Records:	334,000
Who Can Access:	Records are available to the general public.
Search Requirements:	This repository maintains all "fingerprintable charges," meaning, essentially, all felony records and misdemeanor offenses including DUI and domestic violence. Include the following in your request: set of fingerprints, signed release, full name. DOB, SSN, sex and race are helpful.
What Is Released:	Records without dispositions are not released, unless an approved waiver is submitted. The following data is not released: sealed records or juvenile records.
Indexing & Storage:	40% of all arrests in database have final dispositions recorded, approximately 25% for those arrests within last 5 years. Records are indexed on on computer. Records are records maintained indefinitely, unless purged due to court order. Records are available from 1987 on computer.
Access By:	Mail, in person.
Mail Search:	Turnaround time is 15 working days. No self addressed stamped envelope is required.
In Person Search:	Records are still returned by mail.
Fee & Payment:	The fingerprint search fee is $15.00 per individual. If the search requires an FBI fingerprint check (for record checks on occupations concerning children or the elderly, per state stutute), the fee is $39.00. Fee payee: Nevada Highway Patrol. Prepayment required. Cash, money order or cashier's check required. No credit cards or personal checks accepted.

Sexual Offender Registry

A sex offender registry is not available online to the public. Submit phone or mail requests with name, DOB, DL or SSN to the agency listed above. Responses take one week, fee is $8.00. The 3,400 sex offender records go back to 1998. They will only release where, when and of what conviction.

State Incarceration Records Agency

Nevada Department of Corrections   **Phone:** 775-887-3207

Correctional Case Records Manager

P.O. Box 7011   **Web:**   www.ndoc.state.nv.us/ncis/

Carson City, NV 89702

Access by:	Phone, mail, online. For a search, you must provide full name and DOB, or Inmate ID number.
What is released:	Information on current and former inmates is available. Location, conviction and sentencing information, case number, and release dates are released.
Search Notes:	No fee for search. Searches can be done back to 1864, with varing results.

State Court System

Court Structure:	There are 17 District Courts within 9 judicial districts. The 45 Justice Courts are named for the township of jurisdiction. Note that, due to their small populations, some townships no longer have Justice Courts.
Find Felony Records:	District Court
Misdemeanor Records:	District Court, Justice Court
Online Access:	Some Nevada Courts have internal online computer systems, but only Clark County has online access available to the public. A statewide court automation system is being implemented.
Searching Hints:	Many Nevada Justice Courts are small and have very few records. Their hours of operation vary widely and contact is difficult. It is recommended that requesters call ahead for information prior to submitting a written request or attempting an in-person retrieval.
Court Administrator:	For add'l questions about the state's court system, visit the web site at http://silver.state.nv.us/elec_judicial.htm, or contact: Supreme Court of Nevada, Administrative Office of the Courts, 201 S Carson St, #250, Carson City, NV 89701-4702, phone: 775-684-1700.

New Hampshire

If You Are an Employer—

By state statute, vendors may only report 7 years of criminal conviction information to employers. However, this time limit is waived if the applicant is reasonably expected to make $20,000 or more annually.

State Criminal Records Agency

State Police Headquarters
Criminal Records
James H. Hayes Bldg, 10 Hazen Dr
Concord, NH 03305

Phone: 603-271-2538.
Fax: 603-271-2339

Web: http://www.state.nh.us/nhsp/cr.html

Total Records: 618,000

Who Can Access: Requester must have "authorization in writing, duly signed and notarized, explicitly allowing the requester to receive such information." Also specify exactly what information is needed.

Search Requirements: Include the following in your request: notarized release, full name, date of birth, any aliases, sex, race. Fingerprint searches are required for certain occupations (teachers) per state statute. 75% of the records are fingerprint supported. Statutorily-required fingerprint searches include FBI check.

What Is Released: Records without convictions are not released. Records are available from circa 1900.

Indexing & Storage: It takes 1 day before new records are available for inquiry. 80% of all arrests in database have final dispositions recorded, 90% for those arrests within last 5 years.

Access By: Mail, in person.

Mail Search: Turnaround time is 1 week. A self addressed envelope is requested.

In Person Search: In person requests are processed immediately.

Fee & Payment: The search fee is $10.00 per name. When required, FBI fingerprint searches are an additional $24.00 Fee payee: NH State Police. Prepayment required. Personal checks accepted. No credit cards accepted.

Sexual Offender Registry

The Special Investigations Unit of the State Patrol oversees the sex offender data. The information is currently not available online, and limited data is available by phone or mail since the state will only release crimes against victoms of certain ages. We have been told that the list can be accessed through local sheriffs' offices.

State Incarceration Records Agency

New Hampshire Department of Corrections   **Phone:** 603-271-1823

Offender Records Office   **Fax:**   603-271-1867

P.O. Box 14   **Web:**   http://webster.state.nh.us/doc

Concord, NH 03302

Access by:	Phone, fax, mail. For a search, you must provide full name, DOB helpful.
What is released:	Conviction and sentencing information on current and former inmates is available.
Search Notes:	No fee for search. Computer records go back to 1995.

State Court System

Court Structure:	The 11 Superior Courts are the courts of General Jurisdiction. Felony cases include Class A misdemeanors. There are 36 District Courts that mhave limited jurisdiction.
Find Felony Records:	Superior Court
Misdemeanor Records:	District Court
Online Access:	There is no remote online computer access available.
Searching Hints:	A statutory search fee has been implemented in the District Courts, as follows:

- Computer search is $10.00 for up to 10 names in one request; $25.00 for 10 or more names in one request; $25.00 per hour for search time beyond one hour.

- Manual search is $25.00 per hour.

If the search requires both types, the fee is the total for each.

Court Administrator:	For add'l questions about the state's court system, visit the web site at www.state.nh.us/courts/aoc.htm, or contact: Administrative Office of Courts, 2 Noble Dr, Concord, NH 03301-6160, Phone: 603-271-2521.

New Jersey

If You Are an Employer—

If you are not located in New Jersey and wish to search the central state database, it is suggested to contact a local private investigator or a screening firm that has a private investigator's license. Otherwise, your request will be denied.

State Criminal Records Agency

Division of State Police
Records and Identification Section
PO Box 7068
West Trenton, NJ 08628-0068

Phone: 609-882-2000 x2878.
Fax: 609-530-5780
Web: http://www.state.nj.us/njsp

Note: For requesters not living in the state, it is advised to contact a NJ-based investigator to obtain the record.

Total Records: 1,587,000

Who Can Access: Criminal records are not open to the public, but can be obtained by NJ employers, NJ volunteer organizations, NJ private investigators, attorney firms, and the subject. Screening firms are eligible if they have a NJ PI license.

Search Requirements: Include the following in your request: date of birth, Social Security Number. A set of fingerprints is optional. The name must match exactly. All requesters, except attorney firms, must submit Form 212 B which must be signed by the subject. Attorney firms require a subpoena. 100% of the records are fingerprint supported.

What Is Released: All records are released, including those without dispositions. Juvenile records are restricted. Dismissals, acquittals, not-guilty verdicts are also excluded to the general public.

Indexing & Storage: It takes 1 to 5 days before new records are available for inquiry. 85% of all arrests in database have final dispositions recorded, 95% for those arrests within last 5 years. Records are indexed on inhouse computer.

Access By: Mail, in person.

Mail Search: Turnaround time is 5 to 10 working days.

In Person Search: Walk-in requests do not receive priority; they are treated as mail requests. Results are mailed.

Fee & Payment: The fee is $15.00 for a name check and $25.00 for a full check with fingerprints. Will not do FBI fingerprint checks. Fee payee: Division of State Police-SBI. Prepayment required. No personal checks or credit cards accepted.

Sexual Offender Registry

The New Jersey State Police maintain the state's sexual offender data. The database can be searched online at http://www.njsp.org/info/reg_sexoffend.html, but the Police will not release information by mail or phone. Local law enforcement will assist with localized searches.

State Incarceration Records Agency

New Jersey Department of Corrections   **Phone:** 609-777-5753

Central Administrative Offices

P.O. Box 863   **Web:**   www.state.nj.us/corrections/index.html

Trenton, NJ 08625-0863

Access by: Phone. For a search, you must provide full name, DOB and SSN helpful.

What is released: Location information on current and former inmates is available.

Search Notes: No fee for search.

State Court System

Court Structure: Each of the 21 Superior Courts have 2 divisions; one for the Civil Division and another for the Criminal Division. Search requests should be addressed separately to each division. There are 535 Municipal Courts in 21 counties.

                          Special Civil Part of the Superior Court acts like a division of the court, and handles only the smaller civil claims. The small claims limit is $2,000. The Superior Court designation refers to the court where criminal cases and civil claims over $10,000 are heard. Probate is handled by Surrogates.

Find Felony Records: Superior Court

Misdemeanor Records: Municipal Court

Online Access: Online computer access (the ACMS, AMIS, and FACTS systems) is only available for civil, equity, and family records.

                          The fee is $1.00 per minute of use. For further information and/or an Inquiry System Guidebook containing hardware and software requirements and an enrollment form, write to: Superior Court Clerk's Office, Electronic Access Program, 25 Market St, CN971, Trenton NJ 08625, fax 609-292-6564, or call 609-292-4987

Searching Hints: Effective 1/1/95, all court employees became state employees and each section is responsible for its own fees. Note that Cape May County offices are located in the city of "Cape May Court House," and not in the city of "Cape May."

Court Administrator: For add'l questions about the state's court system, visit the web site at www.judiciary.state.nj.us/admin.htm, or contact: Administrative Office of Courts, RJH Justice Complex, PO Box 037, Courts Bldg, 7th Floor, Trenton, NJ 08625, Phone: 609-984-0275.

New Mexico

State Criminal Records Agency

Department of Public Safety
Records Bureau
PO Box 1628
Santa Fe, NM 87504-1628

Phone: 505-827-9181

Fax: 505-827-3388

Web: http://www.dps.nm.org/

Total Records: 360,000

Who Can Access: Requesters must have a state notarized signed release from person of record authorizing the State of New Mexico to release records to requester.

Search Requirements: Include the following in your request: date of birth, Social Security Number, full name. Fingerprint search requests are not available except for checks for childern or elderly-related occupations mandated by state statute. The state's records are 100% fingerprint-supported.

What Is Released: All records are released, including those without dispositions. Records are available from 1935 on.

Indexing & Storage: It takes 2 to 4 weeks before new records are available for inquiry. 33% of all arrests in database have final dispositions recorded, 35% for those arrests within last 5 years. Records are indexed on inhouse computer (93%); historical paper records are added to computer once requested. Records are normally destroyed after 99 years.

Access By: Mail, in person.

Mail Search: Turnaround time is 1 to 2 weeks. Turnaround time is for "no record found." If records exist, turnaround time may be 3 to 4 weeks. A self addressed stamped envelope is requested.

In Person Search: If records are found, they may be available in 5 to 7 working days.

Fee & Payment: The fee is $7.00 per individual. If the FBI fingerprint search is required, then the fee is $31.00. Fee payee: Department of Public Safety. Prepayment required. Must use cashiers check or money order. No credit cards accepted.

Sexual Offender Registry

The Department of Public Safety maintains the state sexual offender list. Access is available online at http://www.nmsexoffender.dps.state.nm.us/, or by phone or mail as listed above.

State Incarceration Records Agency

New Mexico Corrections Department   **Phone:** 505-827-8660

Public Information Officer   **Fax:**   505-827-8220

P.O. Box 27116   **Web:**   www.state.nm.us/corrections

Santa Fe, NM 87502

Access by: Phone, mail. For a search, you must provide first and last name, DOB and SSN helpful.

What is released: Information on current and former inmates is available. Location, conviction and sentencing information, behavior, release dates are provided.

State Court System

Court Structure: The 30 District Courts in 13 districts are the courts of general jurisdiction. Starting July 1, 2001, the Magistrate Courts handle civil cases up to $10,000. Previously, the Magistrate Court limit was $7,500. The Bernalillo Metropolitan Court has jurisdiction in cases up to $5000.

Find Felony Records: District Court

Misdemeanor Records: Magistrate Court, Bernalillo Metropolitan Court

Online Access: The www.nmcourts.com web site offers free access to District and Magistrate Court case information. In general, records are available from June 1997 forward.

     Also, a commercial online service is available for the Metropolitan Court of Bernalillo County. There is a $35.00 set up fee, a connect time fee based on usage. The system is available 24 hours a day. Call 505-345-6555 for more information.

Searching Hints: There are some "shared" courts in New Mexico, with one county handling cases arising in another.

     All Magistrate Courts and the Bernalillo Metropolitan Court have public access terminals to access civil records only.

Court Administrator: For add'l questions about the state's court system, visit the web site at www.nmcourts.com/aoc.htm, or contact: Administrative Office of the Courts, 237 Don Gaspar, Rm 25, Santa Fe, NM 87501, Phone: 505-827-4800.

New York

If You Are an Employer—

By state statute, vendors may only report 7 years of criminal conviction information to employers. However, this time limit is waived if the applicant is reasonably expected to make $25,000 or more annually.

Additionally, New York prohibits employers from reviewing arrest records not connected to a conviction and without a pending charge.

State Criminal Records Agency

Division of Criminal Justice Services   **Phone:**   518-457-6043.
4 Tower Place   **Fax:**   518-457-6550
Albany, NY 12203
                                            Web: http://www.criminaljustice.state.ny.us

Access to Records is Restricted

Total Records: 7,400,000

Search Requirements: Records are only released pursuant to court order, subpoena, to entities authorized by statute, or to person of record. 99% of records are fingerprint supported. The public must search at the county court level. 85% of records have dispositions.

What Is Released: Misdemeanor convictions older than five years cannot be considered unless another crime has been commited during that time. The following data is not released: sealed records and confidential records pursuant to the Criminal Procedure Law or Family Court Act.

Sexual Offender Registry

The Department of Criminal Justice maintains the state sexual offender registry. Sex offender registry Level 3 can be searched at http://www.criminaljustice.state.ny.us/nsor/. The state offers a phone service via 900-288-3838. The fee is $.50 a call, but there is a caveat—your request must include the subject's name and one of the following; address, driver license number, SSN or DOB of the subject.

State Incarceration Records Agency

New York Department of Corrective Services   **Phone:** 505-457-5000

Building 2, 1220 Washington Avenue

Albany, NY 12226-2050   **Web:**   www.docs.state.ny.us

Access by: Phone, mail, online. For a search, you must provide full name; the DOB, SSN, and DIN (inmate number) are helpful.

What is released: Information on current and former inmates is available. Location, DIN number, conviction and sentencing information, and release dates are provided.

Search Notes: No fee for search.

State Court System

Court Structure: "Supreme Courts" are the highest trial courts in the state, equivalent to Circuit or District Courts in other states; note they are not appeals courts.

Records for Supreme and County Courts are maintained by County Clerks. In most counties, the address for the clerk is the same as for the court.

In at least 20 New York counties, misdemeanor records are only available at city, town or village courts. There are over 1250 of such courts in the state. This is also true of small claims and eviction records. Many New York City Courts index by plaintiff only.

Find Felony Records: Supreme Court, City Court

Misdemeanor Records: City Court, District Court, City of NY Criminal Court, Town and Village Justice Courts

Criminal Notes: The New York State Office of Court Administration (address below) will perform an electronic search for criminal history information from a database of criminal case records from the boroughs and counties of Bronx, Dutchess, Erie, Kings, Nassau, New York, Orange, Putnam, Queens, Richmond, Rockland, Suffolk and Westchester. The request must include complete name and date of birth, and, for mail requests, be accompanied by two (2) self addressed stamped return envelopes. The fee, payable by check, is $16.00 per name per county. Mail and in person requests go to:

> Office of Court Administration
> Criminal History Search
> 25 Beaver St, 8th Floor
> New York, NY 10004

Their phone number is 212-428-2810. You may obtain copies of any case dispositions found from the applicable county court.

Online Access: There is no state supported online access is available for criminal records. But, civil case information from the 13 largest counties is available through DataCase, a database index of civil case information publicly available at terminals located at Supreme and County Courts. In addition to the civil case index, DataCase also includes judgment docket and lien information, New York County Clerk system data, and the New York State attorney registration file. Remote access is also available at a fee of $1.00 per minute. Call 800-494-8981 for more remote access information.

Searching Hints: Supreme and County Court records are generally maintained in the County Clerk's Office.

Fees for Supreme and County Courts are generally as follows: $5.00 per 2 year search per name for a manual search, and $16.00 per name for a computer or OCA search; $.50 per page (minimum $1.00) for copies; and $4.00 for certification. City Courts charge $5.00 for certification. Effective 4-1-95, no New York court will accept credit cards for any transaction.

Court Administrator: New York State has two administrative locations, as listed below. Also, for add'l questions about the state's court system, visit the web site at www.courts.state.ny.us.

- NY State Office of Court Administration, Empire State Plaza, Agency Bldg #4, Suite 2001, Albany, NY 12223, Phone: 518-473-1196.

- Office of Administration, 25 Beaver St, New York NY 10004, and telephone: 212-428-2100.

North Carolina

State Criminal Records Agency

State Bureau of Investigation   **Phone:**   919-662-4500 x300.
Identification Section   **Fax:**   919-662-4380
PO Box 29500
Raleigh, NC 27626   **Web:**   http://sbi.jus.state.nc.us

Access to Records is Restricted

Total Records: 881,983

Search Requirements: Record access is limited to criminal justice and other government agencies authorized by law. Employers are denied access unless subject is in the health or child care business. Contact agency for proper paperwork. Include the following in your request: full name, SSN, DOB. Fingerprints are optional. The state's records are 100% fingerprint supported.

What Is Released: All records are released, including those without dispositions. There are no restrictions for those authorized to receive records.

Sexual Offender Registry

The Division of Criminal Information of the State Bureau of Investigation maintains the state database of sexual offenders. Records are searchable online at http://sbi.jus.state.nc.us/SOR_20/Default.htm. Records may be viewed in person or at local law enforcement agencies. For more information, call the Quality Assurance Unit or e-mail sor@mail.jus.state.nc.us.

State Incarceration Records Agency

North Carolina Department of Corrections   **Phone:** 919-716-3200
Combined Records
2020 Yonkers Road, 4226 MSC   **Web:**   www.doc.state.nc.us
Raleigh, NC 27699-4220

Access by: Phone, mail, online. For a search, you must provide full name, DOB, SSN and DOC number helpful.

What is released: Information on current and former inmates is available. Location, physical identifiers, conviction and sentencing information, and release dates are provided. The online system allows one to search by name or ID number for public information on inmates, probationers or parolees since 1972.

Search Notes: No fee for search. Computer records go back prior to 1972.

State Court System

Court Structure: The Superior Court is the court of general jurisdiction, the District Court is limited. The counties combine the courts, thus searching is done through one court, not two, within the county.

Find Felony Records: Superior Court

Misdemeanor Records: District Court

Online Access: Access the active criminal calendars for most county or on a statewide basis at www.aoc.state.nc.us/www/public/html/calendars.html. Their historical information is not available.

Searching Hints: Most courts perform criminal searches for a $5.00 search fee. Many courts have archived their records prior to 1968 in the Raleigh State Archives, 919-733-5722.

Court Administrator: For add'l questions about the state's court system, visit the web site at www.aoc.state.nc.us/www/public/html/aoc.htm, or contact: Administrative Office of Courts, 2 E Morgan St, Justice Bldg, 4th Floor, Raleigh, NC 27602, Phone: 919-733-7107.

North Dakota

State Criminal Records Agency

Bureau of Criminal Investigation
PO Box 1054
Bismarck, ND 58502-1054

Phone: 701-328-5500.
Fax: 701-328-5510

Web: http://www.ag.state.nd.us

Total Records: 230,400

Who Can Access: Records are available to the general public only with consent of subject.

Search Requirements: Subject will be notified of the request. Include the following in your request: signed release form subject, name, date of birth, current address, Social Security Number. Fingerprints optional, with additional fee. Upon request, the FBI database can be searched also; however, an additional set of fingerpints must be submitted. 100% of the records are fingerprint-supported.

What Is Released: After one year, only records with convictions are released. Charges that are dismissed or sealed are not released. Records are available from 1930 to present.

Indexing & Storage: It takes 6 to 10 days before new records are available for inquiry. 86% of all arrests in database have final dispositions recorded, 78% for those arrests within last 5 years. Records are indexed on computer if DOB is 1940 to present; prior in paper files. Records are maintained indefinitely.

Access By: Mail, in person.

Mail Search: Turnaround time is 3 to 5 days. No self addressed stamped envelope is required.

In Person Search: Turnaround time is merely while you wait.

Fee & Payment: The search fee is $20.00 per name. Fingerprint searches are $22.00; will also do an FBI fingerprint search with fee set by FBI. Fee payee: ND Attorney General. Prepayment required. Personal checks accepted. No credit cards accepted.

Sexual Offender Registry

The Bureau of Criminal Investigation, which is a part of the State Attorney General's Office, maintains the state database of sexual offenders. You can search online at www.ndsexoffender.com, but only the high offender level names are found. The entire list is available for searching by phone or mail at the address listed above.

State Incarceration Records Agency

Department of Correction and Rehabilitation   **Phone:** 701-328-6122

Records Clerk   **Fax:**   701-328-6640

P.O. Box 5521   Web: www.state.nd.us/docr/Directory.htm

Bismark, ND 58506

Access by: Phone, fax, mail. For a search, you must provide full name and DOB.

What is released: Information on current and former inmates is available. Location, conviction and sentencing information, and release dates are provided.

Search Notes: No fee for search. Inmate searching will soon be available online.

State Court System

Court Structure: In 1995, the County Courts merged with the District Courts statewide. County court records are maintained by the 53 District Court Clerks in the 7 judicial districts. We recommend stating "include all County Court cases" in your search requests. There are 76 Municipal Courts that handle traffic cases.

Find Felony Records: District Court

Misdemeanor Records: District Court

Online Access: A statewide computer system for internal purposes only is in operation in most counties.

     You may search North Dakota Supreme Court dockets and opinions at www.ndcourts.com. Search by docket number, party name, or anything else that may appear in the text. Records are from 1991 forward. E-mail notification of new opinions is also available.

Searching Hints: The standard search fee in District Courts is $10.00 per name, and the certification fee is $10.00 per document. Copy fees are set at $.50 per page, but many courts charge only $.25.

Court Administrator: For add'l questions about the state's court system, visit the web site at www.court.state.nd.us, or contact: Court Administrator, North Dakota Supreme Court, 600 E Blvd Ave, Dept 180, Bismarck, ND 58505-0530, Phone: 701-328-4216.

Ohio

State Criminal Records Agency

Ohio Bureau of Investigation   **Phone:**   740-845-2000 (General Info).
Civilian Background Section   **Fax:**   740-845-2633
PO Box 365
London, OH 43140   **Web:** http://www.ag.state.oh.us/bci/bcii.htm

Note:

Total Records: 1,6000,000
Who Can Access: Records are available to the public, but only with consent of subject.
Search Requirements: Include the following in your request: witnessed signed release from subject, fingerprints, name DOB, SSN. 100% of the records are fingerprint supported.
What Is Released: Records without dispositions are not released. Records are available from 1921 on. Records from 1972 on are computerized.
Indexing & Storage: It takes 5 days, 15 with fingerprints, before new records are available for inquiry. 56% of all arrests in database have final dispositions recorded. Records are indexed on inhouse computer. Records are maintained indefinitely. The state has an innovative system over the web for electronic transfer of fingerprints.
Access By: Mail.
Mail Search: Turnaround time is 30 days. No self addressed stamped envelope is required.
Fee & Payment: The search fee is $15.00 per record. Stautorily-required checks may include an FBI fingerprint check for an additional $24.00. Fee payee: Treasurer - State of Ohio. Prepayment required. No credit cards accepted.

Sexual Offender Registry

Ohio's Sex Offender Registration and Notification Law (SORN) is administered within BCI's Identification Division, part of the Attorney General's Office, but there is no public access. Local law enforcement will counduct searches on a localized basis. Cincinnati and a number of counties have posted offenders on web sites.

State Incarceration Records Agency

Ohio Department of Rehabilitation and Correction   **Phone:** 614-752-1159

Bureau of Records Management   **Fax:**   614-752-1086

1050 Freeway Drive, N.   **Web:**   www.drc.state.oh.us

Columbus, OH 43229

Access by: Phone, mail, online. For a search, you must provide first and last name or Offender Number. The DOB and SSN are helpful.

What is released: Information on current and former inmates is available. Location, physical identifiers, conviction and sentencing information, and release dates are provided.

Search Notes: No fee for search. Computer records go back to 1975.

State Court System

Court Structure: The Court of Common Pleas is the general jurisdiction court with one per each of Ohio's 88 counties. The 47 County Courts have limited jurisdiction. There are 118 Municipal Courts and over 395 Mayor's Courts found at the local level.

Since 2001, Ohio Common Pleas Courts may name their own civil action limits, though most of these courts have yet to make changes. In effect, Common Pleas courts may take any civil cases. However, civil maximum limits for Ohio's County Courts and Municipal Courts remains the same at $15,000.

Find Felony Records: Court of Common Pleas

Misdemeanor Records: County Court, Municipal Court, Mayor's Court

Online Access: There is no statewide computer system, but a number of counties offer online access.

Court Administrator: For add'l questions about the state's court system, visit the web site at www.sconet.state.oh.us, or contact: Administrative Director, Supreme Court of Ohio, 30 E Broad St, 3rd Floor, Columbus, OH 43266-0419, Phone: 614-466-2653.

Oklahoma

State Criminal Records Agency

OK State Bureau of Investigation   **Phone:**   405-848-6724.
Criminal History Reporting   **Fax:**   405-879-2503
6600 N Harvey
Oklahoma City, OK 73116   **Web:**   http://www.osbi.state.ok.us

Total Records: 850,000

Who Can Access: Records are available to the general public.

Search Requirements: Include the following in your request: DOB or approximate age. The SSN, sex or race are helpful and provide a better search, but are not required. Fingerprints are optional. 100% of the records are fingerprint-supported. A record request form is available at the web site

What Is Released: Arrest records without dispositions are released if the party was fingerprinted. Computer searches include arrests without dispositions. Records are available from 1925 on.

Indexing & Storage: It takes 5 to 7 days before new records are available for inquiry. 35% of all arrests in database have final dispositions recorded, 47% for those arrests within last 5 years. Records are normally maintained indefinitely.

Access By: Mail, fax, in person.

Mail Search: Turnaround time is 2 weeks. A self addressed stamped envelope is requested.

Fax Search: Use of credit card and their "Credit Card Fax Form" is required. Call to have them first fax you the form.

In Person Search: Name requests take 20 minutes, fingerprint searches take up to ten days to process.

Fee & Payment: The fee for a computer name search is $15.00. The fee for the fingerprint search is $19.00. Fingerprint search does not include FBI fingerprint search; agency will not conduct an FBI search. Copies are $.25 per page. Fee payee: O.S.B.I. Prepayment required. Credit cards accepted: MasterCard, Visa.

Sexual Offender Registry

A sex offender registry is maintained by the Department of Corrections, see below. Mail requests of name searches are available, but this agency does not place the information online. TV Station 9,

WYTV in Oklahoma City maintains a list of offenders on the web, but the list has not been recently updated.

State Incarceration Records Agency

Oklahoma Department of Corrections   **Phone:** 405-425-2880

Records Officer   **Fax:**   405-425-2608

P.O. Box 11400, 3400 Martin Luther King Avenue   **Web:**   www.doc.state.ok.us

Oklahoma City, OK 73136-0400

Access by:	Phone, fax, mail, online. For a search, you must provide first and last name, but the DOB, SSN and DOC number helpful. You can search online by either the name or DOC number. The online system is shut down from 10PM until 10AM.
What is released:	Information on current and former inmates is available. Location, DOC number, physical identifiers, conviction and sentencing information, and release dates are provided.
Search Notes:	No fee for search.

State Court System

Court Structure:	There are 80 District Courts in 26 judicial districts. Cities with populations in excess of 200,000 (Oklahoma City and Tulsa) have Municipal Criminal Courts of Record. Cities with less than 200,000 do not have such courts. For example, there are over 335 Municipal Courts Not of Record.
Find Felony Records:	District Court
Misdemeanor Records:	District Court, Municipal Court of Record
Online Access:	Free Internet access is available for eight District Courts and all Appellate courts at www.oscn.net. Both civil and criminal records are available. The counties are Canadian, Cleveland, Comanche, Garfield, Oklahoma, Payne, Rogers, and Tulsa.
	One can search the Oklahoma Supreme Court Network by single cite or multiple cite (no name searches) from the Internet site.
	Case information is available in bulk form for downloading to computer. For information, call the Administrative Director of Courts, 405-521-2450.
Court Administrator:	For add'l questions about the state's court system, visit the web site at www.oscn.net, or contact: Administrative Director of Courts, 1915 N Stiles, #305, Oklahoma City, OK 73105, Phone: 405-521-2450.

Oregon

State Criminal Records Agency

Oregon State Police, Unit 11   **Phone:**   503-378-3070.
Identification Services Section   **Fax:**   503-378-2121
PO Box 4395   **Web:**   http://www.osp.state.or.us
Portland, OR 97208-4395

Total Records: 1,033,453

Who Can Access: Records are available to the general public.

Search Requirements: Three types of searches exist: open records search, own record search, and statutorily-required search. The latter can include an FBI fingerprint check for an additional $24.00 fee. Include the following in your request: name, date of birth. Submitting the SSN is helpful, but not required. Fingerprints are required only when subject submits the request. If record exists, person of record will be notified of the request and the record will not be released for 14 additional days.

What Is Released: Open record information includes all records with convictions and also all arrests within the past year without disposition. Statutorily-required record searches and own record searches include all records. Records are available from 1941 on and are computerized.

Indexing & Storage: It takes up to 8 days before new records are available for inquiry. Approximately 50% of all arrests in database have final dispositions recorded. Records are indexed on inhouse computer. Records are maintained indefinitely.

Access By: Mail, fax, online.

Mail Search: Clean records are returned in 7-10 days, records with activity take 3 weeks to return.A self addressed stamped envelope is requested.

Fax Search: Requesters must be pre-approved.

Online Search: A web based site is available for requesting and receiving criminal records. Web site is ONLY for high-volume requesters who must be pre-approved. Results are posted as "No Record" or "In Process" ("In Process" means a record will be mailed in 14 days). Use the "open records" link to get into the proper site. Fee is $12.00 per record. Call 503-373-1808, ext 230 to receive the application, or visit the web site.

Fee & Payment: Open record search fee is $15.00 per individual name. If someone is submitting a search on oneself, the fee is $12.00 and fingerprints are required.

Statutorily-required searches are $12.00 plus FBI fingerprint fee, if required. $5.00 fee to notarize. Fee payee: Oregon State Police. Prepayment required. Personal checks accepted. No credit cards accepted.

Sexual Offender Registry

A sex offender registry is not available online. Direct mail and phone inquiries to the State Police, Sex Offender Registration Unit, at the address above or call 503-378-3720.

State Incarceration Records Agency

Oregon Department of Corrections

Central Records Office

2575 Center Street, N.E.

Salem, OR 97301.

Phone: 503-373-1515, ext 509

Fax: 503-373-1629

Web: www.doc.state.or.us

Access by:	Phone, fax, mail. For a search, you must provide full name, DOB and SID# helpful.
What is released:	Information on current and former inmates is available. Location, SID number, physical identifiers, conviction and sentencing information, and release dates are provided.
Search Notes:	No fee for search.

State Court System

Court Structure:	Effective January 15, 1998, the District and Circuit Courts were combined into Circuit Courts. At the same time, three new judicial districts were created by splitting existing ones. Municipal, County, and Justice courts are limited jurisdiction tribunals outside of the state-funded court system and are not subject to its administrative control.
Find Felony Records:	Circuit Court
Misdemeanor Records:	Circuit Court, Justice Court, Municipal Court
Online Access:	Online computer access is available through the Oregon Judicial Information Network (OJIN). OJIN Online includes almost all cases filed in the Oregon state courts. Generally, the OJIN database contains criminal, civil, small claims, probate, and some, but not all, juvenile records. However, it does not contain any records from municipal nor county courts. There is a one-time setup fee of $295.00, plus a monthly usage charge (minimum $10.00) based on transaction type, type of job, shift, and number

of units/pages (which averages $10-13 per hour). For further information and/or a registration packet, write to: Oregon Judicial System, Information Systems Division, ATTN: Technical Support, 1163 State Street, Salem OR 97310, or call 800-858-9658.

Searching Hints: Many Oregon courts indicated that in person searches would markedly improve request turnaround time as court offices are understaffed or spread very thin. Most Circuit Courts that have records on computer do have a public access terminal that will speed up in-person or retriever searches. Most records offices close from Noon to 1PM Oregon time for lunch. No staff is available during that period.

Court Administrator: For add'l questions about the state's court system, visit the web site at www.ojd.state.or.us/osca, or contact: Court Administrator, Supreme Court Bldg, 1163 State St, Salem, OR 97310, Phone: 503-986-5500.

Pennsylvania

If You Are an Employer—

Employers are prohibited from reviewing arrest records not connected to a conviction and without a pending charge. Note that the state repository releases arrest records less than three years old without dispositions.

State Criminal Records Agency

State Police Central Repository
1800 Elmerton Ave
Harrisburg, PA 17110-9758

Phone: 717-783-5494.
Fax: 717-705-8840

Web: http://www.psp.state.pa.us/

Total Records:	1,903,084
Who Can Access:	Records are available to the general public.
Search Requirements:	Must make request on Request Form SP4-164 or the request will be returned. Include the following in your request: full name, date of birth, Social Security Number, sex, race, any aliases. A release is not required. The record database is 100% fingerprint-supported. Statutorily-required fingerprint searches include an FBI fingerprint search.
What Is Released:	Records include felony and misdemeanor convictions, also cases without dispositions less than 3 years old. Records are available from the 1920s. Records are available for all convictions.
Indexing & Storage:	It takes 1 day before new records are available for inquiry. 60% of all arrests in database have final dispositions recorded, 31% for those arrests within last 5 years. Records are indexed on fingerprint cards and inhouse computer. Records are normally 3 years after individual is confirmed deceased by fingerprints.
Access By:	Mail.
Mail Search:	Turnaround time is 2-3 weeks. Turnaround can be 6 weeks if a record has a hit. No self addressed stamped envelope is required.
Fee & Payment:	Fee is $10.00 per name search. Add $24.00 if for a statutorily-required FBI fingerprint check. Fee payee: Commonwealth of Pennsylvania. Prepayment required. No personal checks accepted. No credit cards accepted.

Sexual Offender Registry

The State Police, Megan's Law Unit, oversees the state's sex offender registry. Access is not available online, nor is it available by phone or mail. Local law enforcement are notifed by the State Police about offender activity, so it is suggested to contact local agencies.

State Incarceration Records Agency

Pennsylvania Department of Corrections

Inmate Records Office

P.O. Box 598

Camp Hill, PA 17001-0598

Phone: 717-975-4862

Fax: 717-731-7159

Web: www.cor.state.pa.us

Access by:	Phone, fax, mail, online. For a search, you must provide full name, DOB and SSN helpful.
What is released:	Information on current and former inmates is available by fax, phone and mail. Location, physical identifiers, conviction and sentencing information, and release dates are available. The online system is limited and only provides the physical identifiers and the facility location.
Search Notes:	No fee for search.

State Court System

Court Structure:	The Courts of Common Pleas are the general trial courts, with jurisdiction over both civil and criminal matters and appellate jurisdiction over matters disposed of by the special courts. The civil records Clerk of the Court of Common Pleas is called the Prothonotary. There are 103 courts in 60 districts.
	It is not necessary to check with each Magisterial District Court for misdemeanor records, but rather to check with the Prothonotary for the county.
Find Felony Records:	Court of Common Pleas, Philadelphia Municipal Court
Misdemeanor Records:	Court of Common Pleas, Philadelphia Municipal Court, Pittsburgh City Magistrate Court, Magisterial District Court (Justice Court)
Online Access:	The state's 550 Magisterial District Courts are served by a statewide, automated case management system; online access to the case management system is not available. However, public access to statutorily authorized information is available from the Special Courts, filing offices of Appellate Courts, and from the AOPC. The courts are considering ways to implement

a unified, statewide system in the criminal division of the Courts of Common Pleas.

The Infocon County Access System provides direct dial-up access to criminal (and civil) court record information for 15 counties - Armstrong, Bedford, Blair, Butler, Clarion, Clinton, Erie, Franklin, Huntingdon, Juaniata, Lawrence, Mercer, Mifflin, Pike, and Potter. Set up entails a $25.00 base set-up fee plus $25.00 per county. The monthly usage fee minimum is $25.00, plus time charges. This will be going onto the web in early 2002 at www.ic-access.com. For more information, call Infocon at 814-472-6066.

Searching Hints: Fees vary widely among jurisdictions. Many courts will not conduct searches due to a lack of personnel or, if they do search, turnaround time may be excessively lengthy. Many courts have public access terminals for in-person searches.

Court Administrator: For add'l questions about the state's court system, visit the web site at www.courts.state.pa.us, or contact: Administrative Office of PA Courts, PO Box 229, Mechanicsburg, PA 17055, Phone: 717-795-2000.

Rhode Island

If You Are an Employer—

Employers are prohibited from reviewing arrest records not connected to a conviction and without a pending charge, unless the subject is applying for a job in law enforcement.

State Criminal Records Agency

Department of Attorney General
Bureau of Criminal Identification
150 S Main Street
Providence, RI 02903

Phone: 401-274-4400 x2353.

Web: http://www.riag.state.ri.us

Total Records:	240,000
Who Can Access:	Criminal records are only released to law enforcement agencies, the subject, or to those with a signed notarized authorization from the subject. It is suggested to obtain records at the county level.
Search Requirements:	Include the following in your request: signed notarized release from subject, SSN, picture ID of the requester. Fingerprints are optional. They will call the Notary on the authorization for verification. 100% of the records are fingerprint-supported.
What Is Released:	All arrests and convictions are reported.
Indexing & Storage:	It takes 1 to 7 days before new records are available for inquiry. 60% of all arrests in database have final dispositions recorded.
Access By:	Mail, in person.
Mail Search:	Turnaround time: up to 2 weeks. A self addressed stamped envelope is requested.
In Person Search:	Turnaround time is while you wait.
Fee & Payment:	The fee is $5.00 per name. If required, the FBI fingerprint search is $24.00. Fee payee: Department of Attorney General. Prepayment required. Personal checks accepted. No credit cards accepted.

Sexual Offender Registry

The state sexual offender registry is maintained by the Attorney General's Office and is not available to the public. It is suggested to search at the local level with those enforcement agencies who are notified of offender names and activity.

State Incarceration Records Agency

Rhode Island Department of Corrections

Assistant to the Director

40 Howard Avenue

Cranston, RI 02920

Phone: 401-462-3900

Fax: 401-464-2630

Web: www.doc.state.ri.us

Access by:	Phone, fax, mail. For a search, you must provide first and last name, DOB helpful.
What is released:	Information on current and former inmates is available. Location, physical identifiers, conviction and sentencing information, and release dates are provided.
Search Notes:	No fee for search.

State Court System

Court Structure:	Rhode Island has five counties, but only four Superior/District Court Locations (2nd-Newport, 3rd-Kent, 4th-Washignton, and 6th-Prividence/Bristol Districts). Bristol and Providence counties are completely merged at the Providence location. Civil claims between $5000 and $10,000 may be filed in either Superior or District Court at the discretion of the filer.
Find Felony Records:	Superior Court
Misdemeanor Records:	District Court
Online Access:	The Judiciary offers free access to the adult criminal information database at http://courtconnect.courts.state.ri.us. One may serach by defendant name/business name or by the case identification.
	The Superior (civil, criminal, family) and Appellate courts are online internally for court personnel only.
Court Administrator:	For add'l questions about the state's court system, visit the web site at www.courts.state.ri.us/supreme/index.htm, or contact: Court Administrator, Supreme Court, 250 Benefit St, Providence, RI 02903, Phone: 401-222-3272.

South Carolina

State Criminal Records Agency

South Carolina Law Enforcement Division (SLED)
Criminal Records Section
PO Box 21398
Columbia, SC 29221

Phone: 803-896-7043.
Fax: 803-896-7022

Web: http://www.sled.state.sc.us

Total Records:	1,075,215
Who Can Access:	Records are available to the general public.
Search Requirements:	Include the following in your request: full name, any aliases, date of birth, sex, race. The SSN is optional. Although 100% of the records are fingerprint supported, they will not do fingerprint searches.
What Is Released:	All records are released, including those without dispositions. Records are available from the 1960s.
Indexing & Storage:	It takes 3 to 12 days before new records are available for inquiry. 72% of all arrests in database have final dispositions recorded, 85% for those arrests within last 5 years. Records are indexed on inhouse computer. Records are maintained indefinitely unless expunged.
Access By:	Mail, in person, online.
Mail Search:	Turnaround time is 5 to 7 days. They will return by overnight delivery service if prepaid and materials provided. A self addressed stamped envelope is requested.
In Person Search:	Turnaround time is within minutes.
Online Search:	SLED offers commercial access to criminal record history from 1960 forward on the web site. Fees are $25.00 per screening or $8.00 if for a charitable organization. Credit card ordering accepted. Visit the web site or call 803-896-7219 for details.
Fee & Payment:	The search fee is $25.00 per individual. The fee is $8.00 for non-profit organizations, pre-approval is required. Fee payee: SLED. Prepayment required. Business and company checks are accepted. No credit cards accepted.

Sexual Offender Registry

Sex offender data is available online at www.scattorneygeneral.com (click on "Sex Offender Registry") or local law enforcement. Searches are available by name, city, county or ZIP Code. Records are not available by mail or phone.

State Incarceration Records Agency

Department of Corrections

Inmate Records Branch

4444 Broad River Road

Columbia, SC 29221-1787

Phone: 877-846-3472

Web: www.state.sc.us/scdc

Access by:	Phone. For a search, provide full name, DOB, SSN. The SCDC number is helpful.
What is released:	Information on current and former inmates is available. Location, SCDC number, physical identifiers, conviction and sentencing information, FBI number, and release dates are provided.
Search Notes:	No fee for search. Computer records go back to mid 1970's.

State Court System

Court Structure:	The 46 SC counties are divided among 16 judicial circuits. The Circuit Court is the court of general jurisdiction and consists of a Court of General Sessions (criminal) and a Court of Common Pleas (civil). A family court is also in operation at the county level. The over 340 Magistrate and Municipal Courts only handle misdemeanor cases involving a $500.00 fine and/or 30 days or less jail time.
	The maximum civil claim monetary amount for the Magistrate Courts increased from $5000 to $7500 in 2001.
Find Felony Records:	Circuit Court
Misdemeanor Records:	Circuit Court, Magistrate Court, Municipal Court
Online Access:	The Judicial Department is developing a statewide court case management system. At present, only Charleston County offers Internet access to court records.
Searching Hints:	If requesting a record in writing, it is recommended that the words "request that General Session, Common Pleas, and Family Court records be searched" be included in the request.

Most South Carolina courts will not conduct searches. However, if a name and case number are provided, many will pull and copy the record. Search fees vary widely as they are set by each county individually.

Court Administrator: For add'l questions about the state's court system, visit the web site at www.judicial.state.sc.us/courtadmin/index.cfm, or contact: Court Administration, 1015 Sumter St, 2nd Floor, Columbia, SC 29201, Phone: 803-734-1800.

South Dakota

State Criminal Records Agency

Division of Criminal Investigation   **Phone:** 605-773-3331.
Identification Section   **Fax:**   605-773-4629
500 E Capitol   **Web:**
Pierre, SD 57501-5070   http://www.state.sd.us/attorney/attorney.html

Total Records:	175,000
Who Can Access:	Records are only available with a signed release from the subject.
Search Requirements:	Include the following in your request: date of birth, full name, set of fingerprints, signed release form. The form requires identifying information: color of hair and eyes, height, weight, date of birth, Social Security Number.
What Is Released:	Records without dispositions are not released, unless the case is still open. Records are available for 10 years for misdemeanors and lifetime for felonies. The following data is not released: juvenile records, minor traffic violations or out-of-state or federal charges.
Indexing & Storage:	It takes day before new records are available for inquiry. 98% of all arrests in database have final dispositions recorded. Records are indexed on inhouse computer (90+%); only older records not computerized. Records are normally destroyed after 10 years, if a misdemeanor.
Access By:	Mail.
Mail Search:	Turnaround time: 5 to 10 working days. Upon receipt of those requirements, they will conduct a search of their files and supply a copy of any criminal history that is found or a statement that there is no criminal history. A self addressed stamped envelope is requested.
Fee & Payment:	The fee is $15.00 per name. Statutorily-required fingerprint checks will include an FBI fingerprint check for an additional $24.00. Fee payee: Division of Criminal Investigation. Prepayment required. Personal checks accepted. No credit cards accepted.

Sexual Offender Registry

A search of the sexual offender registry, maintained by the agency mentioned above, is available online at http://www.sddci.com/administration/id/sexoffender/index.htm. Note, however, this is not a statewide database, and one must search by county. Localized searches are also available from local law enforcement.

State Incarceration Records Agency

South Dakota Department of Corrections

Central Records Office

3200 E. Highway 34, 500 E. Capitol Avenue

Pierre, SD 57501-5070

Phone: 605-773-3478

Fax: 605-773-3194

Web:
www.state.sd.us/corrections/corrections.html

Access by:	Phone, fax, mail. For a search, you must provide full name, DOB and SSN helpful.
What is released:	Information on current and former inmates is available. Location, conviction and sentencing information are available.
Search Notes:	No fee for search. Computer records go back to 1986.

State Court System

Court Structure:	The state re-aligned their circuits from 8 to 7 effective June, 2000. The Circuit Court is the court of general jurisdiction, each county also has a Magistrate Court.
Find Felony Records:	Circuit Court
Misdemeanor Records:	Circuit Court, Magistrate Court
Online Access:	There is no statewide online access computer system currently available. Larger courts are being placed on computer systems at a rate of 4 to 5 courts per year. Access is intended for internal use only. Smaller courts place their information on computer cards that are later sent to Pierre for input by the state office.
Searching Hints:	South Dakota has a statewide criminal record search database, administrated by the State Court Administrator's Office in Pierre. All criminal record information from July 1, 1989 forward, statewide, is contained in the database. To facilitate quicker access for the public, the state has designated 10 county record centers to process all mail or ongoing commercial accounts' criminal record requests. All mail requests are forwarded to, and commercial account requests are assigned to one of 10 specific county court clerks for processing a statewide search. Five counties (Buffalo, Campbell, Dewey, McPherson, and Ziebach) do not have computer terminals in-house. The criminal records from these counties are entered into the database by court personnel from another location.

The fee is $15.00 per record. State authorized commercial accounts may order and receive records by fax, there is an additional $5.00 fee unless a non-toll free line is used.

Requesters who wish to set up a commercial account are directed to contact Jill Gusso at the Court Administrator's Office in Pierre at the address mentioned below, or at jill.gusso@ujs.state.sd.us.

Note that walk-in requesters seeking a single or minimum of requests may still obtain a record from their local county court. Most South Dakota courts do not allow the public to perform searches, but rather require the court clerk to do them for the of $15.00 fee. A special Record Search Request Form must be used. Searches will be returned with a disclaimer stating that the clerk is not responsible for the completeness of the search. Clerks are not required to respond to telephone or fax requests. Many courts are not open all day so they prefer written requests.

Court Administrator: For add'l questions about the state's court system, visit the web site at www.state.sd.us/state/judicial, or contact: State Court Administrator, State Capitol Bldg, 500 E Capitol Ave, Pierre, SD 57501-5059, Phone: 605-773-3474.

Tennessee

State Criminal Records Agency

Tennessee Bureau of Investigation

Records and Identification Unit

901 R S Gass Blvd.

Nashville, TN 37216

Phone: 615-744-4000.

Fax: 615-744-4653

Web: http://www.tbi.state.tn.us/

Access to Records is Restricted

Note: The record database is not open to the general public or employers. It can only be accessed by those— mostly state agencies and law enforcement—who have specific authorization per state law. However, there are some vendors who have accumulated a proprietary database of Tennessee criminal docket information. Also, the Department of Corrections maintains a list of those who are on parole or probation but reside in the state, see below.

Total Records: 2,150,000

Sexual Offender Registry

The agency listed above state maintains a web site at http://www.ticic.state.tn.us/ that permits searching of sexual offenders, missing children, and people placed on parole from another state but who reside in TN. Also, you may call 888-837-4170 to search by name or location.

State Incarceration Records Agency

Tennessee Department of Corrections

Rachel Jackson Building

320 6th Avenue, N.

Nashville, TN 37243-0465

Phone: 615-741-1000

Fax: 615-532-1497

Web: www.state.tn.us/correction

Access by: Phone, fax, mail. For a search, you must provide full name; DOB and SSN helpful.

What is released: Information on current and former inmates is available. Location, conviction and sentencing information are provided.

Search Notes: No fee for search. Computer records go back to 1992.

State Court System

Court Structure: Criminal cases are handled by the Circuit Courts and the General Sessions Courts. Criminal Courts were established by the General Assembly to relieve Circuit Courts in areas where are justified by heavy caseloads. They exist in 13 of the State's 31 Judicial Districts. In addition to having jurisdiction over criminal cases, the 29 Criminal Court judges hear misdemeanor appeals from lower courts. In Districts without Criminal Courts, criminal cases are handled at the trial level by Circuit Court judges. There are over 300 Municipal Courts in the state that handle violations of city ordinances.

The Chancery Courts, in addition to handling probate, also hear certain types of equitable civil cases. Combined courts vary by county, and the counties of Davidson, Hamilton, Knox, and Shelby have separate Criminal Courts.

Find Felony Records: Circuit Court

Misdemeanor Records: Circuit Court, General Sessions Court, Criminal Court, Municipal Court

Online Access: The Tennessee Administrative Office of Courts (AOC) has provided computers and CD-ROM readers to state judges, and a computerization project (named TnCIS) to implement statewide court automation.

Court Administrator: For add'l questions about the state's court system, visit the web site at www.tsc.state.tn.us, or contact: Administrative Office of the Courts, Nashville City Center, 511 Union St, Suite 600, Nashville, TN 37219, Phone: 615-741-2687.

Texas

State Criminal Records Agency

Department Of Public Safety   **Phone:** 512-424-2427
Crime Records Service, Correspondence Section
PO Box 15999   **Web:**   http://records.txdps.state.tx.us
Austin, TX 78761-5999

Total Records: 6,400,000

Who Can Access: Conviction only records are available to the general public, otherwise consent is needed.

Search Requirements: To obtain ALL arrest information (conviction and non-conviction), must have a signed release and full set of fingerprints from the person of record. Statutorily-required FBI fingerprint checks are required for Houston City and FD personnel, for instance. To obtain conviction and deferred adjudication data only, submit full name, sex, race, and DOB. The SSN is helpful, but not required. No letter of authorization is needed for the conviction only report. Turnaround time is 24-48 hours.

What Is Released: Fingerprint searches show complete record; name search is conviction only. Since 1/1/93, records include complete information regarding charge, disposition, date of conviction, and county. Data prior to this date may not be complete. Juvenile records are not considered public information and are not released.

Indexing & Storage: It takes 1 day before new records are available for inquiry. 55% of all arrests in database have final dispositions recorded. Records are indexed on inhouse computer. Records are maintained indefinitely.

Access By: Mail, in person, online.

Mail Search: The turnaround time for both fingerprint and name-based searches is approximately three weeks. No self addressed stamped envelope is required.

In Person Search: Records requested at the Dept. of Public Safety Crime Records Service in Austin usually takes 1-2 business days.

Online Search: Records can be pulled from the web site. Requesters may use a credit card or must establish an account and have a pre-paid bank to work from. The fee established by the Department (Sec. 411.135(b)) is $3.15 per request plus a $.57 handling fee.

Fee & Payment: The fee is $15.00 for the full search using fingerprints, and $10.00 for a name-based search. If required, the FBI fingerprint check is an additional

$24.00. Fee payee: Texas Department of Safety. Prepayment required. Credit cards are accepted for online searches only. Personal checks accepted. Credit cards accepted: MasterCard, Visa.

Sexual Offender Registry

Sex offender data is available online at http://records.txdps.state.tx.us/soSearch/soSearch.cfm, you can search by name or local area. There is no charge. The Department of Public Service will perform mail searches, but there is a $10.00 fee.

State Incarceration Records Agency

Texas Department of Criminal Justice

Bureau of Classification and Records

P.O. Box 99

Huntsville, TX 77342-5099

Phone: 936-437-6371

Web: www.tdcj.state.tx.us

Access by:	Phone, mail. For a search, you must provide full name, and DOB. County of conviction or TDCJ number helpful.
What is released:	Information on current and former inmates is available. Location, conviction and sentencing information are provided.
Search Notes:	No fee for search.

State Court System

Court Structure:	The legal court structure for Texas takes up 30 pages in the "Texas Judicial Annual Report." Generally, Texas District Courts have general civil jurisdiction and exclusive felony jurisdiction, along with typical variations such as contested probate, contested elections, and divorce. County Courts handle misdemeanors and general civil cases.
	The County Court structure includes two forms of courts—"Constitutional" and "at Law"—which come in various configurations depending upon the county. County Courts' upper claim limits vary from $5,000 to $100,000. For civil matters up to $5000, we recommend searchers start at the Constitutional County Court as they, generally, offer a shorter waiting time for cases in urban areas. In addition, keep in mind that the Municipal Courts have, per the Texas manual, "limited civil penalties in cases involving dangerous dogs." In some counties the District Court or County Court handles evictions.

Find Felony Records: District Court

Misdemeanor Records: County Court, Justice of the peace Court, Municipal Court

Online Access: Statewide appellate court case information is searchable for free on the Internet at www.info.courts.state.tx.us/appindex/appindex.exe.

A number of individual county courts also offer online access to their records.

Court Administrator: For add'l questions about the state's court system, visit the web site at www.courts.state.tx.us/oca, or contact: Office of Court Administration, PO Box 12066, Austin, TX 78711-2066, Phone: 512-463-1625.

Utah

> **If You Are an Employer—**
>
> Employers are prohibited from reviewing arrest records not connected to a conviction and without a pending charge.

State Criminal Records Agency

Bureau of Criminal Identification
Box 148280
Salt Lake City, UT 84114-8280

Phone: 801-965-4445.
Fax: 801-965-4749

Web: http://www.bci.state.ut.us/

Total Records:	392,800
Who Can Access:	Records are not open to the public or to employers without fingerprints and without the subject's notarized signature. Certain agencies authorized by law do not need to submit fingerprints, but still must have subject's notarized signature.
Search Requirements:	Include the following in your request: name, DOB, SSN, driver's license number, notarized signature of subject, and fingerprints. Records are 100% fingerprint-supported.
What Is Released:	All records are released, including those without dispositions. Records are available back to 1950's.
Indexing & Storage:	It takes 3 to 7 days before new records are available for inquiry. 62% of all arrests in database have final dispositions recorded, approximately 75% for those arrests within last 5 years. Records are maintained indefinitely unless expunged.
Access By:	Mail.
Mail Search:	Turnaround time is 7-10 days.
Fee & Payment:	The fee is $10.00 per name (authorization required); $15.00 for fingerprint searches. Statutorily-required searches may include an FBI fingerprint search, additional $24.00 fee. Fee payee: Utah Bureau of Criminal Investigation Personal checks accepted.

Sexual Offender Registry

Requests of sex offender data are available by mail from the Utah Department of Corrections, Attn: Sex Offenders Registry Program, at 14717 S Minuteman Dr, Draper, UT 84020, or online at http://www.udc.state.ut.us/offenders/sexoffenders/. The online search permits access by name or by ZIP Code.

State Incarceration Records Agency

Utah Department of Corrections

Wasatch Records

P.O. Box 250

Draper, UT 84020

Phone: 801-576-7040

Fax: 801-572-1525

Web: www.cr.ex.state.ut.us

Access by: Phone, fax, mail. For a search, you must provide full name and DOB. The SSN and inmate number are helpful.

What is released: Information on current and former inmates is available. Location, conviction and sentencing information, and release dates are provided.

Search Notes: No fee for search.

State Court System

Court Structure: 41 District Courts are arranged in 8 Judicial Districts. Effective July 1, 1996, each Circuit Court (the lower court) was combined with District Court (the higher court) in each county. It is reported that branch courts in larger counties such as Salt Lake which were formerly Circuit Courts have been elevated to District Courts, with full jurisdiction over felony as well as misdemeanor cases. Many misdemeanors are handled at Justice Courts, which are limited jurisdiction.

Find Felony Records: District Court

Misdemeanor Records: District Court, Justice Court

Online Access: Case information from all Utah District Court locations is available through XChange. Fees include $25.00 registration and $30.00 per month plus $.10 per minute for usage, over 120 minutes. For more information about XChange and the subscription agreement, go to the web site at http://courtlink.utcourts.gov/howto/access or call 801-238-7877. Records go back 7 to 10 years.

Searching Hints: The Administrative Office of Courts provides a fax or mail search service to the public. One can search on a particular case or the case history of individuals. Information on this service is at http://courtlink.utcourts.gov/. Include the county or geographic region.

UT Code Rule 4-202.08 sets fees for record searches at $21.00 per hour, billed on 15 minute increments, with the first 15 minutes free and the copy fee at $.25 per page.

Court Administrator: For add'l questions about the state's court system, visit the web site at http://courtlink.utcourts.gov, or contact: Court Administrator, 450 S State, Salt Lake City, UT 84114, Phone: 801-578-3800.

Vermont

State Criminal Records Agency

State Repository
Vermont Criminal Information Center
103 S. Main St.
Waterbury, VT 05671-2101

Phone: 802-244-8727.
Fax: 802-241-5552

Web: http://www.dps.state.vt.us

Access to Records is Restricted

Note: Records are not available to the public and can only be access by those authorized by law and the subject, for personal review. Those authorized can include employers with employees working with children, the elderly, or the disabled. Otherwise, search at the county level.

Total Records: 179,000

Search Requirements: Non-criminal justice agencies must present a signed release form, by the subject. The VCIC Release Form is recommended. 35% of records are fingerprint supported. 96% of records have dispositions.

What Is Released: All records are released to law enforcement. Only conviction data is released to others.

Searching Hints: There is no fee for those authorized by law.

Sexual Offender Registry

The state sex offender registry is maintained by the agency listed above and is not available to the public. Local law enforcement agencies will perform localized name searches.

State Incarceration Records Agency

Vermont Department of Corrections   **Phone:** 802-241-2276

Inmate Information Request   **Fax:**   802-241-2565

103 S. Main Street   **Web:**   www.doc.state.vt.us

Waterbury, VT 05671-1001

Access by:	Phone, fax, mail. For a search, you must provide first and last name, DOB, SSN helpful.
What is released:	Information on current and former inmates is available. Location, conviction and sentencing information, and release dates are provided.
Search Notes:	No fee for search. Computer records go back to 1988.

State Court System

Court Structure:	Generally, the District Court handles all criminal cases and the Superior Court handles all civil cases. The Vermont Judicial Bureau has jurisdiction over Traffic, Municipal Ordinance, and Fish and Game, Minors in Possession, and hazing.
Find Felony Records:	District Court
Misdemeanor Records:	District Court
Online Access:	There is no online computer access available to the public; however, some courts offer calendar data over the Internet.
Searching Hints:	All counties have a diversion program in which first offenders go through a process that includes a letter of apology, community service, etc. and, after 2 years, the record is expunged. These records are never released.
	There are statewide certification and copy fees, as follows: Certification Fee - $5.00 per document plus copy fee; Copy Fee - $.25 per page with a $1.00 minimum.
Court Administrator:	For add'l questions about the state's court system, visit the web site at www.state.vt.us/courts/admin.htm, or contact: Court Administrator, Administrative Office of Courts, 111 State St, Montpelier, VT 05609-0701, Phone: 802-828-3278.

Virginia

If You Are an Employer—

Employers are prohibited from reviewing arrest records not connected to a conviction and without a pending charge.

State Criminal Records Agency

Virginia State Police
CCRE
PO Box 85076
Richmond, VA 23261-5076

Phone: 804-674-2084.

Web: http://www.vsp.state.va.us/

Total Records: 1,245,900

Who Can Access: Section 19.2-389 Code of Virginia outlines the non-criminal entities that can receive conviction only records. Certain state agencies may receive complete records. The web site gives complete details.

Search Requirements: Include the following in your request: full name, date of birth, Social Security Number, sex, race. Turnaround time: 4-6 weeks. The general public and employers not covered by statute must have a signed release form from person of record, including notarized signatures for both subject and requester. These requesters must use Form SP-167, which is downloadable from the web site.

What Is Released: Arrest records over one year old without a disposition are not released to the general public. Certain agencies receive complete records, but non-criminal justice entities receive conviction only records. Records are available from 1966.

Indexing & Storage: It takes 1 to 3 days before new records are available for inquiry. 83% of all arrests in database have final dispositions recorded.

Access By: Mail, online.

Mail Search: Turnaround time 4 to 6 weeks. A self addressed stamped envelope is requested.

Online Search: Certain entities, including screening companies, are entitled to online access. The system is ONLY available to IN-STATE accounts. Fees are same as manual submission with exception of required software package purchase. The system is windows oriented, but will not handle networks. The PC user must be a stand alone system. There is a minimum usage requirement of 25 requests per month. Turnaround time is 24-72 hours. Fee is $15.00 per record.

Fee & Payment: The fee is $15.00 per name. Statutorily-required fingerprint checks are $13.00; $37 if the FBI fingerpirnt check is also required. Statutorily-required "name search only" turnaround time is 72 hours. Fee payee: Virginia State Police. Prepayment required. Pay by certified check or money order. MasterCard and Visa are accepted.

Sexual Offender Registry

The State Police maintains the state's sexual offender registry, but the data is divided into two separate searchable databases. The "Violent Sex Offender" database is available online at at http://sex-offender.vsp.state.va.us/cool-ICE/. The "Sex Offender" is available for mail inquiry at the state police address above, Attention Sex Offender Registry.

State Incarceration Records Agency

Virginia Department of Corrections   **Phone:** 804-674-3209

Central Criminal Records Section

6900 Atmore Drive   **Web:**   www.vadoc.state.va.us

Richmond, VA 23225

Access by: For a search, phone or e-mail (clasrec@vadoc.state.va.us) and provide full name, DOB and SSN helpful. The web site provides an *Inmate Locator* to ascertain where an inmate is located. This is not designed to provide complete inmate records nor is it a database of all inmates past and present in the system.

What is released: Information on current and former inmates is available by mail. Location, conviction and sentencing information, and release dates are provided.

Search Notes: No fee for search. Online search only reveals location. Computer records go back to early 1980's.

State Court System

Court Structure: 117 Circuit Courts in 31 Judicial Districts are the courts of general jurisdiction and handle felony cases. There are 123 District Courts of limited jurisdiction that handle misdemeanor cases. Please note that a district can comprise either a county or a city. Records of civil action from $3000 to $15,000 can be at either the Circuit or District Court, as either can have jurisdiction. It is necessary to check both record locations since there is no concurrent database nor index.

The upper limit for civil actions in District Court was raised from $10,000 to $15,000 as of July 1, 1997.

Find Felony Records: Circuit Court

Misdemeanor Records: District Court

Online Access: Two online, statewide public access computer systems are available. The first is the Law Office Public Access System (LOPAS). The system allows remote access to the court case indexes and abstracts from most of the state's courts. In order to determine which courts are on LOPAS, you must obtain an ID and password (instructions below), and search on the system. A summary list of included courts is not available. Searching is by specific court; there is no combined index.

LOPAS contains opinions from the Supreme Court and the Court of Appeals as well as criminal and civil case information from Circuit and District Courts. The number of years of information provided varies widely from court to court, depending on when the particular court joined the Courts Automated Information System (CAIS). There are no sign-up or other fees to use LOPAS. Access is granted on a request-by-request basis. Anyone wishing to establish an account or receive information on LOPAS must contact Ken Mittendorf, Director of MIS, Supreme Court of Virginia, 100 N 9th St, Richmond VA 23219 or by phone at 804-786-6455 or Fax at 804-786-4542.

Also, Virginia offers the "Circuit Court Case Information Pilot Project" which includes free Internet access to records from these Circuit Courts: Arlington, Augusta, Bedford, Botetourt, Carroll, Chesapeake City, Danville City, Dickenson, Fauquier, Floyd, Franklin City, Fredericksburg City, Gloucester, Hampton City, Henry, Hopewell City, Isle of Wight, King George, Louisa, Martinsville City, Nelson, Newport News City, Norfolk City, Nottoway, Orange, Petersburg City, Pulaski, Radford City, Richmond City, Roanoke City, Rockingham, Russell, Tazewell, Warren, Waynesboro City, Williamsburg/James City, Winchester, Wise, York. Use the web site listed below.

Searching Hints: In most jurisdictions, the certification fee is $2.00 per document plus copy fee. The copy fee is $.50 per page.

Court Administrator: For add'l questions about the state's court system, visit the web site at www.courts.state.va.us, or contact: Executive Secretary, Administrative Office of Courts, 100 N 9th St, 3rd Floor, Richmond, VA 23219, Phone: 804-786-6455.

Washington

State Criminal Records Agency

Washington State Patrol
Identification Section
PO Box 42633
Olympia, WA 98504-2633

Phone: 360-705-5100.
Fax: 360-570-5275

Web: http://www.wa.gov/wsp/wsphome.htm

Total Records:	1,044,880
Who Can Access:	Records are available to the general public.
Search Requirements:	Include the following in your request: date of birth, Social Security Number, sex, race, name and address of subject. Fingerprints are optional. Records are 100% fingerprint-supported.
What Is Released:	Records without dispositions are not released, unless the arrest is less than 1 year old. Records are available from 1974.
Indexing & Storage:	It takes 30 to 45 days before new records are available for inquiry. 79% of all arrests in database have final dispositions recorded, 70% for those arrests within last 5 years. Criminal history information is retained at the Identification Section until the offender is age seventy, or ten years from the last date of arrest, whichever is longer.
Access By:	Mail, in person, online.
Mail Search:	Turnaround time: 7 to 10 days. No self addressed stamped envelope is required.
Online Search:	WSP offers access through a system called WATCH, which can be accessed from their web site. The fee per search is $10.00. The exact DOB and exact spelling of the name are required. Credit cards are accepted. To set up a WATCH account, call (360) 705-5100 or e-mail to crimhis@wsp.gov.

Fee & Payment: The fee for a name check is $10.00 per individual. For a fingerprint check, the fee is $25.00 per individual. Will not conduct FBI fingerprint checks. Fee payee: Washington State Patrol. Money orders or cashier's checks preferred. Personal checks accepted.

Sexual Offender Registry

The Washington State Patrol (WSP) maintains the sexual offender database. Information is not readily available to the public, but there are plans to have statewide data available at the web site above. Mail requests are directed to the Public Record Manager at the WSP or e-mail to questions@wsp.wa.gov.

State Incarceration Records Agency

Washington Department of Corrections   **Phone:** 360-753-3317

Office of Correctional Operations

410 W. 5th   **Web:**   www.wa.gov/doc.

Olympia, WA 98504-1118

Access by: Phone, mail. For a search, you must provide full name, the DOB and SSN are helpful.

What is released: Information on current and former inmates is available. Location, CCO, parole review data, and counselor are released.

Search Notes: No fee for search.

State Court System

Court Structure: 39 Superior Courts are organized in 29 Judicial Districts and are the courts of general jurisdiction. The 65 District Courts and 131 Municipal Courts are limited jurisdiction courts. District Courts retain civil records for 10 years from date of final disposition, then the records are destroyed. District Courts retain criminal records forever.

Find Felony Records: Superior Court

Misdemeanor Records: District Court, Municipal Court

Online Access: Appellate, Superior, and District Court records are available online. The Superior Court Management Information System (SCOMIS), the Appellate Records System (ACORDS) and the District/Municipal Court Information System (DISCIS) all reside on the Judicial Information System's JIS-Link. Case records available through JIS-Link from 1977 include criminal, civil, domestic, probate, and judgments. JIS-Link is generally available 24-hours daily. Equipment requirements include a PC running Windows or MS-DOS. There is a one-time installation fee of $100.00 per site, and a connect time charge of $25.00 per hour (approximately $.42 per minute), plus a surcharge of $.85 per session. For additional information and/or a registration packet, contact: JISLink Coordinator, Office of the Administrator for the Courts, 1206 S Quince St., PO Box 41170, Olympia WA 98504-1170, 360-357-2407 or visit the web site at www.courts.wa.gov/jislink

Searching Hints: SASE is required in every jurisdiction that responds to written search requests.

Court Administrator: For add'l questions about the state's court system, visit the web site at www.courts.wa.gov, or contact: Court Administrator, Temple of Justice, PO Box 41174, Olympia, WA 98504-1174, Phone: 360-357-2121.

West Virginia

State Criminal Records Agency

State Police
Criminal Identification Bureau, Records Section
725 Jefferson Rd
South Charleston, WV 25309

Phone: 304-746-2277.
Fax: 304-746-2402
Web: http://www.wvstatepolice.com

Total Records:	501,043
Who Can Access:	Records are only available to the general public with consent of the subject.
Search Requirements:	Certain statutorily-required searches require fingerprints, also FBI fingerprint checks; standard name searches do not. Include the following in your request: signed release of subject, SSN, DOB, race, sex, and thumbprint. You must use their "39A Card." All records are returned by mail. Search can be initiated in person, results mailed. 100% of the records are fingerprint-supported.
What Is Released:	All records are released, including those without dispositions. Records are available from 1938 on computer.
Indexing & Storage:	It takes 3 days before new records are available for inquiry. 70% of all arrests in database have final dispositions recorded. Records are indexed on in house computer (100% of names). Approximately 30% of arrest data is computerized. Records are normally destroyed after the person reaches age 80.
Access By:	Mail.
Mail Search:	Turnaround time: 5 to 10 days.
Fee & Payment:	The search fee is $20.00 per record. Certain statutorily-required searches are $10.00, plus an addition FBI fingercheck can be conducted for an additional $24.00. A total record check (fingerprints/FBI/arrest data) is $44.00. Fee payee: West Virginia State Police. Prepayment required. Personal checks accepted. No credit cards accepted. **Note:** The state will also sell an "incident report" of a specific criminal action for $15.00, call 304-746-2178.

Sexual Offender Registry

The West Virginia State Police maintains the state's sex offender data. Access is available online at http://www.wvstatepolice.com/sexoff/ with both a name and county search available. Less serious offenders are not found on the online search, but local law enforcement agencies have extensive localized lists available.

State Incarceration Records Agency

West Virginia Division of Corrections

Records Room

112 California Avenue, 3rd floor

Charleston, WV 25305

Phone: 304-558-2037

Fax: 304-558-5934

Web: www.state.wv.us/wvdoc/default.htm

Access by: Phone, fax, mail. For a search, you must provide full name; the DOB and SSN are helpful.

What is released: Information on current and former inmates is available. Location, conviction and sentencing information, and release dates are provided.

Search Notes: No fee for search. Phone is preferred method to search.

State Court System

Court Structure: The 55 Circuit Courts are courts of general jurisdiction, the 55 Magistrate Courts are courts of limited jurisdiction. There are over 120 local Municipal Courts in the state. Effective October 1999, a family court division was created within the circuit court of each county. Probate is handled by the Circuit Court. Records are held at the County Commissioner's Office.

Find Felony Records: Circuit Court

Misdemeanor Records: Magistrate Court

Online Access: The state's courts are working to develop a statewide system for access to public records. By mid 2000, Magistrate Courts are projected to be on a common server. Several courts's public records are online via private providers. For futher details, contact Kit Thorton, Counsel for Law and Technology at 304-588-0145.

Searching Hints: There is a statewide requirement that search turnaround times not exceed five business days. However, most courts do far better than that limit. Release of public information is governed by WV Code Sec.29B-1-1 et seq.

Court Administrator: For add'l questions about the state's court system, visit the web site at www.state.wv.us/wvsca/AO.htm, or contact: Administrative Office, State Supreme Court of Appeals, 1900 Kanawha Blvd, Bldg 1, Rm E 100, Charleston, WV 25305-0830, Phone: 304-558-0145.

Wisconsin

If You Are an Employer—

Employers are prohibited from reviewing arrest records not connected to a conviction and without a pending charge, unless the applicant is applying for a bondable position. Be aware that the agency below supplies criminal records that may not have dispositions.

State Criminal Records Agency

Wisconsin Department of Justice
Crime Information Bureau, Record Check Unit
PO Box 2688
Madison, WI 53701-2688

Phone: 608-266-5764
Fax: 608-267-4558

Web: http://www.doj.state.wi.us

Total Records: 909,000

Who Can Access: Criminal record information is open to the public per statute 3-21-91.

Search Requirements: Include the following in your request: sex, race, full name, date of birth. Fingerprints are optional, but certain statutorily-required searches require fingerprints. All requests must be in writing.

What Is Released: All records are released, including those without dispositions. Arrests without supporting fingerprints are not included in the database. Records are available from July 1971 (when the agencies were required to save records) and are computerized. The following data is not released: juvenile records. For "caregiver" and "daycare" type requests, the Wisconsin Department of Health and Family Services, effective 5/1/2000, charges an additional $ 2.50 per search to cover their processing costs. The DHFS fee is in addition to the CIB search.

Indexing & Storage: It takes 4 days before new records are available for inquiry. 76% of all arrests in database have final dispositions recorded, 67% for those arrests within last 5 years. Records are indexed on inhouse computer. Records are normally destroyed after (records maintained indefinitely).

Access By: Mail, fax, in person, online.

Mail Search: Turnaround time: 7 to 10 days. A self addressed stamped envelope is requested.

Fax Search: Incoming fax permitted only for customers with accounts. There must be a supply of return envelopes on hand.

In Person Search: Records are returned by mail.

Online Search: The agency offers Internet access at http://wi-recordcheck.org. An account is required, the fees are same as mentioned below. Call the CIB Record Check Unit at 608-266-5764 to set up an account.

Fee & Payment: The fee is $13.00 per individual for a name search, and $10 if a fingerprint search. Non-profits made submit name searches for $2.00 per record. If a statutorily-required search also requires an FBI fingerprint check, add $24.00. Fee payee: Wisconsin Department of Justice. Prepayment required. Personal checks accepted. Credit cards accepted at web site only.

Sexual Offender Registry

As we go to press, the Department of Corrections is in the process of placing the sexual offender database online at http://widocoffenders.org. Requests for information can be e-mailed to bopadmin@doc.state.wi.us, or mailed to Dept. of Corrections, Attn: SORP, PO Box 7925, Madison WI 53707.

State Incarceration Records Agency

Wisconsin Department of Corrections   **Phone:** 608-240-5000

Central Records Unit

P.O. Box 8986   **Web:**   www.wi-doc.com

Madison, WI 53704

Access by: Phone, mail. For a search, you must provide full name and DOB.

What is released: Information on current and former inmates is available. Location, conviction and sentencing information, and release dates are provided.

Search Notes: No fee for search. Computer records go back to 1961.

State Court System

Court Structure: The Circuit Court is the court of general jurisdiction, with 74 courts in 69 circuits. There are over 225 Municipal Courts in the state. The Register in Probate maintains guardianship and mental health records, most of which are sealed but may be opened for cause with a court order. In some counties, the Register also maintains termination and adoption records, but practices vary widely across the state.

Find Felony Records: Circuit Court

Misdemeanor Records: Circuit Court

Online Access: Wisconsin Circuit Court Access (WCCA) allows users to view circuit court case information at http://ccap.courts.state.wi.us/internetcourtaccess which is the Wisconsin court system web site. Data is available from all counties except Outagamie and Walworth. Searches can be conducted statewide or county by county. WCCA provides detailed information about circuit cases and for civil cases, the program displays judgment and judgment party information. WCCA also offers the ability to generate reports. In addition, public access terminals are available at each court. Due to statutory requirements, WCCA users will not be able to view restricted cases. There are probate records for all counties except Outagamie, Milwaukee and Walworth. Portage County offers probate records only online.

Searching Hints: The statutory fee schedule for the Circuit Courts is as follows: Search Fee - $5.00 per name; Copy Fee - $1.25 per page; Certification Fee - $5.00. In about half the Circuit Courts, no search fee is charged if the case number is provided. There is normally no search fee charged for in-person searches.

Court Administrator: For add'l questions about the state's court system, visit the web site at www.courts.state.wi.us, or contact: Director of State Courts, Supreme Court, PO Box 1688, Madison, WI 53701-1688, Phone: 608-266-6828.

Wyoming

State Criminal Records Agency

Division of Criminal Investigation
Criminal Record Unit
316 W 22nd St
Cheyenne, WY 82002

Phone: 307-777-7523.
Fax: 307-777-7252

Web:
http://attorneygeneral.state.wy.us/dci/index.html

Total Records: 102,678

Who Can Access: A signed release is requirement before a record is released to the general public.

Search Requirements: First, obtain a Request for Criminal Record Packet ($15.00) from address above or phone. Include the following in your request: notarized waiver from subject, name, set of fingerprints, date of birth, Social Security Number, number of years to search. Use the standard 8" x 8" orange fingerprint card. Must also fill out waiver that is on the back of this office's fingerprint card.

What Is Released: Records include all felony and major misdemeanor arrests and convictions. Records are available from 1941 on. The following data is not released: juvenile records.

Indexing & Storage: It takes up to 10 days before new records are available for inquiry. 79% of all arrests in database have final dispositions recorded, 65% for those arrests within last 5 years. Records are indexed on inhouse computer.

Access By: Mail, in person.

Mail Search: Turnaround time: 2 to 4 weeks. A self addressed stamped envelope is requested.

In Person Search: Proper forms are required to be filled out.

Fee & Payment: The search fee is $15.00 plus an additional $5.00 if this office must perform the fingerprinting. The fee is $10.00 if the applicant is providing volunteer services, plus the fingerprinting fee if applicable. The FBI fingerprint check is an add'l $24.00. Fee payee: Office of the Attorney General. Prepayment required. Money order, cash or certified checks only. No credit cards accepted.

Sexual Offender Registry

State law limits disclosure of registered sex offenders to the criminal justice system unless the County or District Attorney petitions the court to disclose registered sex offender information to the public. If a registered sex offender is classified as a high risk of re-offense, information regarding the sex offender can be released to the public via the Internet. This information includes name, address, date and place of birth, date and place of conviction, crime for which convicted, photograph and physical description. Access is at http://attorneygeneral.state.wy.us/dci/so/so_registration.html. Records are maintained by the Division of Criminal Investigation, 307-777-7181.

State Incarceration Records Agency

Wyoming Department of Corrections

Herschler Building

700 W. 21st Street

Cheyenne, WY 82002

Phone: 307-777-7405

Fax: 307-777-7479

Web: http://doc.state.wy.us/corrections.html.

Access by:	Fax. For a search, you must provide full name, DOB and SSN helpful.
What is released:	Information on current and former inmates is available. Location, conviction and sentencing information, and release dates are provided.
Search Notes:	No fee for search.

State Court System

Court Structure:	Each county has a District Court ("higher" jurisdiction) and for their "lower" jurisdiction court, some counties have Circuit Courts and others have Justice Courts. Circuit Courts handle civil claims up to $7,000 while Justice Courts handle civil claims up to $3,000. The District Courts take cases over the applicable limit in each county. There are 80 Municipal Courts in the state.
	Three counties have two Circuit Courts each: Fremont, Park, and Sweetwater. Cases may be filed in either of the two court offices in those counties, and records requests are referred between the two courts.
	The Park and Sublette County Justice Courts were eliminated on January 2, 1995 and were replaced by Circuit Courts, where the Justice Court records are now located.
	Probate is handled by the District Court.
Find Felony Records:	District Court
Misdemeanor Records:	Circuit Court, Justice of the Peace, Municipal Court

Online Access: Wyoming's statewide case management system is for internal use only. Planning is underway for a new case management system that will ultimately allow public access.

Court Administrator: For add'l questions about the state's court system, visit the web site at www.courts.state.wy.us, or contact: Court Administrator, Supreme Court Bldg, 2301 Capitol Ave, Cheyenne, WY 82002, Phone: 307-777-7480.

Chapter 18

U.S. District Courts

Federal criminal records are a result of an individual committing a federal crime. Federal criminal records in the United States result from Federal District Courts and Federal Appellate Courts. There are ninety-four Federal Judicial Districts. A state may have one or more districts, usually designated by geographic direction, i.e. Eastern, Southern, etc. Additionally, a district may be subdivided into divisions, which are designated by the location city name. Please refer to Chapter 7 - *Criminal Records at the Federal Level* for details on how U.S. District Courts organize and maintain records.

How to Access Records by Mail or Phone

The fees for record searching are standard throughout all Judicial Districts. The standard fee for a mailed request is $20.00 per item (one party name or case number). The standard certification fee is $7.00. A few courts will release limited information or docket information by phone. Copies are $.50 a page if done by the court, $.15 if done in-person by the searcher. As a rule, little information is available by telephone. Data appearing on the docket sheet is released by many courts, but you may need to supply the case number.

Online Access to Records

In ninety-three of the ninety-four US Federal Judicial Districts locations, criminal docket sheets are available online. The only Judicial District not offering the records online is South Dakota. Most online access is through PACER via the Internet. However, a small number of District Courts offer records searching online for free. These are:

- Arkansas Western District at www.arwd.uscourts.gov/mailform.html
- Idaho District at www.id.uscourts.gov/wconnect/wc.dll?usdc_racer~main
- Indiana Southern District at www.insd.uscourts.gov/casesearch.htm
- Pennsylvania Eastern District at www.paed.uscourts.gov

PACER Access

As mentioned on page 48, PACER is a service of United States Judiciary. All the basic case information is entered onto docket sheets and into computerized systems like **PACER**.

PACER, the acronym for **P**ublic **A**ccess to **E**lectronic **C**ourt **R**ecords, provides docket information online for open cases at most US District courts and all US Bankruptcy courts. Cases for the US Court of Federal Claims are also available.

The PACER Service Center is operated by the Administrative Office of the United States Courts. PACER information and registration is available at the PACER Service Center in San Antonio Texas. This centralized registration, billing, and technical support center can be reached at P.O. Box 780549, San Antonio, TX 78278-0549, 800-676-6856, and on the Internet at http://pacer.psc.uscourts.gov/.

The user fee for PACER on the Internet is $.07 per page. Additionally, PACER is accessible by remote dial-up service. Users of this telephone system are billed $.60 per minute and dial PACER directly using communication software and a modem. The toll-free number for PACER dial-up information is 800-676-6856.

Within PACER, each court maintains its own databases with case information. Because PACER database systems are maintained within each court, each jurisdiction will have a different URL or modem number. Accessing and querying information from each service is comparable; however, the format and content of information provided may differ slightly. US District Courts that offer access to records through PACER, PACER dial-up modem, CM/ECF, or on the Web are noted in the profiles to follow.

U.S. Party/Case Index

To locate a case number, which is essential for searching in the US Court System, the system provides the US Party/Case Index. Access the US Party/Case Index on the internet at http://pacer.uspci.uscourts.gov. To access the US Party/Case Index by dial-up modem, the toll-free dial-up number is 800-974-8896. Or, talk to the PACER Service Center at 800-676-6856. Requests for archived cases must be made at the court where the case was heard.

CM/ECF—Case Management/Electronic Case Files

As described in Chapter 7, Case Management/Electronic Case Files (CM/ECF) is the growing court-sponsored system that enables attorneys and litigants to electronically submit pleadings and docket entries to the court via the Internet. This system is searchable, but *only* includes case information that is filed electronically into the system, thus it does not offer a complete search of the participating court's case files. The key here is that *Document Images* are available, as well as docket sheets. However, this is going away for the general public, as outlined on page 49. For further information on CM/ECF, visit http://pacer.psc.uscourts.gov/cmecf.

Federal Records Centers and the National Archives

After a federal case is closed, the documents are held by Federal Courts themselves for a number of years, then stored at a designated Federal Records Center (FRC). After 20 to 30 years, the records are then transferred from the FRC to the regional archives offices of the National Archives and Records Administration (NARA). The length of time between a case being closed and its being moved to an FRC varies widely by district. Each court has its own transfer cycle and determines access procedures to its case records, even after they have been sent to the FRC.

When case records are sent to an FRC, the boxes of records are assigned accession, location and box numbers. These numbers, which are called case locator information, **must be obtained from the originating court in order to retrieve documents from the FRC.** Some courts will provide such information over the telephone, but others require a written request.

Locations of the U.S. District Courts

Each of the 296 District and Divisional Courts listed below is show with their respective address, telephone, and the counties that comprise the particular division or district. The web site and type of PACER service is indicated at the beginning of each District. Note that all the records for all Divisional Courts within a specific Judicial District are co-mingled.

Alabama

Middle District of Alabama

http://www.almd.uscourts.gov **Special access:** PACER dial-up.
-Dothan Div. c/o Montgomery Division. **Counties:** Coffee, Dale, Geneva, Henry, Houston.
-Montgomery Div. Records Search, PO Box 711, Montgomery, AL 36101-0711 (physical address: 15 Lee St, Montgomery, AL 36104), 334-223-7308. **Counties:** Autauga, Barbour, Bullock, Butler, Chilton, Coosa, Covington, Crenshaw, Elmore, Lowndes, Montgomery, Pike.
-Opelika Div. c/o Montgomery Division. **Counties:** Chambers, Lee, Macon, Randolph, Russell, Tallapoosa.

Northern District of Alabama

http://www.alnd.uscourts.gov **Special access:** phone, PACER dial-up, PACER online.
-Birmingham Div. Room 104, US Courthouse, 1729 5th Ave N, Birmingham, AL 35203 (physical address: same as mail address), 205-278-1700. **Counties:** Bibb, Blount, Calhoun, Clay, Cleburne, Greene, Jefferson, Pickens, Shelby, Sumter, Talladega, Tuscaloosa.
-Florence Div. PO Box 776, Florence, AL 35630 (physical address: 210 Court St, Florence, AL 35631), 205-760-5815. **Counties:** Colbert, Franklin, Lauderdale.
-Gadsden Div. c/o Birmingham Division, Room 140 **Counties:** Cherokee, De Kalb, Etowah, Marshall, St. Clair.
-Huntsville Div. Clerk's Office, US Post Office & Courthouse, 101 Holmes Ave NE, Huntsville, AL 35801 (physical address: same as mail address), 205-534-6495. **Counties:** Cullman, Jackson, Lawrence, Limestone, Madison, Morgan.
-Jasper Div. c/o Birmingham Division, Room 140 **Counties:** Fayette, Lamar, Marion, Walker, Winston.

Southern District of Alabama

http://www.als.uscourts.gov **Special access:** PACER dial-up, PACER online, or on the web.
-Mobile Div. Clerk, 113 St Joseph St, Mobile, AL 36602 (physical address: same as mail address), 334-690-2371. **Counties:** Baldwin, Choctaw, Clarke, Conecuh, Escambia, Mobile, Monroe, Washington.

-Selma Div. c/o Mobile Division **Counties:** Dallas, Hale, Marengo, Perry, Wilcox.

Alaska
District of Alaska

http://www.akd.uscourts.gov **Special access:** phone, PACER dial-up.

-Anchorage Div. Box 4, 222 W 7th Ave, Anchorage, AK 99513-7564 (physical address: same as mail address), 907-677-6100. **Counties:** Aleutian Islands-East, Aleutian Islands-West, Anchorage Borough, Bristol Bay Borough, Kenai Peninsula Borough, Kodiak Island Borough, Matanuska-Susitna Borough, Valdez-Cordova.

-Fairbanks Div. Box 1, 101 12th Ave, Fairbanks, AK 99701 (physical address: same as mail address), 907-451-5791. **Counties:** Bethel, Fairbanks North Star Borough, North Slope Borough, Northwest Arctic Borough, Southeast Fairbanks, Wade Hampton, Yukon-Koyukuk.

-Juneau Div. PO Box 020349, Juneau, AK 99802-0349 (physical address: Room 979, Federal Bldg-US Courthouse, 709 W 9th, Juneau, AK 99802), 907-586-7458. **Counties:** Haines Borough, Juneau Borough, Prince of Wales-Outer Ketchikan, Sitka Borough, Skagway-Hoonah-Angoon, Wrangell-Petersburg.

-Ketchikan Div. 648 Mission St, Room 507, Ketchikan, AK 99901 (physical address: same as mail address), 907-247-7576. **Counties:** Ketchikan Gateway Borough.

-Nome Div. PO Box 130, Nome, AK 99762 (physical address: 2nd Floor, Federal Bldg, Front St, Nome, AK 99762), 907-443-5216. **Counties:** Nome.

Arizona
District of Arizona

http://www.azd.uscourts.gov **Special access:** phone (dockets or basic information only), PACER dial-up, PACER online.

-Phoenix Div. Room 1400, 230 N 1st Ave, Phoenix, AZ 85025-0093 (physical address: same as mail address), 602-514-7101. **Counties:** Gila, La Paz, Maricopa, Pinal, Yuma. Some Yuma cases handled by San Diego Division of the Southern District of California.

-Prescott Div. c/o Phoenix Division **Counties:** Apache, Coconino, Mohave, Navajo, Yavapai.

-Tucson Div, 405 W. Congress, Tucson, AZ 85701-1711 (physical address: same as mail address), 520-205-4200. **Counties:** Cochise, Graham, Greelee, Pima,

Santa Cruz. The Globe Division was closed effective January 1994, and all case records for that division are now found here.

Arkansas
Eastern District of Arkansas

http://www.are.uscourts.gov **Special access:** phone, PACER dial-up, or on the web.

-Batesville Div. c/o Little Rock Division **Counties:** Cleburne, Fulton, Independence, Izard, Jackson, Sharp, Stone.

-Helena Div. c/o Little Rock Division **Counties:** Cross, Lee, Monroe, Phillips, St. Francis, Woodruff.

-Jonesboro Div. PO Box 7080, Jonesboro, AR 72403 (physical address: Federal Office Bldg, Room 312, 615 S Main St, Jonesboro, AR 72401), 870-972-4610. **Counties:** Clay, Craighead, Crittenden, Greene, Lawrence, Mississippi, Poinsett, Randolph.

-Little Rock Div. Room 402, 600 W Capitol, Little Rock, AR 72201 (physical address: same as mail address), 501-324-5351. **Counties:** Conway, Faulkner, Lonoke, Perry, Pope, Prairie, Pulaski, Saline, Van Buren, White, Yell.

-Pine Bluff Div. PO Box 8307, Pine Bluff, AR 71611-8307 (physical: US Post Office & Courthouse, 100 E 8th St, Room 3103, Pine Bluff, AR 71601), 870-536-1190. **Counties:** Arkansas, Chicot, Cleveland, Dallas, Desha, Drew, Grant, Jefferson, Lincoln.

Western District of Arkansas

http://www.arwd.uscourts.gov **Special access:** phone, fax, PACER dial-up, or on the web.

-El Dorado Div. PO Box 1566, El Dorado, AR 71731 (physical address: Room 205, 101 S Jackson, El Dorado, AR 71731), 870-862-1202. **Counties:** Ashley, Bradley, Calhoun, Columbia, Ouachita, Union.

-Fayetteville Div. PO Box 6420, Fayetteville, AR 72702 (physical address: Room 510, 35 E Mountain, Fayetteville, AR 72701), 501-521-6980. **Counties:** Benton, Madison, Washington.

-Fort Smith Div. PO Box 1547, Fort Smith, AR 72902 (physical address: Judge Isaac C. Parker Federal Bldg #1038, 6th & Rogers Ave, Fort Smith, AR 72901), 501-783-6833. **Counties:** Crawford, Franklin, Johnson, Logan, Polk, Scott, Sebastian.

-Hot Springs Div. PO Drawer I, Hot Springs, AR 71902 (physical address: Federal Bldg Room 347, 100 Reserve, Hot Springs, AR 71901), 501-623-6411. **Counties:** Clark, Garland, Hot Springs, Montgomery, Pike.

-Texarkana Div. PO Box 2746, Texarkana, AR 75504-2746 (physical address: 500 State Line Ave, Texarkana, AR 71854), 870-773-3381. **Counties:** Hempstead, Howard, Lafayette, Little River, Miller, Nevada, Sevier.

California

Central District of California

http://www.cacd.uscourts.gov **Special access:** fax, PACER dial-up, PACER online. Opinions available at http://www.cacd.uscourts.gov.
-Los Angeles (West) Div. US Courthouse, Attn: Correspondence, 312 N Spring St, Room G-8, Los Angeles, CA 90012 (physical address: same as mail address), 213-894-5261. **Counties:** Los Angeles, San Luis Obispo, Santa Barbara, Ventura.
-Riverside (East) Div. US District Court, PO Box 13000, Riverside, CA 92502-3000 (physical address: 3470 12th St, Riverside, CA 92501), 909-328-4450. **Counties:** Riverside, San Bernardino.
-Santa Ana (South) Div. 411 W 4th St Rm 1053, Santa Ana, CA 92701-4516 (physical address: same as mail address), 714-338-4750. **Counties:** Orange.

Eastern District of California

http://www.caed.uscourts.gov **Special access:** phone, PACER dial-up, PACER online, or on the web. Opinions available at http://www.caed.uscourts.gov.
-Fresno Div. US Courthouse, Room 5000, 1130 "O" St, Fresno, CA 93721-2201 (physical address: same as mail address), 559-498-7483. **Counties:** Fresno, Inyo, Kern, Kings, Madera, Mariposa, Merced, Stanislaus, Tulare, Tuolumne.
-Sacramento Div. 501 I St, Sacramento, CA 95814 (physical address: same as mail address), 916-930-4000. **Counties:** Alpine, Amador, Butte, Calaveras, Colusa, El Dorado, Glenn, Lassen, Modoc, Mono, Nevada, Placer, Plumas, Sacramento, San Joaquin, Shasta, Sierra, Siskiyou, Solano, Sutter, Tehama, Trinity, Yolo, Yuba.

Northern District of California

http://www.cand.uscourts.gov **Special access:** phone, PACER dial-up, PACER online, CM/ECF.
-Oakland Div. 1301 Clay St, Ste 400S, Oakland, CA 94612-5212 (physical address: same as mail address), 510-637-3530. **Counties:** Alameda, Contra Costa(Note: Cases may be filed here or at San Francisco Div.; records available electronically at either; the 1st number of the case number indicates the file location: 3=SF, 4=Oak, 5=SJ.

-San Francisco Div. 450 Golden Gate Ave, 16th Fl, San Francisco, CA 94102 (physical address: same as mail address), 415-522-2000. **Counties:** Del Norte, Humboldt, Lake, Marin, Mendocino, Napa, San Francisco, San Mateo, Sonoma(Note: Cases may be filed here or at Oakland Div; records available electronically at either; the 1st number of the case number indicates the file location: 3=SF, 4=Oak, 5=SJ.
-San Jose Div. Room 2112, 280 S 1st St, San Jose, CA 95113 (physical address: same as mail address), 408-535-5364. **Counties:** Monterey, San Benito, Santa Clara, Santa Cruz.

Southern District of California

http://www.casd.uscourts.gov **Special access:** PACER dial-up, PACER online, or on the web. Room 4290, 880 Front St, San Diego, CA 92101-8900 (physical address: same as mail address), 619-557-5600. **Counties:** Imperial, San Diego. Court also handles cases from Yuma County, AZ.

Colorado

District of Colorado

http://www.co.uscourts.gov **Special access:** phone, PACER dial-up, PACER online. US Courthouse, Room C-145, 1929 Stout St, Denver, CO 80294-3589 (physical address: same as mail address), 303-844-3433. **Counties:** All in Colorado.

District of Columbia

District of Columbia

www.dcd.uscourts.gov **Special access:** phone, PACER dial-up, PACER online, CM/ECF. Opinions available at http://www.dcd.uscourts.gov. US Courthouse, Clerk's Office, Room 1225, 333 Constitution Ave NW, Washington, DC 20001 (physical address: same as mail address), 202-727-2947. **Counties:**.

Connecticut

District of Connecticut

http://www.ctd.uscourts.gov **Special access:** phone, PACER dial-up, PACER online.
-Bridgeport Div. Office of the clerk, Room 400, 915 Lafayette Blvd, Bridgeport, CT 06604 (physical address: same as mail address), 203-579-5861. **Counties:** Fairfield (prior to 1993). Since January 1993, cases from any county may be assigned to any of the divisions in the district.
-Hartford Div. 450 Main St, Hartford, CT 06103 (physical address: same as mail address), 860-240-

3200. **Counties:** Hartford, Tolland, Windham (prior to 1993). Since 1993, cases from any county may be assigned to any of the divisions in the district.

-New Haven Div. 141 Church St, New Haven, CT 06510 (physical address: same as mail address), 203-773-2140. **Counties:** Litchfield, Middlesex, New Haven, New London (prior to 1993). Since 1993, cases from any county may be assigned to any of the divisions in the district.

Delaware
District of Delaware

http://www.ded.uscourts.gov **Special access:** phone, PACER dial-up, PACER online. Opinions available at http://www.lawlib.widener.edu/pages/deopind.htm. US Courthouse, Lock Box 18, 844 N King St, Wilmington, DE 19801 (physical address: US Courthouse, 844 N King St, Clerk's Office, 4th Floor, Room 4209, Wilmington, DE 19801), 302-573-6170. **Counties:** All in Delaware.

Florida
Middle District of Florida

http://www.flmd.uscourts.gov **Special access:** phone, PACER dial-up, PACER online.

-Fort Myers Div. 2110 First St, Room 2-194, Fort Myers, FL 33901 (physical address: same as mail address), 941-461-2000. **Counties:** Charlotte, Collier, De Soto, Glades, Hendry, Lee.

-Jacksonville Div. PO Box 53558, Jacksonville, FL 32201 (physical address: Suite 110, 311 W Monroe St, Jacksonville, FL 32202), 904-549-1900. **Counties:** Baker, Bradford, Clay, Columbia, Duval, Flagler, Hamilton, Nassau, Putnam, St. Johns, Suwannee, Union.

-Ocala Div. c/o Jacksonville Division **Counties:** Citrus, Lake, Marion, Sumter.

-Orlando Div. Room 218, 80 North Hughey Ave, Orlando, FL 32801 (physical address: same as mail address), 407-835-4200. **Counties:** Brevard, Orange, Osceola, Seminole, Volusia.

-Tampa Div. Office of the clerk, 801 N Florida Ave #223, Tampa, FL 33602-4500 (physical address: same as mail address), 813-301-5400. **Counties:** Hardee, Hernando, Hillsborough, Manatee, Pasco, Pinellas, Polk, Sarasota.

Northern District of Florida

http://www.flnd.uscourts.gov **Special access:** phone, PACER dial-up, PACER online.

-Gainesville Div. 401 SE First Ave, Room 243, Gainesville, FL 32601 (physical address: same as mail address), 352-380-2400. **Counties:** Alachua, Dixie, Gilchrist, Lafayette, Levy. Records for cases prior to July 1996 are maintained at the Tallahassee Division.

-Panama City Div. 30 W. Government St, Panama City, FL 32401 (physical address: same as mail address), 850-769-4556. **Counties:** Bay, Calhoun, Gulf, Holmes, Jackson, Washington.

-Pensacola Div. US Courthouse, 1 N Palafox St, #226, Pensacola, FL 32501 (physical address: same as mail address), 850-435-8440. **Counties:** Escambia, Okaloosa, Santa Rosa, Walton.

-Tallahassee Div. Suite 122, 110 E Park Ave, Tallahassee, FL 32301 (physical address: same as mail address), 850-942-8826. **Counties:** Franklin, Gadsden, Jefferson, Leon, Liberty, Madison, Taylor, Wakulla.

Southern District of Florida

http://www.flsd.uscourts.gov **Special access:** phone (dockets or basic information only), PACER dial-up, PACER online.

-Fort Lauderdale Div. 299 E Broward Blvd, Fort Lauderdale, FL 33301 (physical address: same as mail address), 954-769-5400. **Counties:** Broward.

-Fort Pierce Div. c/o Miami Division, 305-523-5210. **Counties:** Highlands, Indian River, Martin, Okeechobee, St. Lucie.

-Key West Div. 301 Simonton St, Key West, FL 33040 (physical address: same as mail address), 305-295-8100. **Counties:** Monroe.

-Miami Div. Room 150, 301 N Miami Ave, Miami, FL 33128-7788 (physical address: same as mail address), 305-523-5700. **Counties:** Dade.

-West Palm Beach Div. Room 402, 701 Clematis St, West Palm Beach, FL 33401 (address: same as mail address), 561-803-3400. **Counties:** Palm Beach.

Georgia
Middle District of Georgia

http://www.gamd.uscourts.gov **Special access:** phone, PACER dial-up, PACER online.

-Albany/Americus Div. PO Box 1906, Albany, GA 31702 (physical address: Room 106, 345 Broad Ave, Albany, GA 31701), 229-430-8432. **Counties:** Baker, Ben Hill, Calhoun, Crisp, Dougherty, Early, Lee, Miller, Mitchell, Schley, Sumter, Terrell, Turner, Webster, Worth. Ben Hill and Crisp were transferred from the Macon Division as of October 1, 1997.

-Athens Div. PO Box 1106, Albany, GA 30603 (physical address: Room 106, 345 Broad Ave, Albany,

GA 31701), 229-430-1094. **Counties:** Clarke, Elbert, Franklin, Greene, Hart, Madison, Morgan, Oconee, Oglethorpe, Walton. Closed cases before April 1997 are located in the Macon Division.

-Columbus Div. PO Box 124, Columbus, GA 31902 (physical address: Room 216, 120 12th St, Columbus, GA 31901), 706-649-7816. **Counties:** Chattahoochee, Clay, Harris, Marion, Muscogee, Quitman, Randolph, Stewart, Talbot, Taylor.

-Macon Div. PO Box 128, Macon, GA 31202-0128 (physical address: 475 Mulberry, Suite 216, Macon, GA 31201), 912-752-3497. **Counties:** Baldwin, Ben Hill, Bibb, Bleckley, Butts, Crawford, Crisp, Dooly, Hancock, Houston, Jasper, Jones, Lamar, Macon, Monroe, Peach, Pulaski, Putnam, Twiggs, Upson, Washington, Wilcox, Wilkinson.Athens Division cases closed before April 1997 are also located here.

-Thomasville Div. c/o Valdosta Division, 912-226-3651. **Counties:** Brooks, Colquitt, Decatur, Grady, Seminole, Thomas.

-Valdosta Div. PO Box 68, Valdosta, GA 31603 (physical address: Room 212, 401 N Patterson, Valdosta, GA 31601), 912-242-3616. **Counties:** Berrien, Clinch, Cook, Echols, Irwin, Lanier, Lowndes, Tift.

Northern District of Georgia

http://www.gand.uscourts.gov **Special access:** phone, PACER dial-up, PACER online.

-Atlanta Div. 2211 US Courthouse, 75 Spring St SW, Atlanta, GA 30303-3361 (physical address: same as mail address), 404-215-1660. **Counties:** Cherokee, Clayton, Cobb, De Kalb, Douglas, Fulton, Gwinnett, Henry, Newton, Rockdale.

-Gainesville Div. Federal Bldg, Room 201, 121 Spring St SE, Gainesville, GA 30501 (physical address: same as mail address), 678-450-2760. **Counties:** Banks, Barrow, Dawson, Fannin, Forsyth, Gilmer, Habersham, Hall, Jackson, Lumpkin, Pickens, Rabun, Stephens, Towns, Union, White.

-Newnan Div. PO Box 939, Newnan, GA 30264 (physical address: 18 Greenville St, #352, Newnan, GA 30263), 678-423-3060. **Counties:** Carroll, Coweta, Fayette, Haralson, Heard, Meriwether, Pike, Spalding, Troup.

-Rome Div. PO Box 1186, Rome, GA 30162-1186 (physical address: 600 E 1st St, Room 304, Rome, GA 30161), 706-291-5629. **Counties:** Bartow, Catoosa, Chattooga, Dade, Floyd, Gordon, Murray, Paulding, Polk, Walker, Whitfield.

Southern District of Georgia

http://www.gasd.uscourts.gov **Special access:** phone, PACER dial-up, PACER online.

-Augusta Div. PO Box 1130, Augusta, GA 30903 (physical address: same as mail address, 500 E Ford St, First Floor), 706-849-4400. **Counties:** Burke, Columbia, Glascock, Jefferson, Lincoln, McDuffie, Richmond, Taliaferro, Warren, Wilkes.

-Brunswick Div. PO B 1636, Brunswick, GA 31521 (courie: Room 222, 801 Glouchester, Brunswick, GA 31520), 912-280-1330. **Counties:** Appling, Camden, Glynn, Jeff Davis, Long, McIntosh, Wayne.

-Dublin Div. c/o Augusta Division. **Counties:** Dodge, Johnson, Laurens, Montgomery, Telfair, Treutlen, Wheeler.

-Savannah Div. PO Box 8286, Savannah, GA 31412 (physical address: Room 306, 125 Bull St, Savannah, GA 31401), 912-650-4020. **Counties:** Bryan, Chatham, Effingham, Liberty.

-Statesboro Div. c/o Savannah Division. **Counties:** Bulloch, Candler, Emanuel, Evans, Jenkins, Screven, Tattnall, Toombs.

-Waycross Div. c/o Savannah Division. **Counties:** Atkinson, Bacon, Brantley, Charlton, Coffee, Pierce, Ware.

Hawaii

District of Hawaii

http://www.hid.uscourts.gov **Special access:** PACER dial-up, PACER online. 300 Ala Moana Blvd, Rm C-338, Honolulu, HI 96850 (physical address: same as mail address), 808-541-1300. **Counties:** All.

Idaho

District of Idaho

http://www.id.uscourts.gov **Special access:** phone, fax, or on the web. Opinions available at http://www.id.uscourts.gov.

-Boise Div. MSC 039, Federal Bldg, 550 W Fort St, Room 400, Boise, ID 83724 (physical address: same as mail address), 208-334-1361. **Counties:** Ada, Adams, Blaine, Boise, Camas, Canyon, Cassia, Elmore, Gem, Gooding, Jerome, Lincoln, Minidoka, Owyhee, Payette, Twin Falls, Valley, Washington.

-Coeur d' Alene Div. c/o Boise Division. **Counties:** Benewah, Bonner, Boundary, Kootenai, Shoshone.

-Moscow Div. c/o Boise Division. **Counties:** Clearwater, Latah, Lewis, Nez Perce.

-Pocatello Div. Boise Division, 801 E Sherman, Pocatello, ID 83201 (physical address: same as mail address), 208-478-4123. **Counties:** Bannock, Bear Lake, Bingham, Bonneville, Butte, Caribou, Clark, Custer, Franklin, Fremont, Idaho, Jefferson, Lemhi, Madison, Oneida, Power, Teton.

Illinois

Central District of Illinois

http://www.ilcd.uscourts.gov **Special access:** phone, PACER dial-up, PACER online.

-Danville/Urbana Div. 201 S Vine, Room 218, Urbana, IL 61801 (physical address: same as mail address), 217-373-5830. **Counties:** Champaign, Coles, Douglas, Edgar, Ford, Iroquois, Kankakee, Macon, Moultrie, Piatt, Vermilion.

-Peoria Div. US District Clerk's Office, 309 Federal Bldg, 100 NE Monroe St, Peoria, IL 61602 (physical address: same as mail address), 309-671-7117. **Counties:** Bureau, Fulton, Hancock, Knox, Livingston, McDonough, McLean, Marshall, Peoria, Putnam, Stark, Tazewell, Woodford.

-Rock Island Div. US District Clerk's Office, Room 40, Post Office Bldg, 211 19th St, Rock Island, IL 61201 (physical address: same as mail address), 309-793-5778. **Counties:** Henderson, Henry, Mercer, Rock Island, Warren.

-Springfield Div. Clerk, 151 US Courthouse, 600 E Monroe, Springfield, IL 62701 (physical address: same as mail address), 217-492-4020. **Counties:** Adams, Brown, Cass, Christian, De Witt, Greene, Logan, Macoupin, Mason, Menard, Montgomery, Morgan, Pike, Sangamon, Schuyler, Scott, Shelby.

Northern District of Illinois

http://www.ilnd.uscourts.gov **Special access:** phone (dockets or basic information only), PACER dial-up, PACER online.

-Chicago (Eastern) Div. 20th Floor, 219 S Dearborn St, Chicago, IL 60604 (physical address: same as mail address), 312-435-5698. **Counties:** Cook, Du Page, Grundy, Kane, Kendall, Lake, La Salle, Will.

-Rockford Div. Room 211, 211 S Court St, Rockford, IL 61101 (physical address: same as mail address), 815-987-4355. **Counties:** Boone, Carroll, De Kalb, Jo Daviess, Lee, McHenry, Ogle, Stephenson, Whiteside, Winnebago.

Southern District of Illinois

http://www.ilsd.uscourts.gov **Special access:** phone, PACER dial-up, PACER online.

-Benton Div. 301 W Main St, Benton, IL 62812 (physical address: same as mail address), 618-439-7760. **Counties:** Alexander, Clark, Clay, Crawford, Cumberland, Edwards, Effingham, Franklin, Gallatin, Hamilton, Hardin, Jackson, Jasper, Jefferson, Johnson, Lawrence, Massac, Perry, Pope, Pulaski, Richland, Saline, Union, Wabash, Wayne, White, Williamson. Cases mayalso be allocated to the Benton Division.

-East St Louis Div. PO Box 249, East St Louis, IL 62202 (physical address: 750 Missouri Ave, East St Louis, IL 62201), 618-482-9371. **Counties:** Bond, Calhoun, Clinton, Fayette, Jersey, Madison, Marion, Monroe, Randolph, St. Clair, Washington. Cases for these counties may also be allocated to Benton Div..

Indiana

Northern District of Indiana

http://www.innd.uscourts.gov **Special access:** phone, PACER dial-up, PACER online.

-Fort Wayne Div. Room 1108, Federal Bldg, 1300 S Harrison St, Fort Wayne, IN 46802 (physical address: same as mail address), 219-424-7360. **Counties:** Adams, Allen, Blackford, DeKalb, Grant, Huntington, Jay, Lagrange, Noble, Steuben, Wells, Whitley.

-Hammond Div. Room 101, 507 State St, Hammond, IN 46320 (physical address: same as mail address), 219-937-5235. **Counties:** Lake, Porter.

-Lafayette Div. PO Box 1498, Lafayette, IN 47902 (physical address: 230 N 4th St, Lafayette, IN 47901), 765-420-6250. **Counties:** Benton, Carroll, Jasper, Newton, Tippecanoe, Warren, White.

-South Bend Div. Room 102, 204 S Main, South Bend, IN 46601 (physical address: same as mail address), 219-246-8000. **Counties:** Cass, Elkhart, Fulton, Kosciusko, La Porte, Marshall, Miami, Pulaski, St. Joseph, Starke, Wabash.

-Evansville Div. 304 Federal Bldg, 101 NW Martin Luther King Blvd, Evansville, IN 47708 (physical address: same as mail address), 812-465-6426. **Counties:** Daviess, Dubois, Gibson, Martin, Perry, Pike, Posey, Spencer, Vanderburgh, Warrick.

Southern District of Indiana

http://www.insd.uscourts.gov **Special access:** phone, CM/ECF, or on the web.

-Indianapolis Div. Clerk, Room 105, 46 E Ohio St, Indianapolis, IN 46204 (physical address: same as mail address), 317-229-3700. **Counties:** Bartholomew, Boone, Brown, Clinton, Decatur, Delaware, Fayette, Fountain, Franklin, Hamilton, Hancock, Hendricks, Henry, Howard, Johnson, Madison, Marion, Monroe, Montgomery, Morgan, Randolph, Rush, Shelby, Tipton, Union, Wayne.

-New Albany Div. Room 210, 121 W Spring St, New Albany, IN 47150 (physical address: same as mail address), 812-948-5238. **Counties:** Clark, Crawford, Dearborn, Floyd, Harrison, Jackson, Jefferson, Jennings, Lawrence, Ohio, Orange, Ripley, Scott, Switzerland, Washington.

-Terre Haute Div. 207 Federal Bldg, 30 N 7th St, Terre Haute, IN 47808 (courier: same as mail address), 812-234-9484. **Counties:** Clay, Greene, Knox, Owen, Parke, Putnam, Sullivan, Vermillion, Vigo.

Iowa

Northern District of Iowa

http://www.iand.uscourts.gov **Special access:** phone, PACER dial-up, PACER online.

-Cedar Rapids Div. Court Clerk, PO Box 74710, Cedar Rapids, IA 52407-4710 (physical address: Federal Bldg, US Courthouse, 101 1st St SE, Room 313, Cedar Rapids, IA 52401), 319-286-2300. **Counties:** Benton, Cedar, Cerro Gordo, Grundy, Hardin, Iowa, Jones, Linn, Tama.

-Dubuque Div. c/o Cedar Rapids Division. **Counties:** Allamakee, Black Hawk, Bremer, Buchanan, Chickasaw, Clayton, Delaware, Dubuque, Fayette, Floyd, Howard, Jackson, Mitchell, Winneshiek.

-Sioux City Div. Room 301, Federal Bldg, 320 6th St, Sioux City, IA 51101 (courier: same as mail address), 712-233-3900. **Counties:** Buena Vista, Cherokee, Clay, Crawford, Dickinson, Ida, Lyon, Monona, O'Brien, Osceola, Plymouth, Sac, Sioux, Woodbury.

Southern District of Iowa

http://www.iasd.uscourts.gov **Special access:** phone, PACER dial-up, PACER online, or on the web.

-Council Bluffs (West) Div. PO Box 307, Council Bluffs, IA 51502 (physical address: Room 313, 8 S 6th St, Council Bluffs, IA 51501), 712-328-0283. **Counties:** Audubon, Cass, Fremont, Harrison, Mills, Montgomery, Page, Pottawattamie, Shelby.

-Davenport (East) Div. PO Box 256, Davenport, IA 52805 (physical address: Room 215, 131 E 4th St, Davenport, IA 52801), 563-322-3223. **Counties:** Henry, Johnson, Lee, Louisa, Muscatine, Scott, Van Buren, Washington.

-Des Moines (Central) Div. PO Box 9344, Des Moines, IA 50306-9344 (physical address: 123 E. Walnut St, Rm. 300, Des Moines, IA 50306-9344), 515-284-6248. **Counties:** Adair, Adams, Appanoose, Boone, Clarke, Clinton, Dallas, Davis, Decatur, Des Moines, Greene, Guthrie, Jasper, Jefferson, Keokuk, Lucas, Madison, Mahaska, Marion, Marshall, Monroe, Polk, Poweshiek, Ringgold, Story, Taylor, Union, Wapello, Warren, Wayne.

Kansas

District of Kansas

http://www.ksd.uscourts.gov **Special access:** phone (dockets or basic information only), PACER dial-up, PACER online.

-Kansas City Div. Clerk, 500 State Ave, Kansas City, KS 66101 (physical address: same as mail address), 913-551-6719. **Counties:** Atchison, Bourbon, Brown, Cherokee, Crawford, Doniphan, Johnson, Labette, Leavenworth, Linn, Marshall, Miami, Nemaha, Wyandotte.

-Topeka Div. Clerk, US District Court, Room 490, 444 SE Quincy, Topeka, KS 66683 (physical address: same as mail address), 785-295-2610. **Counties:** Allen, Anderson, Chase, Clay, Cloud, Coffey, Dickinson, Douglas, Franklin, Geary, Jackson, Jewell, Lincoln, Lyon, Marion, Mitchell, Morris, Neosho, Osage, Ottawa, Pottawatomie, Republic, Riley, Saline, Shawnee, Wabaunsee, Washington, Wilson, Woodson.

-Wichita Div. 204 US Courthouse, 401 N Market, Wichita, KS 67202-2096 (physical address: same as mail address), 316-269-6491. **Counties:** All in Kansas. Cases may be heard from counties in other division.

Kentucky

Eastern District of Kentucky

http://www.kyed.uscourts.gov **Special access:** phone, PACER dial-up, PACER online.

-Ashland Div. Suite 336, 1405 Greenup Ave, Ashland, KY 41101 (physical address: same as mail address), 606-329-8652. **Counties:** Boyd, Carter, Elliott, Greenup, Lawrence, Lewis, Morgan, Rowan.

-Covington Div. Clerk, PO Box 1073, Covington, KY 41012 (physical address: US Courthouse, Room 201, 35 W 5th St, Covington, KY 41011), 859-392-7925. **Counties:** Boone, Bracken, Campbell, Gallatin, Grant, Kenton, Mason, Pendleton, Robertson.

-Frankfort Div. Room 313, 330 W Broadway, Frankfort, KY 40601 (physical address: same as mail address), 502-223-5225. **Counties:** Anderson, Carroll, Franklin, Henry, Owen, Shelby, Trimble.

-Lexington Div. PO Box 3074, Lexington, KY 40588 (physical address: Room 206, 101 Barr St, Lexington, KY 40507), 859-233-2503. **Counties:** Bath, Bourbon, Boyle, Clark, Estill, Fayette, Fleming, Garrard, Harrison, Jessamine, Lee, Lincoln, Madison,

Menifee, Mercer, Montgomery, Nicholas, Powell, Scott, Wolfe, Woodford.

-London Div. PO Box 5121, London, KY 40745-5121 (physical address: 124 US Courthouse, 300 S Main, London, KY 40741), 606-864-5137. **Counties:** Bell, Clay, Harlan, Jackson, Knox, Laurel, Leslie, McCreary, Owsley, Pulaski, Rockcastle, Wayne, Whitley.

-Pikeville Div. Office of the clerk, 203 Federal Bldg, 110 Main St, Pikeville, KY 41501 (physical address: same as mail address), 606-437-6160. **Counties:** Breathitt, Floyd, Johnson, Knott, Letcher, Magoffin, Martin, Perry, Pike. Lee and Wolfe Counties were part of this division until 10/31/92, when they were moved to the Lexington Division.

Western District of Kentucky

http://www.kywd.uscourts.gov **Special access:** phone, PACER dial-up, PACER online, CM/ECF. Opinions available at http://www.kywd.uscourts.gov.

-Bowling Green Div. US District Court, 241 E Main St, Room 120, Bowling Green, KY 42101-2175 (physical address: same as mail address), 270-781-1110. **Counties:** Adair, Allen, Barren, Butler, Casey, Clinton, Cumberland, Edmonson, Green, Hart, Logan, Metcalfe, Monroe, Russell, Simpson, Taylor, Todd, Warren.

-Louisville Div. Clerk, US District Court, 450 US Courthouse, 601 W Broadway, Louisville, KY 40202 (physical address: same as mail address), 502-625-3500. **Counties:** Breckinridge, Bullitt, Hardin, Jefferson, Larue, Marion, Meade, Nelson, Oldham, Spencer, Washington.

-Owensboro Div. Federal Bldg, Room 126, 423 Frederica St, Owensboro, KY 42301 (physical address: same as mail address), 270-683-0221. **Counties:** Daviess, Grayson, Hancock, Henderson, Hopkins, McLean, Muhlenberg, Ohio, Union, Webster.

-Paducah Div. 127 Federal Building, 501 Broadway, Paducah, KY 42001 (physical address: same as mail address), 270-443-1337. **Counties:** Ballard, Caldwell, Calloway, Carlisle, Christian, Crittenden, Fulton, Graves, Hickman, Livingston, Lyon, McCracken, Marshall, Trigg.

Louisiana

Eastern District of Louisiana

http://www.laed.uscourts.gov **Special access:** phone (dockets or basic information only), PACER dial-up, PACER online. Clerk, Room 151, 500 Camp St, New Orleans, LA 70130 (physical address: same as mail address), 504-589-7650. **Counties:** Assumption Parish, Jefferson Parish, Lafourche Parish, Orleans Parish, Plaquemines Parish, St. Bernard Parish, St. Charles Parish, St. James Parish, St. John the Baptist Parish, St. Tammany Parish, Tangipahoa Parish, Terrebonne Parish, Washington Parish.

Middle District of Louisiana

http://www.lamd.uscourts.gov **Special access:** phone, PACER dial-up, PACER online. PO Box 2630, Baton Rouge, LA 70821-2630 (physical address: 777 Florida St, #139, Baton Rouge, LA 70801), 225-389-3500. **Counties:** Ascension Parish, East Baton Rouge Parish, East Feliciana Parish, Iberville Parish, Livingston Parish, Pointe Coupee Parish, St. Helena Parish, West Baton Rouge Parish, West Feliciana Parish.

Western District of Louisiana

http://www.lawd.uscourts.gov **Special access:** phone, PACER dial-up, PACER online.

-Alexandria Div. PO Box 1269, Alexandria, LA 71309 (physical address: 515 Murray, Alexandria, LA 71301), 318-473-7415. **Counties:** Avoyelles Parish, Catahoula Parish, Concordia Parish, Grant Parish, La Salle Parish, Natchitoches Parish, Rapides Parish, Winn Parish.

-Lafayette Div. Room 113, Federal Bldg, 705 Jefferson St, Lafayette, LA 70501 (physical address: same as mail address), 337-593-5000. **Counties:** Acadia Parish, Evangeline Parish, Iberia Parish, Lafayette Parish, St. Landry Parish, St. Martin Parish, St. Mary Parish, Vermilion Parish.

-Lake Charles Div. 611 Broad St, Suite 188, Lake Charles, LA 70601 (physical address: same as mail address), 337-437-3870. **Counties:** Allen Parish, Beauregard Parish, Calcasieu Parish, Cameron Parish, Jefferson Davis Parish, Vernon Parish.

-Monroe Div. PO Drawer 3087, Monroe, LA 71210 (physical address: Room 215, 201 Jackson St, Monroe, LA 71201), 318-322-6740. **Counties:** Caldwell Parish, East Carroll Parish, Franklin Parish, Jackson Parish, Lincoln Parish, Madison Parish, Morehouse Parish, Ouachita Parish, Richland Parish, Tensas Parish, Union Parish, West Carroll Parish.

-Shreveport Div. US Courthouse, Suite 1167, 300 Fannin St, Shreveport, LA 71101-3083 (physical address: same as mail address), 318-676-4273. **Counties:** Bienville Parish, Bossier Parish, Caddo Parish, Claiborne Parish, De Soto Parish, Red River Parish, Sabine Parish, Webster Parish.

Maine

District of Maine

http://www.med.uscourts.gov **Access:** phone, PACER dial-up, PACER online.
-Bangor Div. Court Clerk, PO Box 1007, Bangor, ME 04402-1007 (physical address: Room 357, 202 Harlow St, Bangor, ME 04401), 207-945-0575. **Counties:** Aroostook, Franklin, Hancock, Kennebec, Penobscot, Piscataquis, Somerset, Waldo, Washington.
-Portland Div. Court Clerk, 156 Federal St, Portland, ME 04101 (physical address: same as mail address), 207-780-3356. **Counties:** Androscoggin, Cumberland, Knox, Lincoln, Oxford, Sagadahoc, York.

Maryland

Northern District of Maryland

http://www.mdd.uscourts.gov **Special access:** phone, PACER dial-up, PACER online. Opinions available at http://www.mdd.uscourts.gov. Clerk, 4th Floor, Room 4415, 101 W Lombard St, Baltimore, MD 21201 (physical address: same as mail address), 410-962-2600. **Counties:** Allegany, Anne Arundel, Baltimore, City of Baltimore, Caroline, Carroll, Cecil, Dorchester, Frederick, Garrett, Harford, Howard, Kent, Queen Anne's, Somerset, Talbot, Washington, Wicomico, Worcester.

Southern District of Maryland

http://www.mdd.uscourts.gov **Special access:** phone, fax, PACER dial-up, PACER online. Opinions available at http://www.mdd.uscourts.gov. Clerk, Room 240, 6500 Cherrywood Lane, Greenbelt, MD 20770 (physical address: same as mail address), 301-344-0660. **Counties:** Calvert, Charles, Montgomery, Prince George's, St. Mary's.

Massachusetts

District of Massachusetts

http://www.mad.uscourts.gov **Special access:** PACER dial-up, PACER online.
-Boston Div. US Courthouse, 1 Courthouse Way, Boston, MA 02210 (physical address: same as mail address), 617-748-9152. **Counties:** Barnstable, Bristol, Dukes, Essex, Middlesex, Nantucket, Norfolk, Plymouth, Suffolk.
-Springfield Div. 1550 Main St, Springfield, MA 01103 (physical address: same as mail address), 413-785-0214. **Counties:** Berkshire, Franklin, Hampden, Hampshire.

-Worcester Div. 595 Main St, Room 502, Worcester, MA 01608 (physical address: same as mail address), 508-793-0552. **Counties:** Worcester.

Michigan

Eastern District of Michigan

http://www.mied.uscourts.gov **Special access:** phone, PACER dial-up, PACER online.
-Ann Arbor Div. PO Box 8199, Ann Arbor, MI 48107 (physical address: 200 E Liberty, Room 120, Ann Arbor, MI 48104), 734-741-2380. **Counties:** Jackson, Lenawee, Monroe, Oakland, Washtenaw, Wayne. Civil cases in these counties are assigned randomly to the Detroit, Flint or Port Huron Divisions. Case files are maintained where the case is assigned.
-Bay City Div. 1000 Washington Ave Rm 304, PO Box 913, Bay City, MI 48707 (physical address: same as mail address), 989-894-8800. **Counties:** Alcona, Alpena, Arenac, Bay, Cheboygan, Clare, Crawford, Gladwin, Gratiot, Huron, Iosco, Isabella, Midland, Montmorency, Ogemaw, Oscoda, Otsego, Presque Isle, Roscommon, Saginaw, Tuscola.
-Detroit Div. 231 W Lafayette Blvd, Detroit, MI 48226 (physical address: same as mail address), 313-234-5050. **Counties:** Macomb, St. Clair, Sanilac. Civil cases for these counties are assigned randomly among the Flint, Ann Arbor and Detroit divisions. Port Huron cases may also be assigned here. Case files are kept where the case is assigned.
-Flint Div. Clerk, Federal Bldg, Room 140, 600 Church St, Flint, MI 48502 (physical address: same as mail address), 810-341-7840. **Counties:** Genesee, Lapeer, Livingston, Shiawassee. This office handles all criminal cases for these counties. Civil cases are assigned randomly among the Detroit, Ann Arbor and Flint divisions.

Western District of Michigan

http://www.miwd.uscourts.gov **Special access:** phone, PACER dial-up, PACER online, CM/ECF.
-Grand Rapids Div. PO Box 3310, Grand Rapids, MI 49501 (physical address: Gerald Ford Federal Building, 110 Michigan St NW, Rm 299, Grand Rapids, MI 49503), 616-456-2693. **Counties:** Antrim, Barry, Benzie, Charlevoix, Emmet, Grand Traverse, Ionia, Kalkaska, Kent, Lake, Leelanau, Manistee, Mason, Mecosta, Missaukee, Montcalm, Muskegon, Newaygo, Oceana, Osceola, Ottawa, Wexford. The Lansing and Kalamazoo Divisions also handle cases from these counties.

-Kalamazoo Div. 410 W Michigan, Rm B-35, Kalamazoo, MI 49007 (physical address: same as mail address), 616-349-2922. **Counties:** Allegan, Berrien, Calhoun, Cass, Kalamazoo, St. Joseph, Van Buren. Also handle cases from the counties in the Grand Rapids Division.

-Lansing Div. 113 Federal Building, 315 W Allegan, Rm 101, Lansing, MI 48933 (physical address: same as mail address), 517-377-1559. **Counties:** Branch, Clinton, Eaton, Hillsdale, Ingham. Also handle cases from the counties in the Grand Rapids Division.

-Marquette-Northern Div. PO Box 909, Marquette, MI 49855 (physical address: 202 W Washington, Room 229, Marquette, MI 49855), 906-226-2117. **Counties:** Alger, Baraga, Chippewa, Delta, Dickinson, Gogebic, Houghton, Iron, Keweenaw, Luce, Mackinac, Marquette, Menominee, Ontonagon, Schoolcraft.

Minnesota

District of Minnesota

http://www.mnd.uscourts.gov **Special access:** phone, PACER dial-up, PACER online.

-Duluth Div. Clerk's Office, 417 Federal Bldg, Duluth, MN 55802 (physical address: same as mail address), 218-529-3500. **Counties:** Aitkin, Becker*, Beltrami*, Benton, Big Stone*, Carlton, Cass, Clay*, Clearwater*, Cook, Crow Wing, Douglas*, Grant*, Hubbard*, Itasca, Kanabec, Kittson*, Koochiching, Lake, Lake of the Woods*, Mahnomen*, Marshall*, Mille Lacs, Morrison, Norman*, Otter*,Tail, Pennington*, Pine, Polk*, Pope*, Red Lake*, Roseau*, Stearns*, Stevens*, St. Louis, Todd*, Traverse*, Wadena*, Wilkin*. From March 1, 1995, to 1998, cases from the counties marked with an asterisk (*) were heard here.Before and after that period, cases were and are allocated between St. Paul and Minneapolis.

-Minneapolis Div. Court Clerk, Room 202, 300 S 4th St, Minneapolis, MN 55415 (physical address: same as mail address), 612-664-5000. **Counties:** All not covered by the Duluth Division. Cases are allocated between Minneapolis and St Paul.

-St Paul Div. 700 Federal Bldg, 316 N Robert, St Paul, MN 55101 (physical address: same as mail address), 651-848-1100. **Counties:** All not covered by the Duluth Division. Cases are allocated between Minneapolis and St Paul.

Mississippi

Northern District of Mississippi

http://www.msnd.uscourts.gov **Special access:** PACER dial-up, PACER online. Opinions available at http://sunset.backbone.olemiss.edu/~llibcoll/ndms.

-Aberdeen-Eastern Div. PO Box 704, Aberdeen, MS 39730 (physical address: 301 W Commerce, Room 310, Aberdeen, MS 39730), 662-369-4952. **Counties:** Alcorn, Attala, Chickasaw, Choctaw, Clay, Itawamba, Lee, Lowndes, Monroe, Oktibbeha, Prentiss, Tishomingo, Winston.

-Clarksdale/Delta Div. c/o Oxford-Northern Division. **Counties:** Bolivar, Coahoma, De Soto, Panola, Quitman, Tallahatchie, Tate, Tunica.

-Greenville Div. PO Box 190, Greenville, MS 38702-0190 (physical address: US Post Office & Federal Bldg, 305 Main, Greenville, MS 38701), 662-335-1651. **Counties:** Carroll, Humphreys, Leflore, Sunflower, Washington.

-Oxford-Northern Div. PO Box 727, Oxford, MS 38655 (physical address: Suite 369, 911 Jackson Ave, Oxford, MS 38655), 662-234-1971. **Counties:** Benton, Calhoun, Grenada, Lafayette, Marshall, Montgomery, Pontotoc, Tippah, Union, Webster, Yalobusha.

Southern District of Mississippi

http://www.mssd.uscourts.gov **Special access:** phone (dockets or basic information only), PACER dial-up, PACER online.

-Biloxi-Southern Div. Room 243, 725 Dr. Martin Luther King Jr. Blvd, Biloxi, MS 39530 (physical address: same as mail address), 228-432-8623. **Counties:** George, Hancock, Harrison, Jackson, Pearl River, Stone.

-Hattiesburg Div. Suite 200, 701 Main St, Hattiesburg, MS 39401 (physical address: same as mail address), 601-583-2433. **Counties:** Covington, Forrest, Greene, Jefferson Davis, Jones, Lamar, Lawrence, Marion, Perry, Walthall.

-Jackson Div. Suite 316, 245 E Capitol St, Jackson, MS 39201 (physical address: same as mail address), 601-965-4439. **Counties:** Amite, Copiah, Franklin, Hinds, Holmes, Leake, Lincoln, Madison, Pike, Rankin, Scott, Simpson, Smith.

-Meridian Div. c/o Jackson Division. **Counties:** Clarke, Jasper, Kemper, Lauderdale, Neshoba, Newton, Noxubee, Wayne.

-Vicksburg Div. c/o Jackson Division. **Counties:** Adams, Claiborne, Issaquena, Jefferson, Sharkey, Warren, Wilkinson, Yazoo.

Missouri

Eastern District of Missouri

http://www.moed.uscourts.gov **Special access:** phone, PACER dial-up, PACER online.

-Cape Girardeau Div. 339 Broadway, Room 240, Cape Girardeau, MO 63701 (physical address: same as mail address), 573-335-8538. **Counties:** Bollinger, Butler, Cape Girardeau, Carter, Dunklin, Madison, Mississippi, New Madrid, Pemiscot, Perry, Reynolds, Ripley, Scott, Shannon, Stoddard, Wayne.

-Hannibal Div. 801 Broadway, Hannibal, MO 63401 (physical address: same as mail address), 573-221-0757. **Counties:** Adair, Audrain, Chariton, Clark, Knox, Lewis, Linn, Macon, Marion, Monroe, Montgomery, Pike, Ralls, Randolph, Schuyler, Scotland, Shelby.

-St Louis Div. 111 S. 10th St, Ste 3.300, St Louis, MO 63102 (physical address: same as mail address), 314-244-7900. **Counties:** Crawford, Dent, Franklin, Gasconade, Iron, Jefferson, Lincoln, Maries, Phelps, St. Charles, Ste. Genevieve, St. Francois, St. Louis, Warren, Washington, City of St. Louis.

Western District of Missouri

http://www.mow.uscourts.gov **Special access:** phone, PACER dial-up, PACER online, CM/ECF.

-Jefferson City-Central Div. 131 W High St, Jefferson City, MO 65101 (physical address: same as mail address), 573-636-4015. **Counties:** Benton, Boone, Callaway, Camden, Cole, Cooper, Hickory, Howard, Miller, Moniteau, Morgan, Osage, Pettis.

-Joplin-Southwestern Div. c/o Kansas City Division. **Counties:** Barry, Barton, Jasper, Lawrence, McDonald, Newton, Stone, Vernon.

-Kansas City-Western Div. Clerk of Court, 201 US Courthouse, Rm 1056, 400 E 9th St, Kansas City, MO 64106 (physical address: same as mail address), 816-512-5000. **Counties:** Bates, Carroll, Cass, Clay, Henry, Jackson, Johnson, Lafayette, Ray, St. Clair, Saline.

-Springfield-Southern Div. 222 N John Q Hammons Pkwy, Suite 1400, Springfield, MO 65806 (physical address: same as mail address), 417-865-3869. **Counties:** Cedar, Christian, Dade, Dallas, Douglas, Greene, Howell, Laclede, Oregon, Ozark, Polk, Pulaski, Taney, Texas, Webster, Wright.

-St Joseph Div. PO Box 387, 201 S 8th St, St Joseph, MO 64501 (physical address: same as mail address,),. **Counties:** Andrew, Atchison, Buchanan, Caldwell, Clinton, Daviess, De Kalb, Gentry, Grundy, Harrison, Holt, Livingston, Mercer, Nodaway, Platte, Putnam, Sullivan, Worth.

Montana

District of Montana

Special access: phone, fax, PACER dial-up.

-Billings Div. Clerk, Room 5405, Federal Bldg, 316 N 26th St, Billings, MT 59101 (physical address: same as mail address), 406-247-7000. **Counties:** Big Horn, Carbon, Carter, Custer, Dawson, Fallon, Garfield, Golden Valley, McCone, Musselshell, Park, Petroleum, Powder River, Prairie, Richland, Rosebud, Stillwater, Sweet Grass, Treasure, Wheatland, Wibaux, Yellowstone, Yellowstone National Park.

-Butte Div. Room 303, Federal Bldg, Butte, MT 59701 (physical address: same as mail address), 406-782-0432. **Counties:** Beaverhead, Deer Lodge, Gallatin, Madison, Silver Bow.

-Great Falls Div. Clerk, PO Box 2186, Great Falls, MT 59403 (physical address: 215 1st Ave N, Great Falls, MT 59401), 406-727-1922. **Counties:** Blaine, Cascade, Chouteau, Daniels, Fergus, Glacier, Hill, Judith Basin, Liberty, Phillips, Pondera, Roosevelt, Sheridan, Teton, Toole, Valley.

-Helena Div. Federal Bldg, 301 S. Park Ave, Rm 542, Helena, MT 59626 (physical address: Room 542, 301 S Park Ave, Helena, MT 59626), 406-441-1355. **Counties:** Broadwater, Jefferson, Lewis and Clark, Meagher, Powell.

-Missoula Div. Russell Smith Courthouse, PO Box 8537, Missoula, MT 59807 (physical address: 201 E Broadway, Missoula, MT 59802), 406-542-7260. **Counties:** Flathead, Granite, Lake, Lincoln, Mineral, Missoula, Ravalli, Sanders.

Nebraska

District of Nebraska

http://www.ned.uscourts.gov **Special access:** PACER dial-up, PACER online, CM/ECF.

-Lincoln Div. PO Box 83468, Lincoln, NE 68501 (physical address: 593 Federal Bldg, 100 Centennial Mall N, Lincoln, NE 68508), 402-437-5225. **Counties:** Nebraska cases may be filed in any of the three courts at the option of the attorney, except that filings in the North Platte Division must be during trial session.

-North Platte Div. c/o Lincoln Division. **Counties:** Some case records may be in the Omaha Division as well as Lincoln.

-Omaha Div. 111 S 18th Plaza, Ste 1152, Omaha, NE 68102 (physical address: same as mail address), 402-661-7350. **Counties:** Nebraska cases may be filed in any of the three courts at the option of the attorney, except that filings in the North Platte Division must be during trial session.

Nevada

District of Nevada

http://www.nvd.uscourts.gov **Special access:** phone, PACER online.
-Las Vegas Div. Room 4425, 300 Las Vegas Blvd S, Las Vegas, NV 89101 (physical address: same as mail address), 702-464-5400. **Counties:** Clark, Esmeralda, Lincoln, Nye.
-Reno Div. Room 301, 400 S Virginia St, Reno, NV 89501 (physical address: same as mail address), 775-686-5800. **Counties:** Carson City, Churchill, Douglas, Elko, Eureka, Humboldt, Lander, Lyon, Mineral, Pershing, Storey, Washoe, White Pine.

New Hampshire

District of New Hampshire

http://www.nhd.uscourts.gov **Special access:** phone, PACER dial-up, PACER online. Warren B Rudman Courthouse, 55 Pleasant St, #110, Concord, NH 03301 (physical address: same as mail address), 603-225-1423. **Counties:** Belknap, Carroll, Cheshire, Coos, Grafton, Hillsborough, Merrimack, Rockingham, Strafford, Sullivan.

New Jersey

District of New Jersey

http://pacer.njd.uscourts.gov **Special access:** phone, PACER dial-up, PACER online. Opinions available at http://lawlibrary.rutgers.edu/fed/search.html.
-Camden Div. Clerk, PO Box 2797, Camden, NJ 08101 (physical address: Room 1050, 4th & Cooper Sts, Camden, NJ 08101), 856-757-5021. **Counties:** Atlantic, Burlington, Camden, Cape May, Cumberland, Gloucester, Salem.
-Newark Div. ML King, Jr Federal Bldg. & US Courthouse, 50 Walnut St, Room 4015, Newark, NJ 07101 (physical address: same as mail address), 973-645-3730. **Counties:** Bergen, Essex, Hudson, Middlesex, Monmouth, Morris, Passaic, Sussex, Union. Monmouth County was transferred from Trenton Division in late 1997; closed cases remain in Trenton.
-Trenton Div. Clerk, US District Court, Room 2020, 402 E State St, Trenton, NJ 08608 (physical address: same as mail address), 609-989-2065. **Counties:** Hunterdon, Mercer, Ocean, Somerset, Warren.

Monmouth County was transferred to Newark and Camden Division in late 1997; closed Monmouth cases remain in Trenton.

New Mexico

District of New Mexico

http://www.nmcourt.fed.us/dcdocs **Special access:** phone, CM/ECF. 333 Lomas Blvd NW #270, Albuquerque, NM 87102-2274 (physical address: same as mail address), 505-348-2000. **Counties:** All in New Mexico. Cases may be assigned to any of its three divisions.

New York

Eastern District of New York

http://www.nyed.uscourts.gov **Special access:** PACER dial-up, PACER online, CM/ECF.
-Brooklyn Div. Brooklyn Courthouse, 225 Cadman Plaza E, Room 130, Brooklyn, NY 11201 (physical address: same as mail address), 718-260-2600. **Counties:** Kings, Queens, Richmond. Cases from Nassau and Suffolk may also be heard here.
-Central Islip Div. 100 Federal Plaza, Central Islip, NY 17722-4438 (physical address: same as mail address), 613-712-6000. **Counties:** Nassau, Suffolk.

Northern District of New York

http://www.nynd.uscourts.gov **Special access:** PACER dial-up.
-Albany Div. 445 Broadway, Room 222, James T Foley Courthouse, Albany, NY 12207-2924 (physical address: same as mail address), 518-257-1800. **Counties:** Albany, Clinton, Columbia, Essex, Greene, Rensselaer, Saratoga, Schenectady, Schoharie, Ulster, Warren, Washington.
-Binghamton Div. 15 Henry St, Binghamton, NY 13901 (physical address: same as mail address), 607-773-2893. **Counties:** Broome, Chenango, Delaware, Franklin, Jefferson, Lewis, Otsego, St. Lawrence, Tioga.
-Syracuse Div. PO Box 7367, Syracuse, NY 13261-7367 (physical address: 100 S Clinton St, Syracuse, NY 13261-7367), 315-234-8500. **Counties:** Cayuga, Cortland, Fulton, Hamilton, Herkimer, Madison, Montgomery, Onondaga, Oswego, Tompkins.
-Utica Div. Alexander Pirnie Bldg, 10 Broad St, Utica, NY 13501 (physical address: same as mail address), 315-793-8151. **Counties:** Oneida.

Southern District of New York

http://www.nysd.uscourts.gov **Special access:** phone (dockets or basic information only), PACER dial-up, CM/ECF. Opinions available at http://www.nysd.uscourts.gov/courtweb.
-New York City Div. 500 Pearl St, New York, NY 10007 (physical address: same as mail address), 212-805-0136. **Counties:** Bronx, New York. Some cases from the counties in the White Plains Division are also assigned to the New York Division.
-White Plains Div. 300 Quarropas St, White Plains, NY 10601 (physical address: same as mail address), 914-390-4000. **Counties:** Dutchess, Orange, Putnam, Rockland, Sullivan, Westchester. Some cases may be assigned to New York Division.

Western District of New York

http://www.nywd.uscourts.gov **Special access:** PACER dial-up, PACER online.
-Buffalo Div. Room 304, 68 Court St, Buffalo, NY 14202 (courier: same as mail address), 716-551-4211. **Counties:** Allegany, Cattaraugus, Chautauqua, Erie, Genesee, Niagara, Orleans, Wyoming.
-Rochester Div. Room 2120, 100 State St, Rochester, NY 14614 (physical address: same as mail address), 716-263-6263. **Counties:** Chemung, Livingston, Monroe, Ontario, Schuyler, Seneca, Steuben, Wayne, Yates.

North Carolina

Eastern District of North Carolina

http://wwnced.uscourts.gov **Special access:** PACER dial-up.
-Elizabeth City Div. c/o Raleigh Division. **Counties:** Bertie, Camden, Chowan, Currituck, Dare, Gates, Hertford, Northampton, Pasquotank, Perquimans, Tyrrell, Washington.
-Greenville-Eastern Div. Room 209, 201 S Evans St, Greenville, NC 27858-1137 (physical address: same as mail address), 252-830-6009. **Counties:** Beaufort, Carteret, Craven, Edgecombe, Greene, Halifax, Hyde, Jones, Lenoir, Martin, Pamlico, Pitt.
-Raleigh Div. Clerk's Office, PO Box 25670, Raleigh, NC 27611 (physical address: Room 574, 310 New Bern Ave, Raleigh, NC 27601), 919-856-4370. **Counties:** Cumberland, Franklin, Granville, Harnett, Johnston, Nash, Vance, Wake, Warren Wayne, Wilson.
-Wilmington Div. PO Box 338, Wilmington, NC 28402 (physical address: Room 239, 2 Princess St, Wilmington, NC 28401), 910-815-4663. **Counties:**

Bladen, Brunswick, Columbus, Duplin, New Hanover, Onslow, Pender, Robeson, Sampson.

Middle District of North Carolina

http://www.ncmd.uscourts.gov **Special access:** phone (dockets or basic information only), PACER dial-up, PACER online. Clerk's Office, PO Box 2708, Greensboro, NC 27402 (physical address: Room 311, 324 W Market St, Greensboro, NC 27401), 336-332-6000. **Counties:** Alamance, Cabarrus, Caswell, Chatham, Davidson, Davie, Durham, Forsyth, Guilford, Hoke, Lee, Montgomery, Moore, Orange, Person, Randolph, Richmond, Rockingham, Rowan, Scotland, Stanly, Stokes, Surry, Yadkin.

Western District of North Carolina

http://www.ncwd.uscourts.gov **Special access:** phone, PACER dial-up, PACER online.
-Asheville Div. Clerk of the Court, Room 309, US Courthouse Bldg, 100 Otis St, Asheville, NC 28801-2611 (physical address: same as mail address), 828-771-7200. **Counties:** Avery, Buncombe, Haywood, Henderson, Madison, Mitchell, Transylvania, Yancey.
-Bryson City Div. c/o Asheville Division. **Counties:** Cherokee, Clay, Graham, Jackson, Macon, Swain.
-Charlotte Div. Clerk, Room 210, 401 W Trade St, Charlotte, NC 28202 (physical address: same as mail address), 704-350-7400. **Counties:** Anson, Gaston, Mecklenburg, Union.
-Shelby Div. c/o Asheville Division. **Counties:** Burke, Cleveland, McDowell, Polk, Rutherford.
-Statesville Div. PO Box 466, Statesville, NC 28687 (physical address: Room 205, 200 W Broad St, Statesville, NC 28687), 704-883-1000. **Counties:** Alexander, Alleghany, Ashe, Caldwell, Catawba, Iredell, Lincoln, Watauga, Wilkes.

North Dakota

District of North Dakota

http://www.ndd.uscourts.gov **Special access:** phone, PACER dial-up.
-Bismarck-Southwestern Div. PO Box 1193, Bismarck, ND 58502 (physical address: 220 E Rosser Ave, Room 476, Bismarck, ND 58501), 701-530-2300. **Counties:** Adams, Billings, Bowman, Burleigh, Dunn, Emmons, Golden Valley, Grant, Hettinger, Kidder, Logan, McIntosh, McLean, Mercer, Morton, Oliver, Sioux, Slope, Stark.
-Fargo-Southeastern Div. PO Box 870, Fargo, ND 58107 (physical address: 655 1st Ave N, Fargo, ND 58102), 701-297-7000. **Counties:** Barnes, Cass, Dickey, Eddy, Foster, Griggs, La Moure, Ransom,

Richland, Sargent, Steele, Stutsman. Rolette County cases prior to 1995 may be located here.

-Grand Forks-Northeastern Div. c/o Fargo-Southeastern Division, 102 N 4th St, Grand Forks, ND 58201 (physical address: 655 1st Ave N, Fargo, ND 58102), 701-772-0511. **Counties:** Benson, Cavalier, Grand Forks, Nelson, Pembina, Ramsey, Towner, Traill, Walsh.

-Minot-Northwestern Div. c/o Bismarck Division, PO Box 1193, Bismarck, ND 58502 (physical address: 100 1st St SW, Minot, ND 58701), 701-839-6251. **Counties:** Bottineau, Burke, Divide, McHenry, McKenzie, Mountrail, Pierce, Renville, Rolette, Sheridan, Ward, Wells, Williams. Case records from Rolette County prior to 1995 may be located in Fargo-Southeastern Division.

Ohio

Northern District of Ohio

http://www.ohnd.uscourts.gov **Special access:** phone, PACER dial-up, PACER online, CM/ECF.

-Akron Div. 568 Federal Bldg, 2 S Main St, Akron, OH 44308 (physical address: same as mail address), 330-375-5705. **Counties:** Carroll, Holmes, Portage, Stark, Summit, Tuscarawas, Wayne. Cases filed prior to 1995 for counties in the Youngstown Division may be located here.

-Cleveland Div. 201 Superior Ave, NE, Cleveland, OH 44114 (physical address: same as mail address), 216-522-4355. **Counties:** Ashland, Ashtabula, Crawford, Cuyahoga, Geauga, Lake, Lorain, Medina, Richland. Cases prior to July 1995 for the counties of Ashland, Crawford, Medina and Richland are located in the Akron Division. Cases filed prior to 1995 from the counties in theYoungstown Division may be located here.

-Toledo Div. 114 US Courthouse, 1716 Spielbusch, Toledo, OH 43624 (physical address: same as mail address), 419-259-6412. **Counties:** Allen, Auglaize, Defiance, Erie, Fulton, Hancock, Hardin, Henry, Huron, Lucas, Marion, Mercer, Ottawa, Paulding, Putnam, Sandusky, Seneca, Van Wert, Williams, Wood, Wyandot.

-Youngstown Div. 337 Federal Bldg, 125 Market St, Youngstown, OH 44503-1787 (physical address: same as mail address), 330-746-1906. **Counties:** Columbiana, Mahoning, Trumbull. This division was reactivated in the middle of 1995. Older cases will be found in Akron or Cleveland.

Southern District of Ohio

http://www.ohsd.uscourts.gov **Special access:** phone, PACER dial-up, PACER online.

-Cincinnati Div. Clerk, US District Court, 324 Potter Stewart Courthouse, 100 E 5th St, Cincinnati, OH 45202 (physical address: same as mail address), 513-564-7500. **Counties:** Adams, Brown, Butler, Clermont, Clinton, Hamilton, Highland, Lawrence, Scioto, Warren.

-Columbus Div. Office of the clerk, Room 260, 85 Marconi Blvd, Columbus, OH 43215 (physical address: same as mail address), 614-719-3000. **Counties:** Athens, Belmont, Coshocton, Delaware, Fairfield, Fayette, Franklin, Gallia, Guernsey, Harrison, Hocking, Jackson, Jefferson, Knox, Licking, Logan, Madison, Meigs, Monroe, Morgan, Morrow, Muskingum, Noble, Perry, Pickaway, Pike, Ross, Union, Vinton,Washington.

-Dayton Div. Federal Bldg, 200 W 2nd, Room 712, Dayton, OH 45402 (physical address: same as mail address), 937-512-1400. **Counties:** Champaign, Clark, Darke, Greene, Miami, Montgomery, Preble, Shelby.

Oklahoma

Eastern District of Oklahoma

http://www.oked.uscourts.gov **Special access:** phone, PACER dial-up. Clerk, PO Box 607, Muskogee, OK 74401 (physical address: 101 N 5th, Muskogee, OK 74401), 918-687-2471. **Counties:** Adair, Atoka, Bryan, Carter, Cherokee, Choctaw, Coal, Haskell, Hughes, Johnston, Latimer, Le Flore, Love, McCurtain, McIntosh, Marshall, Murray, Muskogee, Okfuskee, Pittsburg, Pontotoc, Pushmataha, Seminole, Sequoyah, Wagoner.

Northern District of Oklahoma

www.oknd.uscourts.gov **Special access:** phone, PACER dial-up, PACER online, or on the web. 411 US Courthouse, 333 W 4th St, Tulsa, OK 74103 (physical address: same as mail address), 918-699-4700. **Counties:** Craig, Creek, Delaware, Mayes, Nowata, Okmulgee, Osage, Ottawa, Pawnee, Rogers, Tulsa, Washington.

Western District of Oklahoma

http://www.okwd.uscourts.gov **Special access:** phone, PACER dial-up, PACER online. Clerk, Room 1210, 200 NW 4th St, Oklahoma City, OK 73102 (physical address: same as mail address), 405-609-5000. **Counties:** Alfalfa, Beaver, Beckham, Blaine, Caddo, Canadian, Cimarron, Cleveland, Comanche, Cotton,

Custer, Dewey, Ellis, Garfield, Garvin, Grady, Grant, Greer, Harmon, Harper, Jackson, Jefferson, Kay, Kingfisher, Kiowa, Lincoln, Logan, McClain, Major, Noble,Oklahoma, Payne, Pottawatomie, Roger Mills, Stephens, Texas, Tillman, Washita, Woods, Woodward.

Oregon
District of Oregon

http://www.ord.uscourts.gov **Special access:** phone, PACER dial-up, PACER online, CM/ECF, or on the web.
-Eugene Div. 100 Federal Bldg, 211 E 7th Ave, Eugene, OR 97401 (physical address: same as mail address), 541-465-6423. **Counties:** Benton, Coos, Deschutes, Douglas, Lane, Lincoln, Linn, Marion.
-Medford Div. 201 James A Redden US Courthouse, 310 W 6th St, Medford, OR 97501 (physical address: same as mail address), 541-776-3926. **Counties:** Curry, Jackson, Josephine, Klamath, Lake. Court set up in April 1994; Cases prior were tried in Eugene.
-Portland Div. Clerk, 740 US Courthouse, 1000 SW 3rd Ave, Portland, OR 97204-2902 (physical address: same as mail address), 503-326-8000. **Counties:** Baker, Clackamas, Clatsop, Columbia, Crook, Gilliam, Grant, Harney, Hood River, Jefferson, Malheur, Morrow, Multnomah, Polk, Sherman, Tillamook, Umatilla, Union, Wallowa, Wasco, Washinton, Wheeler, Yamhill.

Pennsylvania
Eastern District of Pennsylvania

http://www.paed.uscourts.gov **Special access:** PACER dial-up, PACER online, CM/ECF, or on the web. Opinions:
http://www.paed.uscourts.gov/contents.shtml.
-Allentown/Reading Div. c/o Philadelphia Division, Room 2609. **Counties:** Berks, Lancaster, Lehigh, Northampton, Schuylkill.
-Philadelphia Div. Room 2609, US Courthouse, 601 Market St, Philadelphia, PA 19106-1797 (physical address: same as mail address), 215-597-7704. **Counties:** Bucks, Chester, Delaware, Montgomery, Philadelphia.

Middle District of Pennsylvania

http://www.pamd.uscourts.gov **Special access:** fax, PACER dial-up, PACER online, or on the web.
-Harrisburg Div. PO Box 983, Harrisburg, PA 17108-0983 (physical address: US Courthouse & Federal Bldg, 228 Walnut St, Harrisburg, PA 17108),

717-221-3920. **Counties:** Adams, Cumberland, Dauphin, Franklin, Fulton, Huntingdon, Juniata, Lebanon, Mifflin, York.
-Scranton Div. Clerk's Office, William J Nealon Fedearl Bldg & US Courthouse, PO Box 1148, Scranton, PA 18501 (physical address: 235 N Washington Ave, Room 101, Scranton, PA 18503), 570-207-5680. **Counties:** Bradford, Carbon, Lackawanna, Luzerne, Monroe, Pike, Susquehanna, Wayne, Wyoming.
-Williamsport Div. PO Box 608, Williamsport, PA 17703 (physical address: Federal Bldg, ROom 402, 240 W 3rd St, Williamsport, PA 17701), 570-323-6380. **Counties:** Cameron, Centre, Clinton, Columbia, Lycoming, Montour, Northumberland, Perry, Potter, Snyder, Sullivan, Tioga, Union.

Western District of Pennsylvania

http://www.pawd.uscourts.gov **Special access:** phone, PACER dial-up, PACER online.
-Erie Div. PO Box 1820, Erie, PA 16507 (physical address: 102 US Courthouse, 617 State St, Erie, PA 16501), 814-453-4829. **Counties:** Crawford, Elk, Erie, Forest, McKean, Venango, Warren.
-Johnstown Div. Penn Traffic Bldg, Room 208, 319 Washington St, Johnstown, PA 15901 (courier: same as mail address), 814-533-4504. **Counties:** Bedford, Blair, Cambria, Clearfield, Somerset.
-Pittsburgh Div. US Post Office & Courthouse, Room 829, 7th Ave & Grant St, Pittsburgh, PA 15219 (physical address: same as mail address), 412-644-3527. **Counties:** Allegheny, Armstrong, Beaver, Butler, Clarion, Fayette, Greene, Indiana, Jefferson, Lawrence, Mercer, Washington, Westmoreland.

Rhode Island
District of Rhode Island

Special access: phone, PACER dial-up, PACER online. Clerk's Office, Two Exchange Terrace, Federal Bldg, Providence, RI 02903 (physical address: same as mail address), 401-752-7200. **Counties:** All in Rhode Island.

South Carolina
District of South Carolina

http://www.scd.uscourts.gov **Special access:** PACER dial-up, PACER online. Opinions available at http://www.law.sc.edu/dsc/dsc.htm.
-Anderson Div. c/o Greenville Division. **Counties:** Anderson, Oconee, Pickens.

-Beaufort Div. c/o Charleston Division. **Counties:** Beaufort, Hampton, Jasper.

-Charleston Div. PO Box 835, Charleston, SC 29402 (physical address: 85 Broad St, Hollings Judicial Center, Charleston, SC 29401), 843-579-1401. **Counties:** Berkeley, Charleston, Clarendon, Colleton, Dorchester, Georgetown.

-Columbia Div. 1845 Assembly St, Columbia, SC 29201 (physical address: same as mail address), 803-765-5816. **Counties:** Kershaw, Lee, Lexington, Richland, Sumter.

-Florence Div. PO Box 2317, Florence, SC 29503 (physical address: 401 W Evans St, McMillan Federal Bldg, Room 361, Florence, SC 29501), 843-676-3820. **Counties:** Chesterfield, Darlington, Dillon, Florence, Horry, Marion, Marlboro, Williamsburg.

-Greenville Div. PO Box 10768, Greenville, SC 29603 (physical address: 300 E Washington St, Greenville, SC 29601), 864-241-2700. **Counties:** Greenville, Laurens.

-Greenwood Div. c/o Greenville Division. **Counties:** Abbeville, Aiken, Allendale, Bamberg, Barnwell, Calhoun, Edgefield, Fairfield, Greenwood, Lancaster, McCormick, Newberry, Orangeburg, Saluda.

-Spartanburg Div. c/o Greenville Division. **Counties:** Cherokee, Chester, Spartanburg, Union, York.

South Dakota

District of South Dakota

http://www.sdd.uscourts.gov . **Note**: In South Dakota, PACER is not available for criminal records.

-Aberdeen Div. c/o Pierre Division. **Counties:** Brown, Butte, Campbell, Clark, Codington, Corson, Day, Deuel, Edmunds, Grant, Hamlin, McPherson, Marshall, Roberts, Spink, Walworth. Judge Battey's closed case records are located at the Rapid City Division.

-Pierre Div. Federal Bldg & Courthouse, Room 405, 225 S Pierre St, Pierre, SD 57501 (physical address: same as mail address), 605-224-5849. **Counties:** Buffalo, Dewey, Faulk, Gregory, Haakon, Hand, Hughes, Hyde, Jackson, Jerauld, Jones, Lyman, Mellette, Potter, Stanley, Sully, Todd, Tripp, Ziebach.

-Rapid City Div. Clerk's Office, Room 302, 515 9th St, Rapid City, SD 57701 (physical address: same as mail address), 605-342-3066. **Counties:** Bennett, Custer, Fall River, Harding, Lawrence, Meade, Pennington, Perkins, Shannon. Judge Battey's closed cases are located here.

-Sioux Falls Div. P.O. Box 5060, Sioux Falls, SD 57117-5060 (physical address: Room 128, US Courthouse, 400 S Phillips Ave, Sioux Falls, SD 57104-6851), 605-330-4447. **Counties:** Aurora, Beadle, Bon Homme, Brookings, Brule, Charles Mix, Clay, Davison, Douglas, Hanson, Hutchinson, Kingsbury, Lake, Lincoln, McCook, Miner, Minnehaha, Moody, Sanborn, Turner, Union, Yankton.

Tennessee

Eastern District of Tennessee

http://www.tned.uscourts.gov **Special access:** phone, PACER dial-up, PACER online.

-Chattanooga Div. Clerk's Office, PO Box 591, Chattanooga, TN 37401 (physical address: Room 309, 900 Georgia Ave, Chattanooga, TN 37402), 423-752-5200. **Counties:** Bledsoe, Bradley, Hamilton, McMinn, Marion, Meigs, Polk, Rhea, Sequatchie.

-Greeneville Div. 101 Summer St W, Greenville, TN 37743 (physical address: same as mail address), 423-639-3105. **Counties:** Carter, Cocke, Greene, Hamblen, Hancock, Hawkins, Johnson, Sullivan, Unicoi, Washington.

-Knoxville Div. Clerk's Office, 800 Market St, Knoxville, TN 37902 (physical address: same as mail address), 865-545-4279. **Counties:** Anderson, Blount, Campbell, Claiborne, Grainger, Jefferson, Knox, Loudon, Monroe, Morgan, Roane, Scott, Sevier, Union.

-Winchester Div. PO Box 459, Winchester, TN 37398 (physical address: 200 S Jefferson St, Room 201, Winchester, TN 37397), 931-967-1444. **Counties:** Bedford, Coffee, Franklin, Grundy, Lincoln, Moore, Van Buren, Warren.

Middle District of Tennessee

http://www.tnmd.uscourts.gov **Special access:** PACER dial-up, PACER online.

-Columbia Div. c/o Nashville Division. **Counties:** Giles, Hickman, Lawrence, Lewis, Marshall, Maury, Wayne.

-Cookeville Div. c/o Nashville Division. **Counties:** Clay, Cumberland, De Kalb, Fentress, Jackson, Macon, Overton, Pickett, Putnam, Smith, White.

-Nashville Div. 800 US Courthouse, 801 Broadway, Nashville, TN 37203 (physical address: same as mail address), 615-736-5498. **Counties:** Cannon, Cheatham, Davidson, Dickson, Houston, Humphreys, Montgomery, Robertson, Rutherford, Stewart, Sumner, Trousdale, Williamson, Wilson.

Western District of Tennessee

http://www.tnwd.uscourts.gov **Special access:** phone, PACER dial-up.

-Jackson Div. Rm 26, US Courthouse 262, 111 S Highland, Jackson, TN 38301 (physical address: same as mail address), 731-421-9200. **Counties:** Benton, Carroll, Chester, Crockett, Decatur, Gibson, Hardeman, Hardin, Haywood, Henderson, Henry, Lake, McNairy, Madison, Obion, Perry, Weakley.

-Memphis Div. Federal Bldg, Room 242, 167 N Main, Memphis, TN 38103 (physical address: same as mail address), 901-495-1200. **Counties:** Dyer, Fayette, Lauderdale, Shelby, Tipton.

Texas

Eastern District of Texas

http://www.txed.uscourts.gov **Special access:** phone, PACER dial-up, PACER online.

-Beaumont Div. PO Box 3507, Beaumont, TX 77704 (physical address: Room 104, 300 Willow, Beaumont, TX 77701), 409-654-7000. **Counties:** Delta*, Fannin*, Hardin, Hopkins*, Jasper, Jefferson, Lamar*, Liberty, Newton, Orange, Red River. Counties marked with an asterisk are called the Paris Division, case records maintained here.

-Lufkin Div. 104 N. Third St, Lufkin, TX 75901 (physical address: same as mail address), 936-632-2739. **Counties:** Angelina, Houston, Nacogdoches, Polk, Sabine, San Augustine, Shelby, Trinity, Tyler.

-Marshall Div. PO Box 1499, Marshall, TX 75671-1499 (physical address: 100 E Houston, Marshall, TX 75670), 903-935-2912. **Counties:** Camp, Cass, Harrison, Marion, Morris, Upshur.

-Sherman Div. 101 E Pecan St, Sherman, TX 75090 (physical address: same as mail address), 903-892-2921. **Counties:** Collin, Cooke, Denton, Grayson.

-Texarkana Div. Clerk's Office, 500 State Line Ave, Room 301, Texarkana, TX 75501 (physical address: same as mail address), 903-794-8561. **Counties:** Bowie, Franklin, Titus.

-Tyler Div. Clerk, Room 106, 211 W Ferguson, Tyler, TX 75702 (courier: same as mail address), 903-590-1000. **Counties:** Anderson, Cherokee, Gregg, Henderson, Panola, Rains, Rusk, Smith, Van Zandt, Wood.

Northern District of Texas

http://www.txnd.uscourts.gov **Special access:** phone, PACER dial-up, PACER online, CM/ECF.

-Abilene Div. PO Box 1218, Abilene, TX 79604 (physical address: Room 2008, 341 Pine St, Abilene, TX 79601), 915-677-6311. **Counties:** Callahan, Eastland, Fisher, Haskell, Howard, Jones, Mitchell, Nolan, Shackelford, Stephens, Stonewall, Taylor, Throckmorton.

-Amarillo Div. 205 E 5th St, Amarillo, TX 79101 (physical address: same as mail address), 806-324-2352. **Counties:** Armstrong, Briscoe, Carson, Castro, Childress, Collingsworth, Dallam, Deaf Smith, Donley, Gray, Hall, Hansford, Hartley, Hemphill, Hutchinson, Lipscomb, Moore, Ochiltree, Oldham, Parmer, Potter, Randall, Roberts, Sherman, Swisher, Wheeler.

-Dallas Div. Room 14A20, 1100 Commerce St, Dallas, TX 75242 (physical address: same as mail address), 214-753-2200. **Counties:** Dallas, Ellis, Hunt, Johnson, Kaufman, Navarro, Rockwall.

-Fort Worth Div. Clerk's Office, 501 W Tenth St, Room 310, Fort Worth, TX 76102 (physical address: same as mail address), 817-978-3132. **Counties:** Comanche, Erath, Hood, Jack, Palo Pinto, Parker, Tarrant, Wise.

-Lubbock Div. Clerk, Room 209, 1205 Texas Ave, Lubbock, TX 79401 (physical address: same as mail address), 806-472-7624. **Counties:** Bailey, Borden, Cochran, Crosby, Dawson, Dickens, Floyd, Gaines, Garza, Hale, Hockley, Kent, Lamb, Lubbock, Lynn, Motley, Scurry, Terry, Yoakum.

-San Angelo Div. Clerk's Office, Room 202, 33 E Twohig, San Angelo, TX 76903 (physical address: same as mail address), 915-655-4506. **Counties:** Brown, Coke, Coleman, Concho, Crockett, Glasscock, Irion, Menard, Mills, Reagan, Runnels, Schleicher, Sterling, Sutton, Tom Green.

-Wichita Falls Div. PO Box 1234, Wichita Falls, TX 76307 (physical address: Room 203, 1000 Lamar, Wichita Falls, TX 76301), 940-767-1902. **Counties:** Archer, Baylor, Clay, Cottle, Foard, Hardeman, King, Knox, Montague, Wichita, Wilbarger, Young.

Southern District of Texas

http://www.txsd.uscourts.gov **Special access:** phone, PACER dial-up, PACER online.

-Brownsville Div. 600 E Harrison St Rm 101, Brownsville, TX 78520-7114 (physical address: same as mail address, 600 E Harrison St #101), 956-548-2500. **Counties:** Cameron, Willacy.

-Corpus Christi Div. Clerk's Office, 1133 N. Shoreline Blvd, #208, Corpus Christi, TX 78401 (courier: same as mail address), 361-888-3142. **Counties:** Aransas, Bee, Brooks, Duval, Jim Wells, Kenedy, Kleberg, Live Oak, Nueces, San Patricio.

-Galveston Div. Clerk's Office, PO Drawer 2300, Galveston, TX 77553 (physical address: 601 Rosenberg, Room 411, Galveston, TX 77550), 409-

766-3530. **Counties:** Brazoria, Chambers, Galveston, Matagorda.

-Houston Div. PO Box 61010, Houston, TX 77208 (physical address: Room 1217, 515 Rusk, Houston, TX 77002), 713-250-5500. **Counties:** Austin, Brazos, Colorado, Fayette, Fort Bend, Grimes, Harris, Madison, Montgomery, San Jacinto, Walker, Waller, Wharton.

-Laredo Div. PO Box 597, Laredo, TX 78042-0597 (physical address: Room 319, 1300 Matamoros, Laredo, TX 78040), 956-723-3542. **Counties:** Jim Hogg, La Salle, McMullen, Webb, Zapata.

-McAllen Div. Suite 1011, 1701 W Business Hwy 83, McAllen, TX 78501 (physical address: same as mail address), 956-618-8065. **Counties:** Hidalgo, Starr.

-Victoria Div. Clerk US District Court, PO Box 1638, Victoria, TX 77902 (physical address: Room 406, 312 S Main, Victoria, TX 77901), 361-788-5000. **Counties:** Calhoun, De Witt, Goliad, Jackson, Lavaca, Refugio, Victoria.

Western District of Texas

http://www.txwd.uscourts.gov **Special access:** phone, PACER dial-up, PACER online.

-Austin Div. Room 130, 200 W 8th St, Austin, TX 78701 (physical address: same as mail address), 512-916-5896. **Counties:** Bastrop, Blanco, Burleson, Burnet, Caldwell, Gillespie, Hays, Kimble, Lampasas, Lee, Llano, McCulloch, Mason, San Saba, Travis, Washington, Williamson.

-Del Rio Div. Room L100, 111 E Broadway, Del Rio, TX 78840 (physical address: same as mail address), 830-703-2054. **Counties:** Edwards, Kinney, Maverick, Terrell, Uvalde, Val Verde, Zavala.

-El Paso Div. US District Clerk's Office, Room 350, 511 E San Antonio, El Paso, TX 79901 (physical address: same as mail address), 915-534-6725. **Counties:** El Paso.

-Midland Div. Clerk, US District Court, 200 E Wall St, Rm 107, Midland, TX 79701 (physical address: same as mail address), 915-686-4001. **Counties:** Andrews, Crane, Ector, Martin, Midland, Upton.

-Pecos Div. US Courthouse, 410 S Cedar St, Pecos, TX 79772 (physical address: same as mail address), 915-445-4228. **Counties:** Brewster, Culberson, Hudspeth, Jeff Davis, Loving, Pecos, Presidio, Reeves, Ward, Winkler.

-San Antonio Div. US Clerk's Office, 655 E Durango Blvd, Suite G-65, San Antonio, TX 78206 (physical address: same as mail address), 210-472-6550. **Counties:** Atascosa, Bandera, Bexar, Comal,

Dimmit, Frio, Gonzales, Guadalupe, Karnes, Kendall, Kerr, Medina, Real, Wilson.

-Waco Div. Clerk, Room 303, 800 Franklin, Waco, TX 76701 (physical address: same as mail address), 254-750-1501. **Counties:** Bell, Bosque, Coryell, Falls, Freestone, Hamilton, Hill, Leon, Limestone, McLennan, Milam, Robertson, Somervell.

Utah
District of Utah

http://www.utd.uscourts.gov **Special access:** phone, PACER dial-up, PACER online. Clerk's Office, Room 150, 350 S Main St, Salt Lake City, UT 84101-2180 (physical address: same as mail address), 801-524-6100. **Counties:** All in Utah. Although all cases are heard here, the district is divided into Northern and Central Divisions. The Northern Division includes the counties of Box Elder, Cache, Rich, Davis, Morgan and Weber. Central Division is others.

Vermont
District of Vermont

http://www.vtd.uscourts.gov **Special access:** phone, PACER dial-up, or on the web.

-Burlington Div. Clerk's Office, PO Box 945, Burlington, VT 05402-0945 (physical address: Room 506, 11 Elmwood Ave, Burlington, VT 05401), 802-951-6301. **Counties:** Caledonia, Chittenden, Essex, Franklin, Grand Isle, Lamoille, Orleans, Washington. Cases from all counties are assigned randomly to either Burlington or Brattleboro. Brattleboro is a hearing location only, not listed here.

-Rutland Div. PO Box 607, Rutland, VT 05702-0607 (physical address: 151 West St, Rutland, VT 05701), 802-773-0245. **Counties:** Addison, Bennington, Orange, Rutland, Windsor, Windham. However, cases from all counties in the state are randomly assigned to either Burlington or Brattleboro. Rutland is a hearing location only, not listed here.

Virginia
Eastern District of Virginia

http://www.vaed.uscourts.gov **Special access:** phone, PACER dial-up, PACER online.

-Alexandria Div. 401 Courthouse Square, Alexandria, VA 22314 (physical address: same as mail address), 703-299-2100. **Counties:** Arlington, Fairfax, Fauquier, Loudoun, Prince William, Stafford, City of Alexandria, City of Fairfax, City of Falls Church, City of Manassas, City of Manassas Park.

-Newport News Div. Clerk's Office, PO Box 494, Newport News, VA 23607 (physical address: US Post Office Bldg, Room 201, 101 25th St, Newport News, VA 23607), 757-223-4600. **Counties:** Gloucester, James City, Mathews, York, City of Hampton, City of Newport News, City of Poquoson, City of Williamsburg.

-Norfolk Div. US Courthouse, Room 193, 600 Granby St, Norfolk, VA 23510 (physical address: same as mail address), 757-222-7204. **Counties:** Accomack, City of Chesapeake, City of Franklin, Isle of Wight, City of Norfolk,Northampton, City of Portsmouth, City of Suffolk, Southampton, City of Virginia Beach.

-Richmond Div. Lewis F Powell, Jr Courthouse Bldg, 1000 E Main St, Room 305, Richmond, VA 23219-3525 (physical address: same as mail address), 804-916-2200. **Counties:** Amelia, Brunswick, Caroline, Charles City, Chesterfield, Dinwiddie, Essex, Goochland, Greensville, Hanover, Henrico, King and Queen, King George, King William, Lancaster, Lunenburg, Mecklenburg, Middlesex, New Kent, Northumberland, Nottoway, City ofPetersburg, Powhatan, Prince Edward, Prince George, Richmond, City of Richmond, Spotsylvania, Surry, Sussex, Westmoreland, City of Colonial Heights, City of Emporia, City of Fredericksburg, City of Hopewell.

Western District of Virginia

http://www.vawd.uscourts.gov **Special access:** phone, fax, PACER dial-up, PACER online.

-Abingdon Div. Clerk's Office, PO Box 398, Abingdon, VA 24212 (physical address: 180 W Main St, Abingdon, VA 24210), 540-628-5116. **Counties:** Buchanan, City of Bristol, Russell, Smyth, Tazewell, Washington.

-Big Stone Gap Div. PO Box 490, Big Stone Gap, VA 24219 (physical address: 322 Wood Ave E, Room 203, Big Stone Gap, VA 24219), 540-523-3557. **Counties:** Dickenson, Lee, Scott, Wise, Norton City.

-Charlottesville Div. Clerk, Room 304, 255 W Main St, Charlottesville, VA 22902 (physical address: same as mail address), 804-296-9284. **Counties:** Albemarle, Culpeper, Fluvanna, Greene, Louisa, Madison, Nelson, Orange, Rappahannock, City of Charlottesville.

-Danville Div. PO Box 52, Danville, VA 24543-0053 (physical address: Dan Daniel Post Office Bldg, Room 202, 700 Main St, Danville, VA 24541), 804-793-7147. **Counties:** Charlotte, Halifax, Henry, Patrick, Pittsylvania, City of Danville, City of Martinsville, City of South Boston.

-Harrisonburg Div. Clerk, PO Box 1207, Harrisonburg, VA 22801 (physical address: Post Office Bldg, 116 N Main St, Room 314, Harrisonburg, VA 22801), 540-434-3181. **Counties:** Augusta, Bath, Clarke, Frederick, Highland, Page, Rockingham, Shenandoah, Warren, City of Harrisonburg, City of Staunton, City of Waynesboro, City of Winchester.

-Lynchburg Div. Clerk, PO Box 744, Lynchburg, VA 24505 (physical address: Room 212, 1100 Main St, Lynchburg, VA 24504), 804-847-5722. **Counties:** Amherst, Appomattox, Bedford, Buckingham, Campbell, Cumberland, Rockbridge, City of Bedford, City of Buena Vista, City of Lexington, City of Lynchburg.

-Roanoke Div. Clerk, PO Box 1234, Roanoke, VA 24006 (physical address: 210 Franklin Rd SW, Roanoke, VA 24011), 540-857-5100. **Counties:** Alleghany, Bland, Botetourt, Carroll, Craig, Floyd, Franklin, Giles, Grayson, Montgomery, Pulaski, Roanoke, Wythe, City of Covington, City of Clifton Forge, City of Galax, City of Radford, City of Roanoke, City of Salem.

Washington

Eastern District of Washington

http://www.waed.uscourts.gov **Special access:** PACER dial-up, PACER online.

-Spokane Div. PO Box 1493, Spokane, WA 99210-1493 (physical address: Room 840, W 920 Riverside, Spokane, WA 99201), 509-353-2150. **Counties:** Adams, Asotin, Benton, Chelan, Columbia, Douglas, Ferry, Franklin, Garfield, Grant, Lincoln, Okanogan, Pend Oreille, Spokane, Stevens, Walla Walla, Whitman. Some cases from Kittitas, Klickitat, Yakima.

-Yakima Div. PO Box 2706, Yakima, WA 98907 (physical address: Room 215, 25 S 3rd St, Yakima, WA 98901), 509-575-5838. **Counties:** Kittitas, Klickitat, Yakima. Cases assigned primarily to Judge McDonald are here. Some cases from Kittitas, Klickitat and Yakima are heard in Spokane.

Western District of Washington

http://www.wawd.uscourts.gov **Special access:** phone, PACER dial-up, PACER online, CM/ECF.

-Seattle Div. Clerk of Court, 215 US Courthouse, 1010 5th Ave, Seattle, WA 98104 (physical address: same as mail address), 206-553-5598. **Counties:** Island, King, San Juan, Skagit, Snohomish, Whatcom.

-Tacoma Div. Clerk's Office, Room 3100, 1717 Pacific Ave, Tacoma, WA 98402-3200 (physical address: same as mail address), 253-593-6313. **Counties:** Clallam, Clark, Cowlitz, Grays Harbor, Jefferson, Kitsap, Lewis, Mason, Pacific, Pierce,

Skamania, Thurston, Wahkiakum.

West Virginia

Northern District of West Virginia

http://www.wvnd.uscourts.gov **Special access:** phone, PACER dial-up, PACER online.

-Clarksburg Div. PO Box 2857, Clarksburg, WV 26302-2857 (physical address: 500 W Pike St, Rm 301, Clarksburg, WV 26301), 304-622-8513. **Counties:** Braxton, Calhoun, Doddridge, Gilmer, Harrison, Lewis, Marion, Monongalia, Pleasants, Ritchie, Taylor, Tyler.

-Elkins Div. PO Box 1518, Elkins, WV 26241 (physical address: 2nd Floor, 300 3rd St, Elkins, WV 26241), 304-636-1445. **Counties:** Barbour, Grant, Hardy, Mineral, Pendleton, Pocahontas, Preston, Randolph, Tucker, Upshur, Webster.

-Martinsburg Div. Room 207, 217 W King St, Martinsburg, WV 25401 (physical address: same as mail address), 304-267-8225. **Counties:** Berkeley, Hampshire, Jefferson, Morgan.

-Wheeling Div. Clerk, PO Box 471, Wheeling, WV 26003 (physical address: 12th & Chapline Sts, Wheeling, WV 26003), 304-232-0011. **Counties:** Brooke, Hancock, Marshall, Ohio, Wetzel.

Southern District of West Virginia

http://www.wvsd.uscourts.gov **Special access:** phone, fax, PACER dial-up, PACER online.

-Beckley Div. PO Drawer 5009, Beckley, WV 25801 (physical address: 110 N. Heber, Beckley, WV 25801), 304-253-7481. **Counties:** Fayette, Greenbrier, Raleigh, Sumners, Wyoming.

-Bluefield Div. Clerk's Office, PO Box 4128, Bluefield, WV 24701 (physical address: 601 Federal St, Bluefield, WV 24701), 304-327-9798. **Counties:** McDowell, Mercer, Monroe.

-Charleston Div. PO Box 3924, Charleston, WV 25339 (physical address: 300 Virginia St E, #24, Charleston, WV 25339), 304-347-3000. **Counties:** Boone, Clay, Jackson, Kanawha, Lincoln, Logan, Mingo, Nicholas, Putnam, Roane.

-Huntington Div. Clerk of Court, PO Box 1570, Huntington, WV 25716 (physical address: Room 101, 845 5th Ave, Huntington, WV 25701), 304-529-5588. **Counties:** Cabell, Mason, Wayne.

-Parkersburg Div. Clerk of Court, PO Box 1526, Parkersburg, WV 26102 (physical address: Room 5102, 425 Julianna St, Parkersburg, WV 26101), 304-420-6490. **Counties:** Wirt, Wood.

Wisconsin

Eastern District of Wisconsin

http://www.wied.uscourts.gov **Special access:** phone, PACER dial-up, PACER online, CM/ECF. Clerk's Office, Room 362, 517 E Wisconsin Ave, Milwaukee, WI 53202 (physical address: same as mail address), 414-297-3372. **Counties:** Brown, Calumet, Dodge, Door, Florence, Fond du Lac, Forest, Green Lake, Kenosha, Kewaunee, Langlade, Manitowoc, Marinette, Marquette, Menominee, Milwaukee, Oconto, Outagamie, Ozaukee, Racine, Shawano, Sheboygan, Walworth, Washington, Waukesha, Waupaca, Waushara, Winnebago.

Western District of Wisconsin

http://www.wiw.uscourts.gov **Special access:** phone, PACER dial-up, PACER online. PO Box 432, Madison, WI 53701 (physical address: 120 N Henry St, Madison, WI 53703), 608-264-5156. **Counties:** Adams, Ashland, Barron, Bayfield, Buffalo, Burnett, Chippewa, Clark, Columbia, Crawford, Dane, Douglas, Dunn, Eau Claire, Grant, Green, Iowa, Iron, Jackson, Jefferson, Juneau, La Crosse, Lafayette, Lincoln, Marathon, Monroe, Oneida, Pepin, Pierce, Polk,Portage, Price, Richland, Rock, Rusk, Sauk, Sawyer, St. Croix, Taylor, Trempealeau, Vernon, Vilas, Washburn, Wood.

Wyoming

District of Wyoming

http://www.ck10.uscourts.gov/wyoming/district **Special access:** PACER dial-up, PACER online. PO Box 727, Cheyenne, WY 82003 (physical address: Room 2131, 2120 Capitol Ave, Cheyenne, WY 82001), 307-772-2145. **Counties:** All in Wyoming. Some criminal records are held in Casper.

Section 5

Appendix

Appendix 1: State Charts

   - State Membership in Compacts

   - State Criminal Records - Required Data

   - Prohibited Access to State Criminal Records

Appendix 2: Fair Credit Reporting Act Summaries

Appendix 3: Title VII EEOC Notices

Appendix 1

State Membership in Compacts

There are three information sharing compacts that a state may participate in:
1. The Interstate Identification Index, or III. 2. The National Crime Prevention Compact.
3. National Fingerprint File, or NFF.
"X" indicates that state is a participating member.

State	III - Interstate ID Index	Nat. Crime Prevention Compact	NFF	State	III - Interstate ID Index	Nat. Crime Prevention Compact	NFF
Alabama	X			Missouri			
Alaska	X			Montana	X	X	
Arizona	X			Nebraska	X		
Arkansas	X			Nevada	X	X	
California	X			New Hampshire	X		
Colorado	X	X		New Jersey	X		X
Connecticut	X	X		New Mexico	X		
Delaware	X			New York	X		
Dist. of Columbia				North Carolina	X		X
Florida	X	X	X	North Dakota	X		
Georgia	X	X		Ohio	X		
Hawaii				Oklahoma	X		
Idaho	X			Oregon	X		X
Illinois	X			Pennsylvania	X		
Indiana	X			Rhode Island	X		
Iowa	X	X		South Carolina	X	X	
Kansas		X		South Dakota	X		
Kentucky				Tennessee			
Louisiana				Texas	X		
Maine		X		Utah	X		
Maryland				Vermont			
Massachusetts	X			Virginia	X		
Michigan	X			Washington	X		
Minnesota	X			West Virginia	X		
Mississippi	X			Wisconsin	X		
				Wyoming	X		

Appendix 1

State Criminal Records - Required Data

By state statute or agreement, certain data related to criminal records must be submitted for entry into the state central criminal records system.

"X" indicates that the data is required to be submitted to the state criminal records agency.

State	Prosecutor Declinations	Court felony dispositions w/ felony jurisdiction	Admission/ Release of felons - state prisons	Admission/ Release of felons - local jails	Probation Information	Parole information
Alabama		X	X	X		
Alaska	X	X	X	X	X	X
Arizona	X	X	X		X	X
Arkansas	X	X	X	X		X
California	X	X	X	X		X
Colorado		X			X	X
Connecticut		X	X	X	X	X
Delaware	X	X	X	X	X	X
Dist. of Columbia					X	X
Florida	X	X	X		X	X
Georgia	X	X	X		X	X
Hawaii		X			X	
Idaho		X	X	X	X	X
Illinois	X	X	X	X	X	X
Indiana		X	X			
Iowa	X	X	X			
Kansas	X	X	X		X	X
Kentucky	X	X				
Louisiana	X	X	X	X	X	
Maine	X	X				

State	Prosecutor Declinations	Court felony dispositions w/ felony jurisdiction	Admission/ Release of felons - state prisons	Admission/ Release of felons - local jails	Probation Information	Parole information
Maryland	X	X	X	X		
Massachusetts		X			X	X
Michigan	X	X	X		X	X
Minnesota	X	X	X	X	X	X
Mississippi	X	X	X	X	X	X
Missouri	X	X	X		X	X
Montana	X	X			X	
Nebraska	X	X	X	X	X	X
Nevada	X	X				
New Hampshire		X	X			
New Jersey	X	X	X	X	X	X
New Mexico			X	X		
New York	X	X	X	X	X	X
North Carolina	X	X	X		X	X
North Dakota	X	X	X	X	X	X
Ohio	X	X	X	X		
Oklahoma	X	X	X	X	X	X
Oregon		X				
Pennsylvania	X	X			X	X
Rhode Island	X	X				
South Carolina		X	X	X	X	
South Dakota	X	X	X	X	X	X
Tennessee	X	X	X		X	X
Texas	X	X				
Utah	X	X	X	X	X	X
Vermont		X			X	X
Virginia	X	X	X		X	X
Washington	X	X	X			
West Virginia		X	X			
Wisconsin		X	X	X	X	X
Wyoming	X	X	X	X	X	X

Appendix 1

Prohibited Access to State Criminal Records

"X" indicates that employers and employment screeners may not have access to arrest records (without convictions), misdemeanor records, and expunged or sealed records from the state criminal records agency.

Georgia and Massachusetts limit the use of first offense records. Hawaii will not release records over 10 years old. Massachusetts will not release records over 5 years old.

State	May prohibit employer access to arrest records	Prohibits employer access to misdemeanors	Access to expunged or sealed records prohibited
Alabama			
Alaska			
Arizona			
Arkansas			
California	X	X	X
Colorado			X
Connecticut			
Delaware			
Dist. of Columbia			
Florida			
Georgia			
Hawaii	X	X	X
Idaho			
Illinois	X		X
Indiana			
Iowa			
Kansas			
Kentucky			
Louisiana			
Maine			

State	May prohibit employer access to arrest records	Prohibits employer access to misdemeanors	Access to expunged or sealed records prohibited
Maryland			
Massachusetts	X	X	
Michigan	X		
Minnesota		X	
Mississippi			
Missouri			
Montana			
Nebraska			
Nevada	X		
New Hampshire			
New Jersey			
New Mexico			
New York	X	X	
North Carolina			
North Dakota			
Ohio			X
Oklahoma			X
Oregon			X
Pennsylvania	X		
Rhode Island	X		X
South Carolina			
South Dakota			
Tennessee			
Texas			X
Utah	X		
Vermont			
Virginia	X		X
Washington	X		
West Virginia			
Wisconsin	X		
Wyoming			

Appendix 2

Prescribed Summary of Consumer Rights Appendix A to Part 601

The prescribed form for this summary is as a separate document, on paper no smaller than 8x11 inches in size, with text no less than 12-point type (8-point for the chart of federal agencies), in bold or capital letters as indicated. The form in this appendix prescribes both the content and the sequence of items in the required summary. A summary may accurately reflect changes in numerical items that change over time (e.g., dollar amounts, or phone numbers and addresses of federal agencies), and remain in compliance.

A Summary of Your Rights Under the Fair Credit Reporting Act

The federal Fair Credit Reporting Act (FCRA) is designed to promote accuracy, fairness, and privacy of information in the files of every "consumer reporting agency" (CRA). Most CRAs are credit bureaus that gather and sell information about you -- such as if you pay your bills on time or have filed bankruptcy -- to creditors, employers, landlords, and other businesses. You can find the complete text of the FCRA, 15 U.S.C. 1681-1681u, at the Federal Trade Commission's web site (*http://www.ftc.gov*). The FCRA gives you specific rights, as outlined below. You may have additional rights under state law. You may contact a state or local consumer protection agency or a state attorney general to learn those rights.

- **You must be told if information in your file has been used against you.** Anyone who uses information from a CRA to take action against you -- such as denying an application for credit, insurance, or employment -- must tell you, and give you the name, address, and phone number of the CRA that provided the consumer report.

- **You can find out what is in your file.** At your request, a CRA must give you the information in your file, and a list of everyone who has requested it recently. There is no charge for the report if a person has taken action against you because of information supplied by the CRA, if you request the report within 60 days of receiving notice of the action. You also are entitled to one free report every twelve months upon request if you certify that (1) you are unemployed and plan to seek employment within 60 days, (2) you are on welfare, or (3) your report is inaccurate due to fraud. Otherwise, a CRA may charge you up to eight dollars.

- **You can dispute inaccurate information with the CRA.** If you tell a CRA that your file contains inaccurate information, the CRA must investigate the items (usually within 30 days) by presenting to its information source all relevant evidence you submit, unless your dispute is frivolous. The source must review your evidence and report its findings to the CRA. (The source also must advise national CRAs -- to which it has provided the data -- of any error.) The CRA must give you a written report of the investigation, and a copy of your report if the investigation results in any change. If the CRA's investigation does not resolve the dispute, you may add a brief statement to your file. The CRA must normally include a summary of your statement in future reports. If an item is deleted or a dispute statement is filed, you may ask that anyone who has recently received your report be notified of the change.

- **Inaccurate information must be corrected or deleted.** A CRA must remove or correct inaccurate or unverified information from its files, usually within 30 days after you dispute it. **However, the CRA is not required to remove accurate data from your file unless it is outdated (as described below) or cannot be verified.** If your dispute results in any change to your report, the CRA cannot reinsert into your file a disputed item unless the information source verifies its accuracy and completeness. In addition, the CRA must give you a written notice telling you it has reinserted the item. The notice must include the name, address and phone number of the information source.

- **You can dispute inaccurate items with the source of the information.** If you tell anyone -- such as a creditor who reports to a CRA -- that you dispute an item, they may not then report the information to a CRA without including a notice of your dispute. In addition, once you've notified the source of the error in writing, it may not continue to report the information if it is, in fact, an error.

- **Outdated information may not be reported.** In most cases, a CRA may not report negative information that is more than seven years old; ten years for bankruptcies.

- **Access to your file is limited.** A CRA may provide information about you only to people with a need recognized by the FCRA -- usually to consider an application with a creditor, insurer, employer, landlord, or other business.

- **Your consent is required for reports that are provided to employers, or reports that contain medical information.** A CRA may not give out information about you to your employer, or prospective employer, without your written consent. A CRA may not report medical information about you to creditors, insurers, or employers without your permission.

- **You may choose to exclude your name from CRA lists for unsolicited credit and insurance offers.** Creditors and insurers may use file information as the basis for sending you unsolicited offers of credit or insurance. Such offers must include a toll-free phone number for you to call if you want your name and address removed from future lists. If you call, you must be kept off the lists for two years. If you request, complete, and return the CRA form provided for this purpose, you must be taken off the lists indefinitely.

- **You may seek damages from violators.** If a CRA, a user or (in some cases) a provider of CRA data, violates the FCRA, you may sue them in state or federal court.

The FCRA gives several different federal agencies authority to enforce the FCRA:

FOR QUESTIONS OR CONCERNS REGARDING:	PLEASE CONTACT:
CRAs, creditors and others not listed below	Federal Trade Commission Consumer Response Center - FCRA Washington, DC 20580 202-326-3761
National banks, federal branches/agencies of foreign banks (word "National" or initials "N.A." appear in or after bank's name)	Office of the Comptroller of the Currency Compliance Management, Mail Stop 6-6 Washington, DC 20219 800-613-6743
Federal Reserve System member banks (except national banks, and federal branches/agencies of foreign banks)	Federal Reserve Board Division of Consumer & Community Affairs Washington, DC 20551 202-452-3693
Savings associations and federally chartered savings banks (word "Federal" or initials "F.S.B." appear in federal institution's name)	Office of Thrift Supervision Consumer Programs Washington, DC 20552 800-842-6929
Federal credit unions (words "Federal Credit Union" appear in institution's name)	National Credit Union Administration 1775 Duke Street Alexandria, VA 22314 703-518-6360
State-chartered banks that are not members of the Federal Reserve System	Federal Deposit Insurance Corporation Division of Compliance & Consumer Affairs Washington, DC 20429 800-934-FDIC
Air, surface, or rail common carriers regulated by former Civil Aeronautics Board or Interstate Commerce Commission	Department of Transportation Office of Financial Management Washington, DC 20590 202-366-1306
Activities subject to the Packers and Stockyards Act, 1921	Department of Agriculture Office of Deputy Administrator - GIPSA Washington, DC 20250 202-720-7051

Prescribed Notice of Furnisher Responsibilities Appendix B to Part 601

This appendix prescribes the content of the required notice.

NOTICES TO FURNISHERS OF INFORMATION: OBLIGATIONS OF FURNISHERS UNDER THE FCRA

The federal Fair Credit Reporting Act (FCRA), as amended, imposes responsibilities on all persons who furnish information to consumer reporting agencies (CRAs). These responsibilities are found in Section 623 of the FCRA. State law may impose additional requirements. All furnishers of information to CRAs should become familiar with the law and may want to consult with their counsel to ensure that they are in compliance. The FCRA, 15 U.S.C. 1681-1681u, is set forth in full at the Federal Trade Commission's Internet web site (*http://www.ftc.gov*). Section 623 imposes the following duties:

General Prohibition on Reporting Inaccurate Information:

The FCRA prohibits information furnishers from providing information to a consumer reporting agency (CRA) that they know (or consciously avoid knowing) is inaccurate. However, the furnisher is not subject to this general prohibition if it clearly and conspicuously specifies an address to which consumers may write to notify the furnisher that certain information is inaccurate. *Sections 623(a)(1)(A) and (a)(1)(C)*

Duty to Correct and Update Information:

If at any time a person who regularly and in the ordinary course of business furnishes information to one or more CRAs determines that the information provided is not complete or accurate, the furnisher must provide complete and accurate information to the CRA. In addition, the furnisher must notify all CRAs that received the information of any corrections, and must thereafter report only the complete and accurate information. *Section 623(a)(2)*

Duties After Notice of Dispute from Consumer:

If a consumer notifies a furnisher, at an address specified by the furnisher for such notices, that specific information is inaccurate, and the information is in fact inaccurate, the furnisher must thereafter report the correct information to CRAs. *Section 623(a)(1)(B)*

If a consumer notifies a furnisher that the consumer disputes the completeness or accuracy of any information reported by the furnisher, the furnisher may not subsequently report that information to a CRA without providing notice of the dispute. *Section 623(a)(3)*

Duties After Notice of Dispute from Consumer Reporting Agency:

If a CRA notifies a furnisher that a consumer disputes the completeness or accuracy of information provided by the furnisher, the furnisher has a duty to follow certain procedures. The furnisher must:

Conduct an investigation and review all relevant information provided by the CRA, including information given to the CRA by the consumer. *Sections 623(b)(1)(A) and (b)(1)(B)*

Report the results to the CRA, and, if the investigation establishes that the information was, in fact, incomplete or inaccurate, report the results to all CRAs to which the furnisher provided the information that compile and maintain files on a nationwide basis. *Sections 623(b)(1)(C) and (b)(1)(D)*

Complete the above within 30 days from the date the CRA receives the dispute (or 45 days, if the consumer later provides relevant additional information to the CRA). *Section 623(b)(2)*

Duty to Report Voluntary Closing of Credit Accounts:

If a consumer voluntarily closes a credit account, any person who regularly and in the ordinary course of business furnishes information to one or more CRAs must report this fact when it provides information to CRAs for the time period in which the account was closed. *Section 623(a)(4)*

Duty to Report Dates of Delinquencies:

If a furnisher reports information concerning a delinquent account placed for collection, charged to profit or loss, or subject to any similar action, the furnisher must, within 90 days after reporting the information, provide the CRA with the month and the year of the commencement of the delinquency that immediately preceded the action, so that the agency will know how long to keep the information in the consumer's file. *Section 623(a)(5)*

Prescribed Notice of User Responsibilities Appendix C to Part 601

This appendix prescribes the content of the required notice.

NOTICE TO USERS OF CONSUMER REPORTS: OBLIGATIONS OF USERS UNDER THE FCRA

The federal Fair Credit Reporting Act (FCRA) requires that this notice be provided to inform users of consumer reports of their legal obligations. State law may impose additional requirements. This first section of this summary sets forth the responsibilities imposed by the FCRA on all users of consumer reports. The subsequent sections discuss the duties of users of reports that contain specific types of information, or that are used for certain purposes, and the legal consequences of violations. The FCRA, 15 U.S.C. 1681-1681u, is set forth in full at the Federal Trade Commission's Internet web site (*http://www.ftc.gov*).

I. OBLIGATIONS OF ALL USERS OF CONSUMER REPORTS

A. Users Must Have a Permissible Purpose

Congress has limited the use of consumer reports to protect consumers' privacy. All users must have a permissible purpose under the FCRA to obtain a consumer report. Section 604 of the FCRA contains a list of the permissible purposes under the law. These are:

- As ordered by a court or a federal grand jury subpoena. *Section 604(a)(1)*

- As instructed by the consumer in writing. *Section 604(a)(2)*

- For the extension of credit as a result of an application from a consumer, or the review or collection of a consumer's account. *Section 604(a)(3)(A)*

- For employment purposes, including hiring and promotion decisions, where the consumer has given written permission. *Sections 604(a)(3)(B) and 604(b)*

- For the underwriting of insurance as a result of an application from a consumer. *Section 604(a)(3)(C)*

- When there is a legitimate business need, in connection with a business transaction that is initiated by the consumer. *Section 604(a)(3)(F)(i)*

- To review a consumer's account to determine whether the consumer continues to meet the terms of the account. *Section 604(a)(3)(F)(ii)*

- To determine a consumer's eligibility for a license or other benefit granted by a governmental instrumentality required by law to consider an applicant's financial responsibility or status. *Section 604(a)(3)(D)*

- For use by a potential investor or servicer, or current insurer, in a valuation or assessment of the credit or prepayment risks associated with an existing credit obligation. *Section 604(a)(3)(E)*

- For use by state and local officials in connection with the determination of child support payments, or modifications and enforcement thereof. *Sections 604(a)(4) and 604(a)(5)*

In addition, creditors and insurers may obtain certain consumer report information for the purpose of making unsolicited offers of credit or insurance. The particular obligations of users of this "prescreened" information are described in Section V below.

B. Users Must Provide Certifications

Section 604(f) of the FCRA prohibits any person from obtaining a consumer report from a consumer reporting agency (CRA) unless the person has certified to the CRA (by a general or specific certification, as appropriate) the permissible purpose(s) for which the report is being obtained and certifies that the report will not be used for any other purpose.

C. Users Must Notify Consumers When Adverse Actions Are Taken

The term "adverse action" is defined very broadly by Section 603 of the FCRA. "Adverse actions" include all business, credit, and employment actions affecting consumers that can be considered to have a negative impact -- such as unfavorably changing credit or contract terms or conditions, denying or canceling credit or insurance, offering credit on less favorable terms than requested, or denying employment or promotion.

1. Adverse Actions Based on Information Obtained From a CRA

If a user takes any type of adverse action that is based at least in part on information contained in a consumer report, the user is required by Section 615(a) of the FCRA to notify the consumer. The notification may be done in writing, orally, or by electronic means. It must include the following:

The name, address, and telephone number of the CRA (including a toll-free telephone number, if it is a nationwide CRA) that provided the report.

A statement that the CRA did not make the adverse decision and is not able to explain why the decision was made.

A statement setting forth the consumer's right to obtain a free disclosure of the consumer's file from the CRA if the consumer requests the report within 60 days.

A statement setting forth the consumer's right to dispute directly with the CRA the accuracy or completeness of any information provided by the CRA.

2. Adverse Actions Based on Information Obtained From Third Parties Who Are <u>Not</u> Consumer Reporting Agencies

If a person denies (or increases the charge for) credit for personal, family, or household purposes based either wholly or partly upon information from a person other than a CRA, and the information is the type of consumer information covered by the FCRA, Section 615(b)(1) of the FCRA requires that the user clearly and accurately disclose to the consumer his or her right to obtain disclosure of the nature of the information that was relied upon by making a written request within 60 days of notification. The user must provide the disclosure within a reasonable period of time following the consumer's written request.

3. Adverse Actions Based on Information Obtained From Affiliates

If a person takes an adverse action involving insurance, employment, or a credit transaction initiated by the consumer, based on information of the type covered by the FCRA, and this information was obtained from an entity affiliated with the user of the information by common ownership or control, Section 615(b)(2) requires the user to notify the consumer of the adverse action. The notification must inform the consumer that he or she may obtain a disclosure of the nature of the information relied upon by making a written request within 60 days of receiving the adverse action notice. If the consumer makes such a request, the user must disclose the nature of the information not later than 30 days after receiving the request. (Information that is obtained directly from an affiliated entity relating solely to its transactions or experiences with the consumer, and information from a consumer report obtained from an affiliate are not covered by Section 615(b)(2).)

II. OBLIGATIONS OF USERS WHEN CONSUMER REPORTS ARE OBTAINED FOR EMPLOYMENT PURPOSES

If information from a CRA is used for employment purposes, the user has specific duties, which are set forth in Section 604(b) of the FCRA. The user must:

> Make a clear and conspicuous written disclosure to the consumer before the report is obtained, in a document that consists solely of the disclosure, that a consumer report may be obtained.

> Obtain prior written authorization from the consumer.

> Certify to the CRA that the above steps have been followed, that the information being obtained will not be used in violation of any federal or state equal opportunity law or regulation, and that, if any adverse action is to be taken based on the consumer report, a copy of the report and a summary of the consumer's rights will be provided to the consumer.

Before taking an adverse action, provide a copy of the report to the consumer as well as the summary of the consumer's rights. (The user should receive this summary from the CRA, because Section 604(b)(1)(B) of the FCRA requires CRAs to provide a copy of the summary with each consumer report obtained for employment purposes.)

III. OBLIGATIONS OF USERS OF INVESTIGATIVE CONSUMER REPORTS

Investigative consumer reports are a special type of consumer report in which information about a consumer's character, general reputation, personal characteristics, and mode of living is obtained through personal interviews. Consumers who are the subjects of such reports are given special rights under the FCRA. If a user intends to obtain an investigative consumer report, Section 606 of the FCRA requires the following:

> The user must disclose to the consumer that an investigative consumer report may be obtained. This must be done in a written disclosure that is mailed, or otherwise delivered, to the consumer not later than three days after the date on which the report was first requested. The disclosure must include a statement informing the consumer of his or her right to request additional disclosures of the nature and scope of the investigation as described below, and must include the summary of consumer rights required by Section 609 of the FCRA. (The

user should be able to obtain a copy of the notice of consumer rights from the CRA that provided the consumer report.)

The user must certify to the CRA that the disclosures set forth above have been made and that the user will make the disclosure described below.

Upon the written request of a consumer made within a reasonable period of time after the disclosures required above, the user must make a complete disclosure of the nature and scope of the investigation that was requested. This must be made in a written statement that is mailed, or otherwise delivered, to the consumer no later than five days after the date on which the request was received from the consumer or the report was first requested, whichever is later in time.

IV. OBLIGATIONS OF USERS OF CONSUMER REPORTS CONTAINING MEDICAL INFORMATION

Section 604(g) of the FCRA prohibits consumer reporting agencies from providing consumer reports that contain medical information for employment purposes, or in connection with credit or insurance transactions, without the specific prior consent of the consumer who is the subject of the report. In the case of medical information being sought for employment purposes, the consumer must explicitly consent to the release of the medical information in addition to authorizing the obtaining of a consumer report generally.

V. OBLIGATIONS OF USERS OF "PRESCREENED" LISTS

The FCRA permits creditors and insurers to obtain limited consumer report information for use in connection with unsolicited offers of credit or insurance under certain circumstances. *Sections 603(l), 604(c), 604(e), and 615(d)* This practice is known as "prescreening" and typically involves obtaining a list of consumers from a CRA who meet certain pre-established criteria. If any person intends to use prescreened lists, that person must (1) before the offer is made, establish the criteria that will be relied upon to make the offer and to grant credit or insurance, and (2) maintain such criteria on file for a three-year period beginning on the date on which the offer is made to each consumer. In addition, any user must provide with each written solicitation a clear and conspicuous statement that:

- Information contained in a consumer's CRA file was used in connection with the transaction.

- The consumer received the offer because he or she satisfied the criteria for credit worthiness or insurability used to screen for the offer.

- Credit or insurance may not be extended if, after the consumer responds, it is determined that the consumer does not meet the criteria used for screening or any applicable criteria bearing on credit worthiness or insurability, or the consumer does not furnish required collateral.

The consumer may prohibit the use of information in his or her file in connection with future prescreened offers of credit or insurance by contacting the notification system established by the CRA that provided the report. This statement must include the address and toll-free telephone number of the appropriate notification system.

VI. OBLIGATIONS OF RESELLERS

Section 607(e) of the FCRA requires any person who obtains a consumer report for resale to take the following steps:

- Disclose the identity of the end-user to the source CRA.

- Identify to the source CRA each permissible purpose for which the report will be furnished to the end-user.

- Establish and follow reasonable procedures to ensure that reports are resold only for permissible purposes, including procedures to obtain:

    1. the identity of all end-users;

    2. certifications from all users of each purpose for which reports will be used; and

    3. certifications that reports will not be used for any purpose other than the purpose(s) specified to the reseller. Resellers must make reasonable efforts to verify this information before selling the report.

VII. LIABILITY FOR VIOLATIONS OF THE FCRA

Failure to comply with the FCRA can result in state or federal enforcement actions, as well as private lawsuits. *Sections 616, 617, and 621.* In addition, any person who knowingly and willfully obtains a consumer report under false pretenses may face criminal prosecution. *Section 619* .

For More Information About FCRA—

The Federal Trade Commission web site is filled with information, including Staff Opinion Letters, Educational Materials, and a complete copy of the act. Visit http://www.ftc.gov/os/statutes/fcrajump.htm

Appendix 3

Title VII EEOC Notices

The Appendix contains copies of four important notices written by the EEOC. These notices have set the bar so to speak on what an employer and cannot do with criminal records.

- Notice N-915.043 (July, 1989)
- Notice N-915-061 (9/7/90)
- Notice N-915 (7/29/87)
- Notice N-915 (2/4/87)

For more information about the EEOC, visit their web site at www.eeoc.gov.

Notice N-915.043 (July, 1989)

1. SUBJECT: Job advertising and Pre-Employment Inquiries Under the Age Discrimination In Employment Ace (ADEA).

2. PURPOSE: This policy guidance provides a discussion of job advertising and pre-employment inquiries under the ADEA. Additionally, certain defenses are discussed that may be proffered by respondents when impermissible practices appear to be involved.

3. EFFECTIVE DATE: Upon receipt.

4. EXPIRATION DATE: As an exception to EEOC Order 205.001, Appendix B, Attachment 4, § a(5), this Notice will remain in effect until rescinded or superseded.

5. ORIGINATOR: ADEA Division, Office of the Legal Counsel.

6. INSTRUCTIONS: File behind § 801 of Volume II of the Compliance Manual.

7. SUBJECT MATTER:

I. JOB ADVERTISING

A: GENERAL

The ADEA makes it unlawful, unless a specific exemption applies, for an employer to utilize job advertising that discriminates on account of age against persons 40 years of age or older. Specifically, sec. 4(e) of the ADEA provides as follows:

> It shall be unlawful for an employer, labor organization, or employment agency to print of publish, or cause to be printed or published, any notice or advertisement relating to employment by such an employer or membership in or any classification or referral for employment by such a labor organization, or relating to any classification or referral for employment by such an employment agency, indicating any preference, limitation, specification, or discrimination, based on age. 29 USC. § 623(e).

The commission interpretative regulation further develops the statutory language by providing the following guidance.

> When help wanted notices or advertisements contain terms and phrases such as "age 25 to 35," "young," "college student," "recent college graduate," "boy," "girl," or others of a similar nature, such a term or phrase a violation of the Act, unless one of the exceptions applies. Such phrases as "40 to 50," "age over 65," "retired persons," or "supplement your pension" discriminate against others within the protected group and, therefore, are prohibited unless one of the exceptions applies. 29 C.F.R. S 1625.4(a).

Former Secretary of Labor, Willard Wirtz, in his 1965 report to Congress on age discrimination in employment was among the first to recognize a need to carefully assess employers' job advertisements, to assure that older workers are not arbitrarily discriminated against.

> The most obvious kind of discrimination in employment takes the form of employer policies of not haring people over a certain age, without consideration of a particular applicant's individual qualifications. These restrictive practices appear in announced employer policies (e.g., in help-wanted advertisements; or in job orders filed with employment agencies) or in dealing with applicants when they appear in the hiring office.[1]

Congress responded to this concern, in part, by enacting sec. 4(e). Covered entities are limited by sec. 4(e) of the ADEA with respect to the content of their job notices and advertisements. They must be careful to avoid not only explicit age based limitations, but also advertisements that implicitly deter older persons from applying. For example, a "job description can exert a subtle form of discrimination by setting qualifications of education that are completely appropriate for the young employee and completely irrelevant for someone with 30 years experience."[2]

Although the language of sec. 4(e) is relatively straightforward, and judicial and Commission interpretations have added insight as to its application, generally there remains the need for a careful, case-by-case assessment as to whether a particular job advertisement runs afoul of sec. 4(e). The analysis requires an examination not only of the language used in the advertisement but also the context in which it is used to determine whether persons in the protected age group would be discouraged from applying.

In Hodgson v. Approved Personnel Service Inc., 529 F.2d 760 (4th Cir. 1975), the court examined over fifty advertisements published by the defendant, an employment agency. The court held that some of the advertisements violated the ADEA while others did not. The defendant's advertisements used such words and phrases as: "recent college graduate." "those unable to continue in college," "1-2 years out of college," "excellent first job," "any recent degree," "recent high school grad," "young executive," recent technical school grad," "junior secretary," "junior accountant," "athletically inclined," "career girls," "young office group," and "all American type."

The court's analysis of each phrase involved close scrutiny of the advertisement in its entirety to determine whether sec. 4(e) had been violated. Specifically the court stated, "we are inclined to think that the discriminatory effect of an advertisement is determined no solely by "trigger words" but rather

---

[1] *The Older American Worker, Age Discrimination In Employment, Report of the Secretary of Labor to the Congress Under Section 715 of the Civil Rights Act of 1964,* 6 (1965)
[2] *Improving The Age Discrimination Law: A Working Paper, Senate Special Committee on Aging,* 93d Cong., 1st Sess. 6 (1973).

by its context."[3]   In order to determine from its context whether the advertisement is in fact discriminatory, one must read the ad in its entirety, taking into consideration the results of the ad on the employer's hiring practices. The mere presence of "trigger words: does not constitute a violation of the ADEA.

Those words and phrases found by the <u>Hodgson</u> court not to violate the ADEA are as follows: 1) "young executive seeks," refers to the age of the employer and does not state an age requirement for job applicants or suggest that older persons will not be considered; 2) "young office group," certainly carries an implication that an older person might not fit in but it tells the older applicant something he may want to know: that those already employed who will be his work associates are young; 3) "Athletically inclined" or "all American type," state qualifications relating to personal appearance and physical characteristics which can exist in persons at any age; 4) "junior," this adjective when applied to an employee's job description designates the scope of his duties and responsibilities. And does not carry connotations of youth prohibited by the Act; <u>Hodgson</u> at page 767 (Appendix). Of course, in a different context, the outcome with respect to any of the foregoing words and phrases might be different. As stated in the text, a case-by-case fact specific analysis is always required.

Read in context, "trigger words" may be innocent in some advertisements and clearly discriminatory in others. <u>Hodgson</u> at 765. The above concepts are demonstrated by the following examples.

> <u>EXAMPLE 1</u> = CP, a 65 year old, saw an ad in the newspaper for a cashier at a local supermarket ®. R's advertisement specified that "applicant must be young, energetic, and posses excellent customer relations skills. Applicants who are selected would be required to stand long periods of time and to lift 20-30 pounds." CP contacted the Commission to institute a charge against R, local supermarket. In this case the Commission would find a violation. By use of the word "young" the ad specifically indicates a preference, limitation, specification or discrimination based on age. Such an ad would almost certainly deter many qualified older persons from applying. Note that if the same ad appeared with only the word "young" deleted, it would probably be acceptable. Persona of all ages can be energetic and possess excellent customer relations skills. Further, the need to stand for long periods and to lift 20-30 pounds are not age related criteria and, in any event, appear to be legitimate requirements for the job in question.

> <u>EXEMPLE 2</u> – CP, a 57 year old graphic artist, claims that R, Advertising Firm, has discriminated against him based on age by publishing an advertisement which he feels clearly deters older persons from applying. R's ad stated, "Young-thinking, 'new wave' progressive advertising firm has openings for entry level position for graphic artist with no more than 3 years experience. We specialize in music videos and broadcast productions for a youthful audience. Our main focus is in the area of animation. Our clients include famous rock stars. If you have fresh, innovative ideas, and can relate to our audience, send your resume." While the ad does not contain explicit age limitations, read in its entirety, it does appear that persons in the protected age group would be discouraged from applying for the position. The employer contends that it does not discriminate against older persons and would hire a 75 year old applicant if he or she is qualified and willing to work for an entry level salary. However, on further investigation it was found that the employer has no employees over 30 years of age. It was also revealed that the firm recently turned down two

---

[3] *Hodgson v. Approved Personnel Serv.* At 765.

fully qualified graphic artists X and Y, ages 47 and 67, who were willing to work at an entry level salary, though both possessed more that 3 years of experience. In this context the Commission would probably take the position that the ad is designed to deter older persons from applying. The Commission would seek to have R change the ad to read "young-thinking persons of any age with at least 3 years experience and willing to work at an entry level salary." The Commission would also attempt to contact X and Y to investigate the circumstances surrounding the denial of employment for the advertised position. The Commission has provided further specific guidance for investigating such incidents of "subtle" discriminatory advertising. See Volume I, Investigative Procedures Manual, § 8.6(b)(3)(i).

As indicated in sec. 1625.4(a), younger persons in the protected age group, for example, those individuals older than 40 but not old enough to retire, may be victimized by job advertising favoring older persons within the protected age group. The following example illustrates how this situation may occur.

EXAMPLE 3 – CP, a 42 year old individual who is actively seeking part-time employment, contends that she was deterred from applying for a position because of the employer's ad. R, a local Laundromat, advertised in the newspaper as follows: "Opening for a person seeking to supplement pension. Part-time position available for Laundromat Attendant from 9:00 am – 2:00 PM, Monday-Thursday. Responsibilities include dispensing products sold on premises, maintaining washer, dryer, and vending machines. Retired persons preferred." This ad limits the applicant pool by indicating a preference based on age. Persons rarely receive pensions or attain retirement status before 55 and frequently not until age 65. Thus, the ad deters younger persons within the protected age group from applying. Therefore it is a violation of sec. 4(e) unless one of the exceptions to the Act applies.

Note, however, that the Commission would be unlikely to find a violation in situations where an age-neutral advertisement encourages individuals within the protected age group to actively seek the position(s) available.[4]

EXEMPLE 4 – In response to a acute labor shortage that exists throughout the southeast region of the country, R, a large home improvement chain publishes the following advertisement:

WANTED; Individuals of all ages. Day and evening hours available. Full and part-time positions. All inquiries welcomed. Excellent secondary source of income for retirees.

While the ad mentions "retirees," the Commission would not find an illegal age-based discriminatory advertising practice in this instance. Individuals of all ages are welcomed for the employment opportunity. The reference to retirees in the ad does not, on its face, indicate a preference for this sub-grouping of the protected age group. Rather, it notifies them of an opportunity and invites them to

---

[4] Section 2(b) of the ADEA states in pertinent part that "[I]t is therefore the purpose of this Act to promote employment of older persons based on their ability rather than age." See also EEOC Opinion Letter – 1, December 13, 1983 (ADEA rights of retirees).

participate. The language in this ad differs from the language used in Example 3 which suggests that only retired, pension eligible persons are considered for employment.

B. EMPLOYMENT AGENCY ADVERTISEMENTS

Some courts have fashioned an exception to the general rules when the advertising in question is done by an employment agency and is intended to acquaint persons with the agency's services.[5] The Hodgson court held that when employment agencies use such phrases as "recent grad," or others of a similar nature to appeal acquaint such individuals with the agency's services, the ADEA is not violated. However, such an advertisement would seem to clearly indicate a preference, limitation, specifications, or discrimination based on age which is prohibited by the ADEA. The Commission, therefore, would not agree with the exception fashioned in the Hodgson decision. As a general enforcement principle, the Commission will closely scrutinize all ads that use words and phrases that would deter older persons from applying, including those used by employment agencies to inform the public of their services. An employment agency could as easily advertise generally for persons looking for employment by including in the advertisement language making it clear that both young and older applicants are wanted.[6]

In summary, a careful analysis of job advertising practices, whether by an employer or employment agency, is required in determining whether a violation of sec. 4(e) of the ADEA has occurred. If an ADEA charge/complaint raises the issue of an illegal age-based discriminatory advertising practice the following analytical scheme of investigation is suggested.

In some instances an advertisement may use a term or phrase which is listed in 29 C.F.R. § 1625.4(a). If an employer or employment agency resorts to the use of such terminology the advertising practice is per se illegal and a finding of a violation of sec. 4(e) of the ADEA is warranted, unless an exception (e.g., BFOQ) applies.

In many cases, however, the challenged advertisement will not contain direct age-based prohibited specifications or preferences and as such the legality of the advertising practice will depend upon the overall context, application and effect of discouraging individuals within the protected age group from applying or, in the alternative, generally limits, classifies or otherwise discriminates against an individual based on age. Specific attention in such instances should be given but not limited to charging party's/complainant's (1) explanation of why the ad served to discourage him or her from applying; (2) respondent's overall hiring practices, or; (3) a comparative analysis of respondent's applicant flow data with similar size employers using nondiscriminatory advertising practices. See generally Volume I, Investigative Procedures Manual, § 8.6(b)(3)(i)(ii).

C. BONA FIDE OCCUPATIONAL QUALIFICAITON DEFENSE

---

[5] See Hodgson at 766.

[6] C. Edelman & I. Sigler, Federal Age Discrimination in Employment Law, Slowing Down the Gold Watch, 96 (1978). The Commission, for example, would encourage the use of such phrases as "state of the art knowledge" in lieu of "recent college graduate" or recommend to employment agencies the use of a specific disclaimer such as, "While we are skilled in assisting recent grads in finding positions, we encourage applicants of all ages and levels of experience – neither this agency nor any of our clients discriminate on the basis of an applicant's age."

Where an ad is per se discriminatory on the basis of age, a respondent may seek to invoke the :bona fide occupational qualification" defense, hereinafter referred to as "BFOQ," to justify the use of the ad.[7] If, because of the requirements of a job, an employer believes it must limit, specify, or discriminate based on age, an employer has the burden of proving that the position is a BFOQ.[8]

There are several elements which must be met in establishing a BFOQ defense. Whenever this defense is raised an employer must always show that :the age limit is reasonably necessary to the essence of the business."[9] In proving that age must be used as a proxy for ability to perform the job, an employer must next show that either "all or substantially all individuals excluded from the job are in fact disqualified,"[10] or "some of the individuals so excluded possess a disqualifying trait that cannot be ascertained except by reference to age."[11]

Unless the employer can establish the existence of a BFOQ, the ad would have to be modified to eliminate any limitations based upon age.

EXAMPLE 5 – CP, a 43 year old fashion model, contends that she has been discriminated against based on age. R, a modeling agency, advertised in the newspaper as follows:" Experienced models between 20-30 for upcoming spring collection of 'junior sportswear.' Applicants must bring a portfolio and references to our New York Office. Only those persons in the specified age category need apply." CP auditioned and was rejected when the company found out her age. During the investigation, R raises the BFOQ defense and states that the "junior collection requires applicants who have a youthful appearance. R further alleges that traditionally the "junior" fashions are targeted to younger women, generally between 20-30. However, while CP is 43, she appears to be 23. In fact, R was in the process of completing the paperwork necessary to hire CP when its personnel manager noticed the date of birth on her driver's license. R is not able to prove that persons 40 or older have a disqualifying trait that cannot be ascertained except by reference to age. R has not established the existence of a BFOQ and its discriminatory ad must be changed. R has also violated the Act by its failure to hire CP on account of her age.

In sum, the employer has the burden of proving a bona fide occupational qualification. The Commission and the courts construe this defense very narrowly. If, however, the employer satisfies the requirements of the exemption, it can continue to express appropriate age limitations in its job ads.

II. PRE-EMPLOYMENT INQUIRIES

Pursuant to sec. 4(a)(1) of the ADEA, 29 U. S. C. § 623(A)(1), "[I]t shall be unlawful for an employer to fail or refuse to hire or to discharge any individual or otherwise discriminate against any individual with respect to his compensation, terms, conditions, or privileges of employment, because of such individual's age." Although it is almost always unlawful to make employment decisions based on age,

---

[7] Section 4(f)(l) of the ADEA permits an employer "to take any action otherwise prohibited under subsection (a), (b), (c), or (e) of this section where age is a bona fide occupational qualification reasonably necessary to the normal operation of the particular business."

[8] 29 C.F.R.S 1625.6(b)

[9] 29 C.F.R. S 1625.6(b)(3)

[10] 29 C.F.R.S 1625.6(b)(2)

[11] 29 C.F.R. S 1625.6(b)(1)

a pre-employment inquiry on the part of an employer for information such as "Date of Birth" or :State Age" on an application form is not, in itself, a violation of the ADEA.

However, because the request that an applicant state his age may tend to deter older applicants from applying, pre-employment inquires which request such information will be closely scrutinized by the Commission to assure that the request is for a permissible purpose and not for a purpose proscribed by the Act. There must be legitimate, non-discriminatory reasons for seeking the information and the information must not be used for an impermissible purpose.

The Commission has addressed the issue of pre-employment inquiries concerning age in two separate provisions. The first provision, 29 C.F.R. § 1625.4(b), Specifically addresses requests in help-wanted notices or advertisements for age or date of birth. The Commission's position in regard to help-wanted notices and advertisements is that although inquiries regarding age will be closely scrutinized, such inquiries are not per se violations of the Act.

The second provision, 29 C.F.R. § 1625.5, focuses on requests for age on employment application forms. The Commission regulation at 29 C.F.R. § 1625.5 provides in part:

> A request on the art of an employer for information such as "Date of Birth" or "State Age" on an application form is not, in itself, a violation of the Act. But because the request that an applicant state his age may tend to deter older applicants or otherwise discriminate based on age, employment application forms which request such information will be closely scrutinized to assure that the request is for a permissible purpose and not for purposes proscribed by the Act. That the purpose is not one proscribed by the statute should be made known to the applicant. The term "employment applications" refers to all written inquiries about employment or application for employment or promotion including, but not limited to, resumes or other summaries of the applicant's background. It relates not only to written pre-employment inquiries, but to inquiries concerning terms, conditions, or privileges of employment as specified in section 4 of the Act.

The purpose of section 1625.5 is to insure that older applicants are judged on ability rather than age. To assure applicants in the protected age group that an inquiry as to age is for a permissible purpose, employers should include a reference on the application form stating that the employer does not discriminate on the basis of age. Another option would be to explain to each applicant the specific reason why the information concerning age is being requested. Most importantly, of course, employers must not use age related inquiries for an impermissible purpose.

EXAMPLE 6 – CP, a 55 year old radio announcer, sent a resume to R, WZAB, for the position of Program Director. WZAB's format is "hard rock." R responded by forwarding CP an employment application and scheduling an interview. The application requested CP to state his age, and also stated the statutory prohibition against age discrimination in employment. At the interview CP was introduced to the staff, all of whom appeared to be between the ages of 18 and 35. During the interview, CP discussed his past experience and talked at length about how the radio business had changed since he had begun his career. R asked CP if he would be opposed to having a younger supervisor and whether or not CP enjoyed working with younger people. Two days lager CP received a rejection letter from R. CP alleges that he was discriminated against based on age. It was later found that X, a 23 year old who was hired for the position of Program Director, did not submit an application and no inquiry was made as to her age. This evidence conflicted with R's statement that it was a standard practice to ascertain the age of all applicants. Despite the presence of the statutory prohibition against age discrimination on the application form, it would appear that in this particular instance, the inquiry about age was not applied uniformly and was used only to disqualify CP. Thus, even if an employer sets forth the statutory prohibition against age discrimination on the application form, when an age related inquiry is challenged, the employer must show that it has legitimate non-discriminatory reasons for seeking the information.

III. CASE RESOLUTION

The Commission's position is that employment related inquiries requesting an applicant's age or date of birth will be closely scrutinized on a case-by-case basis to assure that they are for a lawful purpose.

Pre-employment inquiries as to age which are used for the purpose of disqualifying persons in the protected age group are prohibited. When the employer's inquiry does not serve any legitimate purpose, or the practice is not uniformly adhered to, it is quite likely that the information is being sought for purposes proscribed by the ADEA.[12]13

[Signed by Clarence Thomas on 07-02-89]

Date: _____   Signed:_____

                                                      Clarence Thomas

                                                      Chairman

---

[12]The ADEA principles and the BFOQ defense discussed in the text apply equally to Title VII. See, e.g., 29 C.F.R. S 1604.7. It should be noted, however, that the BFOQ defense under Title VII is limited to religion, sex, and national origin.

Notice N-915-061 (9/7/90)

1. SUBJECT: Policy Guidance on the Consideration of Arrest Records in Employment Decisions under Title VII of the Civil Rights Act of 1964, as amended, 42 USC. § 2000e et seq. (1982).

2. PURPOSE: This policy guidance sets forth the Commission's procedure for determining whether arrest records may be considered in employment decisions.

3. EFFECTIVE DATE: September 7, 1990.

4. EXPIRATION DATE: As an exception to EEOC Order 205.001, Appendix B, Attachment 4, § a(5), this Notice will remain in effect until rescinded or superseded.

5. ORIGINATOR: Title VII/EPA Division, Office of the Legal Counsel.

6. INSTRUCTIONS: File behind the last Policy Guidance § 604 of Volume II of Compliance Manual.

7. SUBJECT MATTER:

I. Introduction

The question addressed in this policy guidance is "to what extent may arrest records be used in making employment decisions?" The Commission concludes that since the use of arrest records as a absolute bar to employment has a disparate impact on some protected groups, such records alone cannot be used to routinely exclude persons from employment. However, conduct which indicates unsuitability for a particular position is a basis for exclusion. Where it appears that the applicant or employee engaged in the conduct for which he was arrested and that the conduct is job-related and relatively recent, exclusion is justified.

The analysis set forth in this policy guidance is related to two previously issued policy statements regarding the consideration of conviction records in employment decisions: "Policy Statement on the Issue of Conviction Records under Title VII of the Civil Rights Act of 1964, as amended 42 U.S.C. § 2000e et seq. (1982)" (hereinafter referred to as the February 4, 1987 Statement) and "Policy Statement on the use of statistics in charges involving the exclusion of individuals with conviction records from employment" (hereinafter referred to ad July 29, 1987 Statement). The February 4, 1987 Statement states that nationally, Blacks and Hispanics are convicted in numbers which are disproportionate to Whites and that barring people from employment based on their conviction records will therefore disproportionately exclude those groups.[1] Due to this adverse impact, an employer may not base an employment decision on the conviction record of an applicant

---

[1] The July 29 Statement notes that despite national statistics showing adverse impact, an employer may refute this prima facie showing by presenting statistics which are specific to its region or applicant pool. If these statistics demonstrate that the policy has no adverse impact against a protected group, the plaintiff's prima facie case has been rebutted and the employer need not show any business necessity to justify the use of the policy. Statistics relating to arrests should be used in the same manner.

or an employee absent business necessity.[2] Business necessity can be established where the employee or applicant is engaged in conduct which is particularly egregious or related to the position in question.

Conviction records constitute reliable evidence that a person engaged in the conduct alleged since the criminal justice system requires the highest degree of proof ("beyond a reasonable doubt") for a conviction. In contract, arrests alone are not reliable evidence that a person has actually committed a crime. Schware v. Board of Bar Examiners, 353 US 232, 241 (1957) ("[t]he mere fact that a [person] has been arrested has very little, if any, probative value in showing that he has engaged in misconduct.") Thus, the Commission concludes that to justify the use of arrest records, an additional inquiry must be made. Even where the conduct alleged in the arrest record is related to the job at issue, the employer must evaluate whether the arrest record reflects the applicant's conduct. It should, therefore, examine the surrounding circumstances, offer the applicant or employee an opportunity to explain, and, if he or she denies engaging in the conduct, make the follow-up inquiries necessary to evaluate his/her credibility. Since using arrests as a disqualifying criteria can only be justified where it appears that the applicant actually engaged in the conduct for which he/she was arrested and that conduct is job related, the Commission further concludes that an employer will seldom be able to justify making broad general inquiries about an employee's or applicant's arrests.

The following discussion is offered for guidance in determining the circumstances under which an employer can justify excluding an applicant or an employee on the basis of an arrest record.

II. Discussion

A. Adverse Impact of the Use of Arrest Records

The leading case involving an employer's use of arrest records is Gregory v. Litton Systems, 316 F. Supp. 401, 2 EPD ¶ 10,264 (C.D. Cal. 1970), modified on other grounds, 472 F.2d 631, 5 EPD ¶ 8089 (9th Cir. 1972). Litton held that nationally, Blacks are arrested more often than are Whites. Courts and the Commission have relied on the statistics presented in Litton to establish a prima facie case of discrimination against Blacks where arrest records are used in employment decisions.[3] There are, however, more recent statistics, published by the US Department of Justice, Federal Bureau of

---

[2] The policy statements on convictions use the term "business necessity," as used by courts prior to the Supreme Court's decision in Wards Cove Packing Co. v. Atonio, 109 S. Ct. 2115 (1989). In Atonio, the Supreme Court adopted the term "business justification" in place of business necessity, but noted that "although we have phrased the query differently in different cases...the dispositive issue is whether a challenged practice serves, in a significant way, the legitimate employment goals of the employer, "citing, inter alia, Griggs v. Duke Power Co., 401 US 424 (1971). 109 S. Ct. at 2125-2126.

[3] US v. City of Chicago, 385 F. Supp. 543, 556-557 (N.D. Ill. 1974), adopted by reference, 411 F. Supp. 218, aff'd in rel. part, 549 F.2d 415, 432 (7th Cir. 1977); City of Cairo v. Illinois Fair Employment Practice Commission, et al., 8 EPD ! 9682 (Ill. App. Ct. 1974); Commission Decision Nos. 78-03, 77-23, 76-138, 76-87, 76-39, 74-92, 74-90, 74-83, 74-02, CCH EEOC Decisions (1983) !! 6714, 6710, 6700, 6665, 630, 6424, 6423, 6414, 6386 and Commission Decisions Nos. 72-1460, 72-1005, 72-094 and 71-1950, CCH EEOC Decisions (1973) !! 6341, 6357 and 6274 respectively.

Investigation, which are consistent with the <u>Litton</u> finding.[4] It is desirable to use the most current available statistics. In addition, where local statistics are available, it may be helpful to use them, as the court did in <u>Reynolds v. Sheet Metal Workers Local 102</u>, 498 F. Supp. 952, 22 EPD ¶ 30,739 (D.C. 1980), <u>aff'd.</u>, 702 F.2d 221, 25 EPD ¶ 31,706 (D.C. Cir. 1981). In <u>Reynolds,</u> the court found that the use of arrest records in employment decisions adversely affected Blacks since the 1978 Annual Report of the Metropolitan Police of Washington, D.C., stated that 85.5% of persons arrested in the District of Columbia were nonwhite while the nonwhite population constituted 72.4% of the total population. 498 F. Supp. At 960. The Commission has determined that Hispanics are also adversely affected by arrest record inquiries. Commission Decisions Nos. 77-23 and 76-03, CCH EEIC Decisions (1983) ¶¶ 6714 and 6598, respectively.[5] However, the courts have not yet addressed this issue[6] and the FBI's Uniform Crime Reporting Program does not provide information on the arrest records (see July 29, 1987 Statement), the employer may rebut by presenting statistics which are more current, accurate and/or specific to its region or applicant pool than are the statistics presented in the <u>prima facie</u> case.

B. Business Justification

If adverse impact is established, the burden of producing evidence shifts to the employer to show a business justification for the challenged employment practice. <u>Wards Cove Packing Co. v. Atonio</u>, 109 S.Ct. 2115, 2126 (1989).[7] As with conviction records, arrest records may be considered in the employment decision as evidence of conduct which may render an applicant unsuitable for a particular position. However, in the case of arrests, not only must the employer consider the relationship of the charges to the position sought, but also the likelihood that the applicant actually committed the conduct alleged in the charges. <u>Gregory v. Litton Systems</u>, 316 F. Supp. 401; <u>Carter</u>

---

[4] The FBI's Uniform Crime Reporting Program reported that in 1987, 29.5% of all arrests were of Blacks. The US. Census reported that Blacks comprised 11.7% of the national population in 1980 and projected that the figure would reach 12.2% in 1987. Since the national percentage of arrest for Blacks is more that twice the percentage of their representation in the population (whether considering the 1980 figures or the 1987 projections), the <u>Litton</u> presumption of adverse impact, at least nationally, is still valid.

[5] The statistics presented in Decision No. 77-23 pertain only to prison populations in the Southwestern United States. This data would, therefore, probably not constitute a <u>prima facie</u> case of discrimination for other regions of the country. In fact, there is no case law to indicate whether courts would accept this data as evidence of adverse impact for arrest records, even for cases arising in the Southwest, since all arrests do not result in incarceration. Decision No. 76-03 noted that Hispanics are arrested more frequently that are Whites, but no statistics were presented to support this statement.

[6] <u>Cf.</u> <u>EEOC v. Carolina Freight Carriers</u>, 723 F. Supp. 734, 751, 52 EPD ¶ 39, 538 (S.D. Fla. 1989) (EEOC failed to provide statistics for the relevant labor market to prove that trucking company's exclusion of drivers with, convictions for theft crimes had an adverse impact on Hispanics at a particular job site).

[7]Under <u>Atonio</u>, the burden of producing evidence shifts to the employer, but the burden of persuasion remains with the plaintiff at all stages of the Title VII case. 109 S.Ct. at 2116. <u>Atonio</u> thus modifies <u>Griggs</u> and its progeny.

v. Gallagher, 452 F.2d 315, 3 EPD ¶ 8335 (8th Cir. 1971), cert. Denied, 406 U.S. 950, 4 EPD ¶ 7818 (1972); Reynolds v. Sheet Metal Workers Local 102, 498 F. Supp. 952; Dozier v. Chupka, 395 F. Supp. 836 (D.C. Ohio 1975); US. V. City of Chicago, 411 F. Supp. 218 (N.D. Ill. 1974), aff'd. in rel. part, 549 F.2d 415 (7th Cir. 1977); City of Cairo v. Illinois Fair Employment Practice Commission et al., 8 EPD ¶ 9682 (Ill. App. Ct. 1974); Commission Decisions Mos. 78-03, 77-23, 76-138, 76-87, 76-54, 76-39, 76-17, 74-92, 74-83, 76-03, 74-90, 78093, 74025, CCH EEOC Decisions (1983) ¶¶ 6714, 6710, 6700, 6665, 6639, 630, 612, 6424, 6414, 6598, 6423, 6400 and Commission Decisions Nos. 72-0947, 72-1005, 72-1460, CCH EEOC Decisions (1973) ¶¶ 6357, 6350 and 6341, respectively.

1. A Business Justification Can Rarely Be Demonstrated for Blanket Exclusions on the Basis of Arrest Records

Since business justification rests on issues of job relatedness and credibility, a blanket exclusion of people with arrest records will almost never withstand scrutiny. Gregory v. Litton Systems, 316 F. Supp. 401. Litton held that employer's policy of refusing to hire anyone who had been arrested "on a number of occasions" violated Title VII because the policy disproportionately excluded Blacks from consideration and was not justified by business necessity. In Litton, an applicant for a position as a sheet metal worker was disqualified because of this arrest record. The court found no business necessity because the employer had failed to establish a business necessity for its discriminatory policy, it was enjoined from basing future hiring decisions on arrest records. Accord Carter v. Gallagher, 452 F.2d 315 (firefighter); Dozier v. Chupka, 395 F. Supp. 836 (firefighter); City of Cairo v Illinois Fair Employment Practice Commission, et al, 8 EPD ¶ 9682 (police officer).

The Commission has consistently invalidated employment policies which create a blanket exclusion of persons with arrest records. Commission Decision Nos. 78-03, 76-87, 76-39, 76-17, 76-03, 74-90, 74-25, 72-0947, 72-1005, CCH EEOC Decisions (1983) ¶¶ 6714 (laborer), 6665 (police officer), 6630 (cashier), 6612 (credit collector), 6598 (catalogue clerk), 6423 (uniformed guard commissioned by police department), 6400 (firefighter), 6357 (line worker) and 6350 (warehouse worker or driver). In several decisions, it appears that the arrest record inquiry was made on a standard company application which was used by the employer to fill various positions and there was no mention of any particular position sought. Commission Decision Nos. 76-138, 76-54, 74-82, 74-83, 74-02 and 72-1460, CCH EEOC Decisions (1983) ¶¶ 6700, 639, 6424, 6414, 6386 and 6341 and Commission Decision No. 71-1950, CCH EEOC Decisions (1973) ¶ 6274, respectively. An employer may not routinely exclude persons with arrest records based on the assumption that an arrest record will prevent an applicant from obtaining necessary credentials to perform a job without giving the applicant an opportunity to obtain those credentials. For example, in Decision 76-87, the Commission rejected an employer's assertion that employees' arrest records might hinder its ability to maintain fidelity (bond) insurance since it offered no proof to this effect.

Even where there is no direct evidence that an employer used an arrest record in an employment decision, a pre-employment inquiry regarding arrest records may violate Title VII. It is generally presumed that an employer only asks questions which he/she deems relevant to the employment decision. Gregory v. Litton Systems, 316 F. Supp. At 403-404. Noting that information which is obtained is likely to be used, the court in Litton enjoined the employer from making any pre-employment inquiries regarding arrests which did not result in convictions. Id.[8] But see EEOC f.

---

[8] Furthermore, potential applicants who have arrest records may be discouraged from applying for positions which require them to supply this information, thus creating a "chilling effect" on the

Local 638, 532 F.2d 821 (2d Cir. 1976) (inquiry not invalidated where there was no evidence that union actually rejected applicants who had been arrested but not convicted); Jimerson v. Kisco, 404 F. Supp. 338 (E.D. Mo. 1975) (court upheld discharge for falsifying information regarding arrest record on a pre-employment application without considering the inquiry itself violated Title VII).[9] Numerous states have specifically prohibited or advised against pre-employment inquiries in their fair employment laws due to the possible misuse of this information.[10]

2. The Alleged Conduct Must Be Related to the Position Sought

As discussed above, an arrest record may be used as evidence of conduct upon which an employer makes an employment decision. An employer may deny employment opportunities to persons based on any prior conduct which indicates that they would be unfit for the position in question, whether that conduct is evidenced by an arrest, conviction or other information provided to the employer. It is the conduct, not he arrest or conviction per se, which the employer may consider in relation to the position sought. The considerations relevant to the determination of whether the alleged Conduct demonstrates unfitness for the particular job were set forth in Green v. Missouri Pacific Railroad Co., 549 F.2d 1158, 1160, 13 EPD ¶ 11, 579 (8th Cir. 1977) and reiterated in the February 4, 1987 Statement on Convictions, page 2:

1. the nature and gravity of the offense or offenses;

2. the time that has passed since the conviction[11] (or in this case, arrest) .; and

3. the nature of the job held or sought.

See also Carter v. Maloney Trucking and Storage Inc., 631 F.2d 40, 43, 24 EPD ¶ 31,348 (5th Cir. 1980) (employer refused to rehire an ex-employee who had murdered a co-worker, not solely

---

Black applicant pool. Carter v. Gallagher, 452 F.2d at 330-331; Reynolds v. Sheet Metal Workers, Local 102, 498 F. Supp. At 964 n.12, 966 n.13, 967, 973; Commission Decision Nos. 76-138, 76-87, 76-17, 74-90, 74-25 and 74-02, CCH EEOC Decisions (1983) !! 6700, 6665, 612, 6423, 6400, 6386 and Commission Decision Nos. 74-1005 and 71-1950, CCH EEOC Decisions (1973) !! 6350 and 6274, respectively.

9 Note also that in Walls v. City of Petersburg, 895 F.2d 188, 52 EPD ! 39,602 (4th Cir. 1990), the court upheld an employer's policy of making an employment inquiry regarding the arrest records of employees' immediate family members. The court determined that under Atonio, the plaintiff was obligated to show not only that Blacks were more likely to have "negative" responses to this question, but also that the employer made adverse employment decisions based on such responses.

10 New York, Hawaii, Oregon, Wisconsin, New Jersey, Ohio, Virginia, District of Columbia, California, Maryland, Minnesota, Utah, Washington, West Virginia, Arizona, Colorado, Idaho, Massachusetts, Michigan, Mississippi.

11 But see EEOC v. Carolina Freight Carriers, 723 F. Supp. At 753 (court upheld trucking company's lifetime bar to employment of drivers who had been incarcerated for theft crimes since EEOC did not produce evidence that a 5-10 year bar would be an equally effective alternative). Note also that the court in Carolina Freight specifically rejected the Eighth Circuit's reasoning in Green, cautioning that Green could be construed too broadly. 723 F. Supp. At 752.

because of his conviction, but because he was a dangerous person and friends of the murdered man might try to retaliate against him while he was on the job); Osborne v. Cleland, 620 F.2d 195, 22 EPD on a charge of "sexual procurement" was unfit to be a nursing assistant in a psychiatric ward); Lane v. Inman, 509 F.2d 184 (5th Cir. 1975) (city ordinance which prohibited the issuance of taxicab driver permits to persons convicted of smuggling marijuana was "so obviously job related" that "it could not be held to be unlawful race discrimination," irrespective of any adverse impact); EEOC v. Carolina Freight, 723 F. Supp. 734, 52 EPD ¶ (S.D. Fla. 1989) (criminal history was related to position of truck driver who transported valuable property); McCray v. Alexander, 30 EPD ¶ 33,219 (D. Colo. 1982), aff'd 38 EPD ¶35,509 (10th Cir. 1985) (supervisory guard was discharged for killing a motorist, while off-duty, in a traffic dispute because employer concluded that, despite his acquittal, the conduct showed poor judgment on the use of deadly force).

Where the position sought is "security sensitive," particularly where it involves enforcing the law or preventing crime, courts tend to closely scrutinize evidence of prior criminal conduct of applicants. US. V. City of Chicago, 411 F. Supp. 217, 11 EPD ¶ 10,597 (N.D. Ill. 1976), aff'd in rel. part, 549 F.2d 415, 13 EPD ¶ 11,380 (7th Cir. 1977), on remand, 437 F. Supp. 256 (N.D. Ill. 1977) (applicants for the police department were disqualified for prior convictions for "serious" offenses); Richardson v. Hotel Corporation of America, 332 F. Supp. 519, 4 EPD ¶ 7666 (E.D. La. 1971), aff'd mem., 468 F.2d 951, 4 EPD ¶ 7666 (5th Cir. 1972) (bellman was discharged after his conviction for theft and receipt of stolen goods was discovered since bellmen had access to guests; rooms and was not subject to inspection when carrying packages); Haynie v. Chupka, 17 FEP Cases 267, 271 (S.D. Ohio 1976) (police department permissibly made inquires regarding arrest records and other evidence of prior criminal conduct).[12] (See Examples 3 and 4.)

Even where the employment at issue is not a law enforcement position or one which gives the employee easy access to the possessions of others, close scrutiny of an applicant's character and prior conduct is appropriate where an employer is responsible for the safety and/or well being of other persons. Osborne v. Cleland, 620 F.2d 195 (8th Cir. 1975) (psychiatric nursing assistant); Lane v. Inman, 509 F.2d 184 (taxi driver). In these instances, the facts would have to be examined closely in order to determine the probability that an applicant would pose a threat to the safety and well being of others. (See Examples 5 and 6).

3. Evaluating the Likelihood that the Applicant Engaged in the Conduct Alleged

The cases cited above illustrate the job-relatedness of certain conduct to specific positions. In cases alleging race discrimination based on the use of arrest records as opposed to convictions, courts have generally required not only job-relatedness, but also a showing that the alleged conduct was actually committed. In City of Cairo v. Illinois Fair Employment Practice Commission, et al., 8 EPD ¶ 9682, the court held that where applicants sought to become police officers, they could not be absolutely barred from appointment solely because they had been arrested, as distinguished from convicted. See also Commission Decision No. 76-87, CCH EEOC Decisions (1983) ¶ 6665 (potential police officer could not be rejected based on one arrest five years earlier for riding in a stolen car since there was no conviction and the applicant asserted that he did not know that the car was stolen).

---

[12] See also Quarrels v. Brown, 48 EPD ! 38,641 (D.C. Mich. 1988) (recent conviction was related to position of corrections officer). Note however, that this action was brought under 42 USC. S 1983, rather than Title VII, and plaintiff alleged that he was discriminated against because he was an ex-offender, not because the policy adversely affected a protected group.

Similarly, in Decision No. 74083, CCH EEOC Decision (1983) ¶ 6424, the Commission found no business justification for an employer's unconditional termination of all employees with arrest records (all five employees terminated were Black), purportedly to cut down on thefts in the workplace. The employer could produce no evidence that the employee had been involved in any of the thefts or that persons who are arrested, but not convicted, are prone toward crime. Commission Decision No. 74-92, CCH EEOC Decisions (1983) ¶ 6424.

An arrest record does no more than raise a suspicion that an applicant may have engaged in a particular type of conduct.[13] Thus, the investigator must determine whether the applicant is likely to step because it requires the employer either to accept the employee's denial or to attempt to obtain additional information and evaluate his/her credibility. An employer need not conduct an informal "trial" or an extensive investigation to determine an applicant's or employee's guilt or innocence. However, the employer may not perfunctorily "allow the person an opportunity to explain" and ignore the explanation where the person's claims could easily be verified by a phone call, i.e., to a previous employer or a police department. The employer is required to allow the person a meaningful opportunity to explain the circumstances of the arrest(s) and to make a reasonable effort to determine whether the explanation is credible before eliminating him/her from employment opportunities.[14] (See Examples 1, 4, 5 and 6.)

III. Examples

The following examples are provided to illustrate the process by which arrest record charges should be evaluated.

Example 1: Wilma, a Black female, applies to Buss Inc. in Highway City for a position as a bus driver. In response to a pre-employment inquiry, Wilma states that she was arrested two years earlier for driving while intoxicated. Bus Inc. rejects Wilma, despite her acquittal after trial. But Inc. does not accept her denial of the conduct alleged and concludes that Wilma was acquitted only because the breatholizer test which was administered to her at the time of her arrest was not administered in accordance with proper police procedures and was therefore inadmissible at trial. Witnesses at Wilma's trial testified that after being stopped for reckless driving, Wilma staggered from the car and had alcohol on her breath. Wilma's rejection is justified because the conduct underlying the arrest, driving while intoxicated, is clearly related to the safe performance of the duties of a bus driver; it occurred fairly recently; and there was no indication of subsequent rehabilitation.

Contrast Example Number 1 with the facts below.

Example 2: Lola, a Black female, applies to Buss Inc. for a position as a bus driver. In response to an inquiry whether she had ever been arrested, Lola states that she was arrested five years earlier for fraud in unemployment benefits. Lola admits that she committed the crime alleged. She explains that she received unemployment benefits shortly after her husband died and her expenses increased. During this period, she worked part-time for minimum wage because her unemployment check amounted to slightly less than the

---

[13] The employer's suspicion may be raised by an arrest record just as it would be negative comments about an applicant's conduct made by a previous employer or a personal reference.

[14] Although the number of arrests is not determinative (see Litton), it may be relevant in making a credibility determination.

monthly rent for her meager apartment. She did not report the income to the State Unemployment Board for fear that her payments would be reduced and that she would not be able to feed her three young children. After her arrest, she agreed to, and did, repay the state. Bus Inc. rejected Lola. Lola's rejection violated Title VII. The commission of fraud in the unemployment system does not constitute a business justification for the rejection of an applicant for the position of bus driver. The type of crime which Lola committed is totally unrelated to her ability to safely, efficiently and/or courteously drive a bus. Furthermore, the arrest is not recent.

Example 3: Tom, a Black male, applies to Lodge City for a position as a police officer. The arrest rate for Blacks is substantially disproportionate to that of Whites in Lodge City. In response to an arrest record inquiry, Tom states that he was arrested three years earlier for burglary. Tom is interviewed and asked to explain the circumstances surrounding his arrest. Tom admits that although the burglary charge was dismissed for lack of sufficient evidence, he did commit the crime. He claims, however, that he is a changed man, having matured since then. Lodge City rejects Tom. Police officers are: 1) entrusted with protecting the public; 2) authorized to enter nearly and dwelling under the appropriate circumstances; and 3) often responsible for transporting valuables which are confiscated as evidence. The department is, therefore, justified in declining to take the chance that Tom has reformed. Even if the department is completely satisfied that Tom has reformed, it may reject him because his credibility as a witness in court could be severely damaged if he were asked about his own arrest and the surrounding circumstances while testifying against a person whom he has arrested. Since an essential element of police work is the ability to effect an arrest and to credibly testify against the defendant in court, the department would have two separate business justifications for rejecting Tom.

The above example is contracted with circumstances under which an arrest record would not constitute ground for rejection.

Example 4: John, a Black male, applies to Lodge City for the same position as does Tom. John was arrested three years earlier for burglary. The charges were dismissed. Lodge City eliminates John from consideration without further investigation and will not consider the surrounding circumstances of the arrest. If allowed to explain, John could establish that his arrest was a case of mistaken identity and that someone else, who superficially fit John's description, was convicted of the crime for which John was initially charged. Since the facts indicate that John did not commit the conduct alleged in the arrest record, Lodge City has not carried its burden of proving a business justification for John's rejection.

Example 5: David, a Black male, applies for a teaching position in West High School. In response to a pre-employment inquiry, David states that he was arrested two years earlier for statutory rape, having been accused of seducing a seventeen-year old student in his class when he taught at another high school The charges were dismissed. West High rejects David. David relies on Litton to establish a prima facie case of race discrimination, and West High is unable to rebut the case with more current, ac curate or specific statistics. David denies that there is any truth to the charge. West High decides to conduct a further investigation and learns that David was arrested after another teacher found him engaged in sexual activity with Ann, one of his students, in the school's locker room. This event occurred on Ann's eighteenth birthday, but in the confusion of the arrest, no one realized that Ann had just reached the age of majority. Ann's parents and other teachers believed that David had seduced Ann, who has a schoolgirl "crush" on him, prior to her eighteenth birthday. However, since Ann would not testify against David, the charges had been dismissed. West High may reject David. Irrespective of Ann's age, West High is justified in attempting to protect its students from teachers who may make sexual advances toward them. Although he might not have been guilty of statutory rape, his conduct was unbefitting a teacher.

The above example is contracted to the following circumstances.

Example 6: Paul, a Black male, applies for the same position as does David. Paul was arrested two years earlier for statutory rape, having been accused of seducing a seventeen year old student in his class at another high school. West High eliminates Paul from consideration without further investigation and refuses to consider the surrounding circumstances of the arrest. When filing his complaint, Paul states that when he taught at the other high school, he befriended a troubled student in his class, Alice, who was terrified of her disciplinarian parents. Paul insists that he never touched Alice in any improper manner and that on the day before his arrest, Alice confided in him that she had become pregnant by her seventeen-year old boyfriend, Peter, and was afraid to tell her parents for fear that her father would kill him. Paul states that the charges were dismissed because the district attorney did not believe Alice's statements. The district attorney and the principal of the high school, Ms. P., confirm Paul's assessment of Alice. Ms. P; states that Peter confided in her that he was the father of Alice's baby and that Alice had assured him that nothing sexual had ever happened between her and Paul. Ms. P. states that there were indications that Alice's father was abusive, that he had beaten her into giving him the name of someone to blame for the pregnancy and that Alice thought that Paul could handle her father better than could Peter. Since Paul denied committing the conduct alleged and his explanation was well supported by the district attorney and his former employer, West High has not demonstrated a business justification for rejecting Paul.

The examples discussed above demonstrate that whereas an employer may consider a conviction as conclusive evidence that a person has committed the crime alleged, arrests can only be considered as a means of "triggering" further inquiry into that person's character or prior conduct. After considering all of the circumstances, if the employer reasonably concludes that the applicant's or employee's conduct is evidence that he or she cannot be trusted to perform the duties of the position in question, the employer may reject or terminate that person.

9-7-90   *Evan J Kemp, Jr.*

_____   Approved: _____

Date   Evan J Kemp, Jr.

                                                                   Chairman

Notice N-915 (7/29/87)

1. SUBJECT: Policy statement on the use of statistics in charges involving the exclusion of individuals with conviction records from employment

2. PURPOSE: This policy statement sets forth the commission's view as to the appropriate statistics to be used in evaluating an employer's policy of refusing to hire individuals with conviction records.

3. EFFECTIVE DATE: July 29, 1987

4. EXPIRATION DATE: January 29, 1988

5. ORIGINATOR: title VII.EPA Division, Office of Legal Counsel.

6. INSTRUCTIONS: insert behind §S 604 of EEOC Compliance Manual, Volume II

7. SUBJECT MATTER:

INTRODUCTION

Green v. Missouri Pacific Railroad Company, 523 F.2d 1290, 10 EPD ¶ 10,314 (8th Cir. 1975), is the leading Title VII case on the issue of conviction records. In Green, the court held that the defendant's policy of refusing employment to any person convicted of a crime other than a minor traffic offense had an adverse impact on Black applicants and was not justified by business necessity. In a second appeal following remand, the court upheld the district court's injunctive order prohibiting the defendant from using an applicant's conviction record as an absolute bar to employment but allowing it to consider a prior criminal record as long as it constituted a business necessity. Green v. Missouri Pacific Railroad Company,549 F.2d 1158, 1160, 13 EPD ¶ 11,579 (8th Cir. 1977). See also Commission Decision No. 72-1497, CCH EEOC Decisions (1973) ¶ 6352, and Commission Decision Nos. 74-89, 78-10, 78-35, and 80-10, CCH EEOC Decisions (1983) ¶¶ 6418, 6715, 6720, and 6822, respectively.

It is the Commission's position that an employer's policy or practice of excluding individuals from employment on the basis of their conviction records has an adverse impact on Blacks [1] and Hispanics [2] in light of statistics showing that they are convicted at a rate disproportionately greater than their representation in the population. Policy Statement on the Issue of Conviction Records Under Title VII (February 4, 1987). However, when the employer can present more narrowly drawn statistics showing

---

[1] See, e.g., Commission Decision No. 72-1497, CCH EEOC Decisions (1973) ! 6352, and Commission Decision Nos. 74-89, 78-10, 78-35, and 80-10, CCH EEOC Decisions (1983) !! 6418, 6715, 6720, and 6822 respectively.

[2] See Commission Decision No. 78-03, CCH EEOC Decisions (1983) ¶ 6714.

Either that Blacks and Hispanics are not convicted at a disproportionately greater rate or that there is no adverse impact in its own hiring process resulting from the convictions policy, then a no cause determination would be appropriate.

1. Where the Employer's Policy is Not Crime-Specific

An employer's policy of excluding from employment all persons convicted of any crime is likely to create an adverse impact for Blacks and Hispanics based on national and regional conviction rate statistics. However, it is open to the respondent/employer to present more narrow local, regional, or applicant flow data, showing that the policy probably will not have an adverse impact on its applicant pool and/or in fact does not have an adverse impact on the pool. As the Supreme Court has stated,

> Although a statistical showing of disproportionate impact need not always be based on an analysis of the characteristics of actual applicants, Dothard v. Rawlinson, 433 U.S. 321, 330, evidence showing that the figures for the general population might not accurately reflect the pool of qualified job applicants undermines the significance of such figures. Teamsters v. United States, 431 U.S. 324, 340 n. 20.

New York City Transit Authority v. Beazer, 440 U.S. 568, 586 n. 29, 19 EPD ¶ 9027 at p. 6315 (1979). See also Costa v. Markey, 30 EPD ¶ 33,173 at p. 27,638 (1st Cir. 1982), vacated on other grounds, 706 F.2d 796, 32 EPD ¶ 32,622 (1st Cir.), cert. denied, 104 S. Ct. 547, 32 EPD ¶ 33,955 (1983).

If the employer provides applicant flow data, information should be sought to assure that the employer's applicant pool was not artificially limited by discouragement. For example, if many Blacks with conviction records did not apply for a particular job because they knew of the employer's policy and they therefore expected to be rejected, then applicant flow data would not be an accurate reflection of the conviction policy's actual effect. See Dothard v. Rowlinson, 433 US 321, 330 (1977). (Section 608, Recruitment, of Volume II of the Compliance Manual will provide a more detailed discussion of when and how to investigate for discouragement.

2. Where the Employer's Policy is Crime-Specific

In the past, when the Commission has evaluated an employer's "no convictions' policy dealing with a subcategory of crimes; e.g., theft, robbery, or drug-related crimes; the Commission has relied upon national or regional conviction statistics for crimes as a whole. See, e.g., Commission Decision No. 73-0257, CCH EEOC Decisions (1973) ! 6372, and Commission Decision Nos. 76-110 and 80-17, CCH EEOC Decisions (1983) !! 6676 and 6809, respectively. However, these statistics only show a probability of adverse impact for Blacks and Hispanics, while more narrow data may show no adverse impact.

If the employer can present more narrow regional or local data on conviction rates for all crimes showing that Blacks and Hispanics are not convicted at disproportionately higher rates, then a no cause determination would be proper. [3]/ Alternatively, the employer may present national, regional, or local data on conviction rates for the particular crime which is targeted in its crime-specific convictions policy. If such data shows no adverse impact, then a no cause determination would be

---

[3] However, if even more narrow statistics, such as regional or local crime-specific data, show adverse impact, then a cause finding would be appropriate absent a justifying business necessity.

appropriate. Finally, the employer can use applicant flow data to demonstrate that its conviction policy has not resulted in the exclusion from employment of a disproportionately high number of Blacks and Hispanics.

[Signed July 29, 1987 by Clarence Thomas]

_____ Approved_____

Date   Clarence Thomas

                                                        Chairman

Notice N-915 (2/4/87)

1. SUBJECT: Policy Statement on the Issue of Conviction Records under Title VII of the Civil Rights Act of 1964, as amended, 42 U.S.C. § 2000e et seq. (1982).

2. PURPOSE: This policy statement sets forth the Commission's revised procedure for determining the existence of a business necessity justifying, for purposes of Title VII, the exclusion of an individual from employment on the basis of a conviction record.

3. EFFECTIVE DATE: February 27, 1987.

4. EXPIRATION DATE: September 15, 1987.

5. ORIGINATOR: Office of Legal Counsel.

6. INSTRUCTIONS: File behind page 604- 36 of EEOC Compliance Manual, Volume II, Section 604, Theories of Discrimination.

7. SUBJECT MATTER:

At the Commission meeting of November 26, 1985, the Commission approved a modification of its existing policy with respect to the manner in which a business necessity is established for denying an individual employment because of a conviction record. The modification, which is set forth below, does not alter the Commission's underlying position that an employer's policy or practice of excluding individuals from employment on the basis of their conviction records has an adverse impact on Blacks[1] and Hispanics[2] in light of statistics showing that they are convicted at a rate disproportionately greater than their representation in the population. Consequently, the Commission has held and continues to hold that such a policy or practice is unlawful under Title VII in the absence of a justifying business necessity. [3]

However, the Commission has revised the previous requirements for establishing business necessity [4] in the following manner. Where a charge involves an allegation that the Respondent employer [5]

---

[1] See, e.g., Commission Decision No. 72-1497, CCH EEOC Decisions (1973) ¶ 6352, and Commission Decision Nos. 74-89, 78-10, 78-35, and 80-10, CCH EEOC Decisions (1983) ¶¶ 6418, 6715, 6720, and 6822, respectively.

[2] See Commission Decision No. 78-03, CCH EEOC Decisions (1983) ¶ 6714.

[3] See, e.g., Commission decisions cited supra notes 1-2.

[4] Prior to this modification, for an employer to establish a business necessity justifying excluding an individual from employment because of a conviction record, the evidence had to show that the offense for which the applicant or employee was convicted was job-related. If the offense was not job-related, a disqualification based on the conviction alone violated Title VII. However, even if the offense were determined to be job-related, the employer had to examine other relevant factors to determine whether the conviction affected the individual's ability to perform the job in a manner consistent with the safe and efficient operation of the employer's business. The factors identified by the Commission to be considered by an employer included:

failed to hire or terminated the employment of the Charging Party as a result of a conviction policy or practice that has an adverse impact on the protected class to which the Charging Party belongs, The Respondent must show that it considered these three factors to determine whether its decision was justified by business necessity:

1. The nature and gravity of the offense or offenses:

2. The time that has passed since the conviction and/or completion of the sentence; and

3. The nature of the job held or sought. [6]

Footnote 4 continued:

1. The number of offenses and the circumstances of each offense for which the individual was convicted;

2. The length of time intervening between the conviction for the offense and the employment decision;

3. The individual's employment history; and

4. The individual's efforts at rehabilitation.

See, e.g., Commission Decision No. 78-35, CCH EEOC Decisions (1983) ! 6720.

Thus, under the previous procedure, business necessity was established by means of a two-step process: first, by showing that the conviction was job-related; then, by separately demonstrating that the conviction would affect the individual's ability to safety and efficiently perform the job upon consideration of the four factors enumerated above.

[5] Although the term "employer" is used herein, the Commission's position on this issue applies to all entities covered by Title VII. See e.g., Commission Decision No. 77-23, CCH EEOC Decisions (1983) ¶ 6710 (union's policy of denying membership to persons with conviction records unlawfully discriminated against Blacks).

[6] The Commission's revised business necessity analysis follows a decision by the United States Court of Appeals for the Eighth Circuit in the Green v. Missouri Pacific Railroad Company case. Green, 523 F.2d 1290, 10 EPD ¶ 10,314 (8th Cir. 1975), it the leading Title VII case on the issue of conviction records. In that case, the court held that the defendant's absolute policy of refusing employment to any person convicted of a crime other than a minor traffic offense had an adverse impact on Black applicants and was not justified by business necessity. On a second appeal in that case, following remand, the court upheld the district court's injunctive order prohibiting the defendant from using an applicant's conviction record as an absolute bar to employment but allowing it to consider a prior criminal record as a factor in making individual hiring decisions as long as the defendant took into account "the nature and gravity of the offense or offenses, the time that has passed since the conviction and/or completion of sentence, and the nature of the job for which the applicant has applied. Green v. Missouri Pacific Railroad Company, 549 F.2d 1158, 1160, 13 EPD ¶ 11,579 (8th Cir. 1977).

This procedure condenses the Commission's previous standard for business necessity, substituting a one-step analysis for the prior two-step procedure and retaining some but not all of the factors previously considered. [7] The modification principally eliminates the need to consider an individual's employment history and efforts at rehabilitation. However, consideration is still given to the job-relatedness of a conviction, covered by the first and third factors, and to the time frame involved, covered by the second factor. Moreover, the first factor encompasses consideration of the circumstances of the offense(s) for which an individual was convicted as well as the number of offenses.

The Commission continues to hold that, where there is evidence of adverse impact, an absolute bar to employment based on the mere fact that an individual has a conviction record is unlawful under Title VII. [8] The Commission's position on this issue is supported by the weight of judicial authority [9]

It should be noted that the modified procedure does not affect charges alleging disparate treatment on a prohibited basis in an employer's use of a conviction record as a disqualification for employment. A charge brought under the disparate treatment theory of discrimination is one where, for example, an employer allegedly rejects Black applicants who have conviction records but does not reject similarly situated White applicants.

With respect to conviction charges that are affected by this modification—that is, those raising the issue of adverse impact—Commission decisions that apply the previous standard are no longer available as Commission decision precedent for establishing business necessity. To the extent that such prior decisions are inconsistent with the position set forth herein, they are expressly overruled.

Questions concerning the application of the Commission's revised business necessity standard to the facts of a particular charge should be directed to the Regional Attorney for the Commission office in which the charge was filed.

[Signed 2-4-87 by Clarence Thomas]

_____   Approved:_____

Date

                                        Clarence Thomas

                                        Chairman

---

[7] See discussion supra note 4.

[8] See, e.g., Commission Decision No. 78-35, CCH EEOC Decisions (1983) ¶ 6720.

[9] See Green, 523 F.2d at 1298; Carter v. Gallagher, 452 F.2d 315, 3 EPD ¶ 8335 (8th Cir. 1971), cert. denied, 406 US 950, 4 EPD ¶ 7818 (1972) (brought under 42 U.S.C. §§ 1981 and 1983); and Richardson v. Hotel Corporation of America, 332 F. Supp. 519, 4 EPD ¶ 7666 (E.D. La. 1971), aff'd mem., 468 F.2d 951, 5 EPD ¶ 8101 (5th Cir. 1972). See also Hill v. United States Postal Service, 522 F. Supp. 1283 (S.D.N.Y. 1981); Craig v. Department of Health, Education, and Welfare, 508 F. Supp. 1055 (W.D. Mo. 1981); and Cross v. United States Postal Service, 483 F. Supp. 1050 (E.D. Mo. 1979), aff'd in relevant part, 639 F.2d 409, 25 EPD ¶ 31,594 (8th Cir. 1981).

Quick-**Find** *Index*

Facts on Demand Press

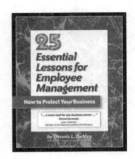

25 Essential Lessons
for Employee Management

25 Essential Lessons for Employee Management cuts through conventional practices and provides managers with easy-to-apply techniques that guide them through five essential processes: hiring, new employee integration, managing employee problems, termination, and compliance with regulations. Included in the book are recommended web sites and 22 essential employment forms.

Dennis l. DeMey • 1-889150-25-8 • 2001 • 320 pgs • $22.95

Public Records Online

How can someone determine which records are available online — who has them and what is available for "free or fee" — without spending time searching endless sources? Use *Public Records Online*. As the only "Master Guide" to online public record searching, *Public Records Online's* third edition details thousands of sites, both government agencies and private sources. This new edition is 80 pages larger, and is easier to use.

Michael Sankey • 1-889150-21-5 • Revised 2001 • 460 pgs • $20.95

Find It Online

Get the information you need as quickly and easily as a professional researcher. *Find it Online* is a practical, how-to-guide written by a non-techno geek and developed for real people. Learn how to quickly find, save, and manage the information you need, find people online, cut through government red tape and put your hands on the vast amounts of information now available on the Internet.

Alan M. Schlein • 1-889150-20-7 • Revised 2001 • 512 pgs • $19.95

Available at Your Local Bookstore!

1-800-929-3811 • Facts on Demand Press • www.brbpub.com